AT THE BBC

BBC

TOM HAGLER

BOWIE

AT THE BBC

A LIFE IN INTERVIEWS

WELBECK

First published in 2023 by Carlton Books Limited

This edition published by Welbeck
An Imprint of HEADLINE PUBLISHING GROUP

1

Cataloguing in Publication Data is available from the British Library

ISBN 978-1-03541-669-1

Printed and bound in Great Britain by Clays Ltd, Elcograf S.p.A

Headline's policy is to use papers that are natural, renewable and recyclable
products and made from wood grown in well-managed forests and other controlled
sources. The logging and manufacturing processes are expected to conform to the
environmental regulations of the country of origin.

HEADLINE PUBLISHING GROUP
An Hachette UK Company
Carmelite House
50 Victoria Embankment
London EC4Y 0DZ

www.headline.co.uk
www.hachette.co.uk

*To my four boys, without whom this book
would have been written far more quickly.*

CONTENTS

INTRODUCTION

At first glance, David Bowie and the British Broadcasting Corporation might appear to be strange bedfellows. Bowie was the ultimate outsider, the great cultural transgressor and the epitome of cool, while the BBC in its early days came across as the exact opposite: a conservative bastion of Cambridge graduates charged with reflecting the country's moral code. Imagine your rebellious nephew hanging out with his ageing 'auntie', as the BBC was commonly called. They certainly had their differences, with Bowie famously failing his first audition at the hands of the corporation's New Talent panel. But, despite initial misgivings, Bowie had a closer relationship with the BBC than with any other broadcaster. Not only did he do more interviews with the BBC than any other outlet, he often spoke more openly and deeply in them. And so, a collection of his BBC interviews provides an unrivalled insight into his thoughts and career.

Would there even have been a David Bowie without 'the Beeb'? It's worth remembering that the BBC had a monopoly on Britain's airwaves throughout most of the sixties, so when its panel barred Bowie from its output – not for being outrageous, but for not being good enough – it effectively ended any chance he had of selling records and making a living. Fortunately for Bowie, DJ John Peel stepped in and insisted the youngster be given a second chance.

It's worth considering what might have happened if there hadn't been maverick individuals within the BBC, like Peel and Bob Harris, championing the seemingly uncommercial outsider. Could Bowie have been forced to stick to his day job at an ad agency, manning the photocopier and writing copy? Almost certainly not. Someone with his determination, talent, ability to suck up the new – and his outright strangeness – was never going to end up doing anything ordinary. But it is possible to imagine his artistic career might have taken a different path. After all, he more than dabbled in acting, directing, painting and writing. Nevertheless, Bowie became so disenchanted with his lack of success in the sixties that he gave up music twice: once to be a Buddhist monk and once to be a mime act.

Jarvis Cocker jokingly tells a story in which he blames John Peel for almost wrecking his life by stopping him going to Oxford University and getting a 'proper' job. Cocker's band Pulp laboured unsuccessfully for over a decade; and always, just at the point they were about to pack it in, Peel would offer to host a session and success would again appear within reach. The same could arguably be said of Bowie. The faith shown in him by a handful of BBC DJs allowed him to keep believing in himself, even when much of the evidence pointed to the contrary. As Peel himself said, 'We kept Bowie alive for a few years.'

There's even an argument to suggest that the BBC helped make Bowie '*Bowie*'. His defining moment happened on *Top of the Pops*; his 1972 performance of 'Starman' was the point when the alien landed and his career took off. The BBC's key role here was its reach – somewhere between 15 and 19 million viewers tuned into that particular episode. Pretty much anyone who bought pop records was watching, and Bowie's performance was beamed directly into their homes. The Starman had arrived. No doubt, Bowie would have gradually seeped into the national consciousness, but it was the white heat of that single performance that would hit the nation like a hand grenade.

It certainly wasn't all one-way traffic. The BBC owes a debt of thanks to the singer. At that time, *Top of the Pops* was packed with music one's grandmother or primary school sibling would have approved of, from Donny Osmond to David Cassidy. Performances like Bowie's gave the show a credibility with younger viewers and a relevance without which its days would surely have been numbered.

The relationship between these two British institutions spanned more than 50 years, and the interviews themselves allowed Bowie himself to stretch out. Less concerned with ratings, gossip or finding a 'scoop', BBC reporters would welcome the chance to delve into the singer's more arcane material, explore his intellectual ideas or play his latest releases – even if they lacked popularity. There were one or two notable exceptions but, by and large, he was treated not just as a musician, but also as one of the country's most significant post-war cultural figures.

One interesting revelation of this research was that his most intensive activity on the BBC was not at the height of his fame, but during his Tin Machine years. Few commercial outlets at that time were interested in giving that particular band the time of day, but the BBC would always find a place for Bowie, whatever the vicissitudes of his career.

The BBC championed him throughout his career, with interviews and with numerous documentaries. This wasn't generosity on the part of the broadcaster; it was because Bowie was the most interesting voice in rock – he simply had more to say and said it better. John Lennon was perhaps the only one who could match him, but Lennon largely locked himself away in the seventies.

Bowie's most revealing BBC interviews are now collected here to show how he evolved, not just as an artist but also as a man, over more than half a century. It is a unique compilation, giving us an opportunity to find out about the life of a complex, enigmatic, ever-changing artist, directly from the man himself and in his very own words.

TONIGHT, BBC TV

INTERVIEWER: CLIFF MICHELMORE

When mums and dads wanted to put their kids to bed in the fifties, TV was their friend rather than enemy. At 6pm on the dot, screens would helpfully go blank for an hour thanks to an official BBC policy called the 'Toddlers' Truce'. It's perhaps easy to see why the BBC was fondly referred to as 'auntie'. That paternalistic policy ended in 1957, and one of the shows that replaced it was *Tonight*, a new type of early evening programme that aimed to mix culture and hard news in a less formal, less 'BBC' way. The host was Cliff Michelmore, a presenter who was told at the start of his career that he was not a 'BBC type', meaning he hadn't gone to public school. It was on *Tonight* in November 1964 that a 17-year-old David Bowie, then Davy Jones, was to provide his first televised interview.

Despite being callow, Bowie had already appeared twice on TV, the first time being that summer on *Juke Box Jury*. Bowie had the unenviable task of being filmed patiently listening backstage as the panellists declared David Jones and the King Bees' first single, 'Liza Jane', a 'miss'. Not that it dented Bowie's confidence. In the dressing room after the show, fellow King Bees bandmate George Underwood recalled the two of them watching Matt Monro, 'the Cockney Sinatra', putting on his socks. 'They were transparent, nylon socks,' said Underwood. "What unusual socks," I said to David. "They must be for rich people."

He laughed and said, "George, you stick with me and you'll be seeing lots more things like that." In David's head, he was already seeing himself as being successful enough to wear see-through socks!'[1]

Bowie appeared on screens again two weeks later when the King Bees played the same song on *Ready Steady Go!* Despite such publicity, the juke box jury was right – the song was such a flop that their manager, Leslie Conn, ended up binning several hundred copies to make space in his garage.

But Bowie's first interview on the BBC had nothing to do with music; it was all about a small, cultish group of men allegedly under threat. As trumpets blared out *Tonight*'s theme tune, a black-and-white image revealed a group of eight teenagers huddled together in a cramped, unadorned studio. The image cut to a close-up of the young man seated in the middle, his smoothly combed, shoulder-length blond hair cascading over his eyebrows. Bowie was already taking centre stage. His tie was neatly done up tight into his buttoned-down collar, his trousers were tapered, his shoes fashionably pointy. While the rest stood around in scarves and heavy coats, like students ready to head off on a protest march, Bowie was already all poise. His right leg was crossed high over his left, one hand rested on his knee, the other on his ankle; such a posture is often described as defensive, but not here. Bowie has thought deeply about this moment. His eyes casually roamed the studio even as the camera zoomed in. He was already ignoring the medium's conventions: sit still, legs down, eyes straight, and pretend you're not in a TV studio. Even in black and white, his flawless, pale skin was striking. He looked every part the rock star he would become. By comparison, Michelmore, balding with a comb-over, half-rimmed glasses on a rotund face, was a man of his time; just 44, he looked 64.

Bowie and his gang were in the studio as members of The Society for the Prevention of Cruelty to Long-Haired Men. Despite the obvious humour, there was a serious element. In Maidstone earlier that year, Bowie had been punched in the face in an unprovoked attack because of his hair. 'This big Herbert walking down the street just knocked me on the pavement and, when I fell, proceeded to kick the shit out of me,' Bowie later said. Shortly before, David Jones and the King Bees had performed their debut at a US Air Force base in Bedfordshire, mainly memorable for the homophobic heckling from the American aircrew.

But there was another reason for the society. Any publicity is good publicity, goes the adage, and, as a young band trying to get known, what better way to get on TV than come up with an outlandish-sounding idea to enrage the older generation?

'Bowie was mad to get as much publicity for himself as he could,' recalled Underwood, who was also present in the *Tonight* studio as one of the society's members. 'One of the people in that group was a complete stranger whom David had asked off the street. But I wouldn't dismiss it as purely a joke. When he put ideas out, there was always passion behind them. I couldn't get served in several local pubs in Bromley because the owners didn't like my long hair. They could turn you away and that was seen as their right. That was a trigger for David thinking, "Well, let's do something about this."'

So, a mixture of seriousness, humour and publicity all rolled into one. So far, so Bowie.

As for the interview, Bowie dismissed Michelmore's suggestion that they were simply copying the hairstyles of The Rolling Stones as 'stupid'. Bowie might have been acting a little disingenuously. He not only loved the Stones, he was also hanging out at the time with their guitarist Brian Jones, and happened to have exactly the same hair style. Although it appears the original inspiration for the hair style may have been Keith Relf, the singer of The Yardbirds, whose long golden hair was the secret, both Joneses (David and Brian) believed, to attracting dozens of attractive Swedish groupies.

Bowie's appearance on *Tonight* would be followed that very evening by a relatively new show called *Top of the Pops* that would feature Val Doonican and German violinist Helmut Zacharias, whose 'Tokyo Medley' was the BBC's theme tune to the 1964 Olympics. Such staid, ageing tastes on a programme designed specifically for a burgeoning youth culture reflected the chasm that still existed between institutions like the BBC and groups like 'the long hairs', the term Michelmore used to describe Bowie and his guests.

CLIFF MICHELMORE: It's all got to stop! They've had enough! The worms are turning. The rebellion of the long hairs is getting underway. They're tired of persecution, they're tired of taunts, they're tired of losing their jobs, they're tired of being sent home from college, they're tired of being sent home from school, they're tired even of being refused the dole. So, with a nucleus of some of his friends, a 17-year-old, Davy Jones, has just founded the Society for the Prevention of Cruelty to Long-Haired Men. Well, here we are. Long-haired men, you've got to have your hair, what, nine inches long before you join?

DAVID BOWIE: Well, I think we've passed over that now.

CM: Have you?

DB: Yes.

CM: Now, exactly, who's been cruel to you?

DB: Well, I think we're all fairly tolerant, but for the last two years we've heard comments like, 'Darling' and 'Can I carry your handbag?' thrown at us, and I think it just has to stop now.

CM: But does it surprise you that you get this kind of comment because, after all, you've got really rather long hair, haven't you?

DB: We have, yes, yeah, it's not too bad really … no, I like it and I think we all like long hair, and we don't see why other people should persecute us because of this.

CM: How are you going to set about this campaign?

MAN NEXT TO DB: Well, I don't know. I think the real sort of thing we should do is to try and get more followers behind us, so that we can march in protest, sort of 'ban the bomb' all over again, only against hair-persecuting people …

DB: [*Laughing*] *Balder*-maston.

CM: Now, you see a lot of people can't tell the difference between a man and a woman, can they, if you've got hair that long?

MAN AT BACK: No, well that's ridiculous. If you can't tell either sex by a few inches of hair, I think it's a pretty poor showing, don't you?

CM: Yeah, I do. Now, why did you grow your hair long in the first place?

SECOND MAN AT BACK: Most of us just like it long. It's nice.

CM: But did you grow it long to stand out in a crowd?

THIRD MAN AT BACK: Mine was an accident. I just forgot to have it cut for some time.

CM: Yeah, for a long time, I should think! [*Laughter*] I mean, did you get this off The Rolling Stones, really?

ALL: Oh no, no. Definitely not.

DB: That's stupid.

CM: But did any of you have your hair growing long more than two years ago or so?

ALL: Oh yeah, yes.

CM: Did you? Before The Rolling Stones ever did?

DB: Well, it takes a long time to get this length, you know.

OFF-CAMERA VOICE: It doesn't grow overnight just because The Rolling Stones did it.

CM: Can I ask you what you say when you're going to the hairdressers? When are you going to the hairdressers?

MOST OF THE MEN: We don't! We don't go.

MAN AT BACK: Mine was last year. [*Laughter*]

CM: Don't you go and have it shampooed and set?

ALL: Oh no, no.

DB: Our mums do it, if anything. [*Laughter*]

CM: Your mothers do it?

DB: Yeah. Why shouldn't they?

CM: Do they?

DB: Yeah, very good at it. Better than I could ever be.

CM: When was the last time that any of you ever went to a barber's?

OFF-CAMERA VOICE: I went last year.

MAN AT BACK: I only did it because I had an operation. [*Laughter*]

CM: Exactly how are you going to stop people being cruel to you? [*Points at DB*] Come on now, it's your idea.

DB: Well, if anybody is chucked out of a factory job or removed from a public bar, we'll get a petition written up and sent to either the LCC [London County Council], the people who hold the pub licence, or …

CM: But do you think any of this will do any good?

DB: Well, it better do good. [*Laughter*]

CM: But do you think many people are on your side, is what I'm saying?

DB: Oh, yes.

CM: All of them with long hair?

OFF-CAMERA VOICE: No. Lots of them would *like* to have long hair.

DB: No, not lots of them. They haven't got permission.

MAN AT BACK: They're just wishing they had got long hair.

MAN WITH SCARF: Either that or the company they work with or their parents don't allow them to have long hair.

CM: No, well, I understand that, can't you? Mind you, I'm talking out of a sense of jealousy in a way, seeing you over there with so much, and I should have gone and got a haircut today. [*Laughter*]

THE DLT SHOW, BBC RADIO

INTERVIEWER: BRIAN MATTHEW

In August 1969, David Bowie's father, Haywood 'John' Jones, died. Aged just 56, he was the single most important influence on David's life up to that point: cheerleader, financial backer, passport into showbiz and port of calm. He bought David his first sax and first Little Richard record. His stories from working at Dr Barnardo's Homes, about the orphans who lived on roofs in Whitechapel, were to inspire Bowie's own take on vagrant children in 'Diamond Dogs'. And it was Bowie's father who first tried to enter the world of entertainment when he invested, and lost, his inherited fortune in forming an acting troupe and trying to make his first wife a star. Second time around, this time with his son, there would be no such failure. 'John' can even claim to have started the famous family tradition: Don't like your name? Change it.

When John died, a large chunk of Bowie's world came crashing down. 'Not now! Not now!' were the words Bowie later used to describe his reaction. 'He just died at the wrong damn time, because there were so many things I'd loved to have said to him and asked him about.' Such remorse was made only worse because those closest to David had decided not to divulge the seriousness of his father's pneumonia for fear of upsetting him.

This period was already emotionally fraught for Bowie. The woman he believed to be the love of his life, Hermione Farthingale, had walked out on him, and he was going through a protracted separation from his other fatherly figure, his manager, Ken Pitt.

While all this was happening, Bowie wrote his second album, two years on from the commercial flop of his first, and was invited on BBC Radio to be interviewed on Dave Lee Travis's *The DLT Show*.

'Space Oddity' had just entered the Top 10, but Bowie decided not to play the record, which clearly perplexed interviewer Brian Matthew. It's tempting to see this as Bowie already being the ever-evolving artist, bored of what he did last month, and keen to get on to the new stuff.

Instead, he chose a newer song whose title, 'Unwashed and Somewhat Slightly Dazed', also reflected his bruised and confused emotional state. He would go on to tell biographer George Tremlett that the song was about trying to capture the surreal feeling in the weeks after his father's death. Bowie claimed that, after the funeral, his phone rang at the same time every day for a week with no one on the other end of the line. Bowie told his friends that this was the spirit of his father trying to let him know that everything was going to be okay.[2]

The radio interview was short and, like most interviews of the time, not intended to be deep or meaningful. Bowie wasn't asked about his father, but he did mention his mother. Ahead of playing 'Let Me Sleep Beside You', Bowie explained that the song had been written several years previously. When the DJ asked why the record had not been released earlier, Bowie said it was because his mother had found the lyrics 'dirty'.

Who could possibly imagine that the man who would go on to become the next decade's great cultural transgressor would be worried about what his mother might think?

BRIAN MATTHEW: David, the record which you have in the charts in Britain at the moment is undoubtedly your biggest success to date, isn't it?

DAVID BOWIE: My *only* success to date.

BM: [*Laughs*] Well, I wouldn't have said that. But tell us a little bit about it. Was it planned a long time ago, or is it fairly recent?

DB: Most people presumed that it was written because of, or anticipating the space shot, but in fact it was started last November, and the recording of it was started last December, and it was finally finished in June, after which it was released within three weeks, which was very good going.

BM: Sure.

DB: Hmm.

BM: Right now, you're not doing it in the studio today.

DB: No.

BM: Why is this?

DB: We'd need about five orchestras to get the right sound, I think.

BM: Yeah?

DB: That's possibly past everybody's budget. [*Laughs*]

BM: [*Laughs*] Yeah, that could be true.

BM: Do you do a live version of it when you're travelling around?

DB: Just with 12-string guitar.

BM: Yeah?

DB: Yeah.

BM: And not with your little electronic gadget?

DB: Yes, I use that thing.

BM: That *thing*? [*Laughs*]

DB: That thing? [*Laughs*] Daren't mention it!

BM: Well, we ought not to really. Have you got anything that you are doing in today's programme that is not on the record?

DB: Oh yeah. We've got a number that we dug up today, which was written about four years ago and it hasn't been out of the house. It's the first airing it's ever had anywhere.

BM: Really?

DB: Mmm.

BM: Why was it not recorded?

DB: Er, well … my mother thought the lyrics were dirty, so …

BM: Are they?

DB: No, not at all.

BM: Oh, dear. [*Laughter*]

DB: They're rather splendid. Very ethereal.

BM: Alright, what's it called?

DB: 'Let Me Sleep Beside You'.

BM: Can we hear it?

DB: Yes.

THE SUNDAY SHOW, BBC RADIO

INTERVIEWER: JOHN PEEL

Mick Ronson met Bowie on a Tuesday, joined his band The Spiders from Mars on the Wednesday and played his first gig with them on the Thursday. Not only that – this wasn't just any gig – the concert was recorded live and listened to by millions.

The fit between the singer and guitarist was immediate. So rapid was the rapport that, within two weeks of this concert, Bowie and Ronson would be back on stage at London's Roundhouse, dressed in an assortment of rainbow-coloured and comically outlandish clothing. The playful seriousness of glam rock had just taken its first colourful bow.

This first recording of these two musicians who would reshape the seventies is, therefore, culturally priceless. What did the BBC do with the tape? It wiped it.

This was not an uncommon practice – there are numerous such instances, involving not just Bowie. To be fair to the BBC, those old reel-to-reel tapes were chunky things that took up space in already enormous and bulging archive vaults. Plus, the organisation's producers were aware, even then, of the need to cut costs and reuse tape. I remember myself grabbing the nearest spool to hand, ignoring the names of several programmes already crossed out on the label, and hitting the record button. But even so.

Given the event's significance in Bowie's career history, imagine fans' delirium when a bootleg recording of the BBC concert of 15 songs came to light in the mid-eighties. Much later, Bowie himself revealed he had kept an original master tape of far better quality, and his recording was released. Typical Bowie. He kept absolutely everything. Even back at the very beginning, he felt the need to document it all for posterity.

The future wasn't yet set in stone, though. When asked if The Spiders from Mars would play more gigs, Bowie seemed genuinely unsure. In fact, it was so early in their relationship that Bowie still referred to Ronson as 'Michael'.

As for John Peel, the DJ had already played a fundamental role in Bowie's career. In the early days, a special BBC New Talent panel would veto singers it thought weren't good enough for its airwaves. Bowie failed his New Talent audition for, famously, having 'no personality' and 'singing wrong notes, out of tune'. It was Peel who campaigned for Bowie to be given a rare second chance, which Bowie passed. Peel played Bowie's records throughout the sixties when almost every other DJ showed little to no interest whatsoever.

As for this concert, appearing as the headline act on BBC Radio was a big deal. Coming just a few months after 'Space Oddity' hit the Top 5, the opportunity promised big things. But the next single, 'The Prettiest Star', was a flop and Bowie was forced back to the drawing board again. He would return with what many regard as his greatest album, *Hunky Dory*.

The venue for this recording was the BBC's 400-capacity Paris Theatre, a relatively intimate setting on London's Regent Street where radio comedy programmes, such as *Dad's Army* and *The Goon Show*, and various panel shows were recorded in front of a live audience. Bowie begins the set on his own with an acoustic guitar and plays a cover song called 'Amsterdam'.

AMSTERDAM

JOHN PEEL: Very tasty, indeed. That's a Jacques Brel song I haven't heard before, actually. 'Port of Amsterdam' [sic], anyway. This second song is one David wrote himself and it's on his LP, which some of you may have may heard, and is named, with a certain kind of charm, and evocatively, *David Bowie*. [*Audience laughs*] Good name for an LP, I think. And the song is called 'God Knows I'm Good'.

GOD KNOWS I'M GOOD

DAVID BOWIE: [*Introducing the next song*] This next one is a comedy number. This one is written by an American called Biff Rose. Biff Rose is a legendary character now. He lives just outside of San Francisco on a mountain, in a cabin, and he's got a bicycle. And he writes a lot of songs, and he cycles down from the cabin to do gigs, in which he never sings; he never sings at any of his gigs. He just talks about shaving and what he saw on the way down from the cabin and how many punctures he's had, and then goes away again, and nobody's really heard him sing. But he does write some good songs, and he's made a couple of LPs, and this is one, one called 'Buzz The Fuzz'.

BUZZ THE FUZZ

JP: A harrowing story indeed. That's a Biff Rose song, 'Buzz the Fuzz'. David made an LP, quite a few years ago now, well three or four years ago, called … I don't know what it was called.

DB: [*Shouting off-mic*] It's called *David Bowie*!

JP: Called what?

DB: *David Bowie*!

JP: Oh, is it? As well?

DB: Yeah.

JP: You pick snappy titles. [*Audience laughter*] The third LP is going to be called … *David Bowie*. The fourth one, *Elvis Presley*, just for variation. Anyway, the first one has just been reissued at a drastically reduced price, and is called *The World of David Bowie*, I think, or *The Wonderful World of David Bowie*, or something similar, and will be re-released on March 6. This is one of the songs on it. It's actually a very good LP, but David isn't too keen on it now, but people never are with their old LPs. This particular song is called 'Karma Man'.

KARMA MAN

JP: And for the next thing that David will be doing, he will be joined by Tony Visconti on bass and John Cambridge on drums. And this is a song which you may remember David doing, oh, a year, a year-and-a-half at least, on *Top Gear* [radio show], and it's called 'London Bye Ta-Ta'. Never quite understood why, but that's what it's called anyway.

LONDON BYE TA-TA

JP: That's the David Bowie Big Band, as it were. [*Laughter*] The next song that the big band will be doing is a track from David's last LP, the one that's called *David Bowie*. [*Laughter*] And this song is 'An Occasional Dream'.

AN OCCASIONAL DREAM

JP: On this next number, in addition to John Cambridge on drums, Tony Visconti on bass and, of course, David on guitar, we have Mick

Ronson, who will be playing lead guitar, and who has recorded on Michael Chapman LPs, one of my favourite singers. And the first thing the full band will be doing is called 'Width of a Circle'.

THE WIDTH OF A CIRCLE

JP: And that was called 'Width of A Circle'. Are you going to be doing gigs with this band?

DB: Well, looking at them, no. [*Laughs*] Yes, we are going to do some gigs. [*DB turns away from the microphone to ask Ronson*] Are we, Michael? Michael doesn't really know, he has just come down from Hull and I met for the first time about two days ago through John, the drummer, who's worked with me once.

JP: I see, but you are planning to go on the road?

DB: Yes, yes, very shortly.

JANINE and WILD EYED BOY FROM FREECLOUD play

JP: Just a while ago, the Pig [Peel's pet name for his wife] and I saw a man, quite well dressed, standing in the middle of Piccadilly Circus, conducting it, as though he were conducting an orchestra, which I thought was rather a nice sight, and I had the idea that I'd be in Lancashire next week conducting the East Lancs Road. [*Laughter*] A pretty nice idea. So, I think the next one could perhaps be for him, and it's called 'Unwashed and Slightly Dazed'.

UNWASHED AND SOMEWHAT SLIGHTLY DAZED

JP: That was a bit of a treat there, actually. That was called 'Unwashed and Slightly Dazed'. David, you have been involved with arts-labby projects [*DB laughs*] in places like Croydon and places. What are you doing with that now?

DB: It's impossible to call it an art lab because of the simple fact that most people won't participate. To a great extent, they prefer to have things fashioned for them, which is unfortunately true.

JP: Yes, that's very true. So, you are not involved?

DB: Well, yes, we are still involved in putting on things, but its futile to call it an arts laboratory because it's much more like a scout patrol unless everybody else joins in.

JP: This is what spoiled the main arts lab here in London.

DB: Exactly, it's the same thing all over. We've heard from other so-called art labs that it's happened all over.

JP: So, you'll carry on?

DB: Oh, I will yeah. As best as we can, yeah.

The band play FILL YOUR HEART, THE PRETTIEST STAR and CYGNET COMMITTEE

TOP OF THE POPS, BBC TV

DAVID BOWIE, 'STARMAN'

Something changed on 6 July 1972, and things would never be quite the same.

The UK in that year appears, in hindsight at least, to have been a drab place ruled by fear and violence. A series of strikes had culminated in a seven-week-long miners' walk-out, while unemployment had topped a million for the first time since the 1930s. In Northern Ireland, the Bloody Sunday killings were followed by a new wave of IRA bombings. The 'Bomb' itself, the nuclear bomb, was on people's minds as the Cold War continued and the Vietnam War escalated. Hooliganism and homophobia were ever-present, while hippie hopes of peace and love were being replaced by scepticism; the recently leaked Pentagon Papers had set in motion a chain of events in the USA that would end in Watergate.

Into this grey world, David Bowie and his colourful men from Mars landed one early evening on terrestrial TV. Their appearance seemed to come not only out of the blue but also from outer space. For anyone wanting 'out', here was their escape route – a world where you could dress as you want, look like you want, be who you want. Boy? Girl? Neither? Gay? Didn't matter.

'At the point where Bowie sang the line, "I had to phone someone, so I picked on you," he pointed directly at the camera, and I knew he was singing that line to me and everyone like me,' said Lol Tolhurst of The Cure. 'It was a call to arms that put me on the path that I would soon follow.'[3]

It wasn't just The Cure who took up the call. Among those who cite this appearance as a pivotal moment in their lives are Bono, Morrissey, Dave Gahan, Ian McCulloch, The Sex Pistols, Boy George, Marc Almond, the Human League, Neil Tennant, Holly Johnson, Siouxsie Sioux, Bauhaus, Gary Numan and pretty much the whole New Romantic movement. This one performance would shape not only the seventies, but it would also inspire those who would define the eighties.

The song talks about a starman messiah whose 'mind-blowing' message is that the world can be saved if we let the children boogie. Well, maybe a touch of the hippie era had survived. But it wasn't so much the song that captivated the young viewers, as their belief that they were in the presence of a genuinely other-worldly being; a fantastical figure who was, paradoxically, compellingly believable. The make-up, the hair, the leotard, the colours, those eyes, that alien, vampiric beauty, the flirtatious arm round Mick Ronson. Where on *Earth* did it all originate from? Watching fathers were heard to say not '*Who* is that?' but '*What* is that?'

To question your sexuality in those days would get you beaten up. To question your gender was not even on the radar. But here Bowie seemed to be questioning whether he was even a member of the same species. Overnight, a devoted army of misfits and outsiders, who now knew that to be different didn't mean to be alone, flocked to join him.

To get a sense of just *how* different this all was, here's a look at some of the other acts appearing on *Top of the Pops* that night. There was Donny Osmond with 'Puppy Love', competing with his teen heart-throb rival David Cassidy (and The Partridge Family); on the floor was the all-female and usually scantily clad dance group Pan's People, while the New Seekers' brand of bland was followed by Dr. Hook's country and western song 'Sylvia's Mother'. With acts like that, surely the question most teenagers were asking was not, 'David, where have you been?', but rather, 'David, why has it taken you so long?!'

The last surviving member of The Spiders from Mars, Woody Woodmansey, spoke about this seminal performance to the author.

*We had been in Trident Studios in Wardour Street doing the album [*The Rise and Fall of*] Ziggy Stardust and The Spiders from Mars. We were really happy and the manager took it to the record company. They said, 'We love it, but we can't release it because you haven't got a single.' I must admit none of us, including David, were thinking singles. He was very much into the concept of the album, and I guess it just didn't cross his mind. So, he said okay. On the Saturday, he was sat in his lounge and wrote 'Starman' and then called us in and said, 'What do you think?' And we said, 'Yeah, that'll do it.' [Laughs] He just knocked it out, basically.*

Top of the Pops for us was really a thing you watched religiously. As a budding musician you were thinking, this is where I want to go; it was the milestone you were headed for. You dreamed about being on it when you were 14. It didn't matter if World War Three was going on, you still watched Top of the Pops. So, when they said, 'We want you to do Top of the Pops', it was like, wow! It was a real high for all of us.

We caused a real reaction from other bands. I can't remember if it was that performance or the next one, but Status Quo were on the same night. We lined up in a little corridor before going out to the staging area and they were on the side opposite us. We were all bright rainbow colours, glittering, sparkling, and they were in denim. It was chalk and cheese, really. I remember Francis Rossi [Quo's guitarist and singer] saying, 'You guys make us feel really old!' We all just cracked up laughing.

We'd come from different musical backgrounds to David. Mick Ronson, myself and Trevor Bolder were into blues and then progressive rock from Hendrix, Led Zeppelin and Cream. Our stage gear was … well, mine was a tie-dye T-shirt, jeans with rips at the knees, patches, moccasins and long hair. That was our streetwear and stage wear. That was me being a real musician!

One day we were watching a film in David's lounge and he was scribbling away doing a little drawing. He passed it over and said, 'What do you think to this, Woody?' It was just a cartoon, kind of looked like Star Trek *figures with wrestling boots. I went 'Yeah', and passed it back to him, not realising what he was getting at. I hadn't really joined up the dots at that point.*

A couple of days later, Mick, David, Angie [Bowie's wife] and myself were in Liberty's material department in London. David was handing down these big rolls of sparkling fabric, saying 'Grab this! Grab this! Oh, this is a good one!' I naively thought we were getting curtains for the flat. [Laughs]

A day later, David brought in his friend, a designer, to measure us up and I thought, Ah, okay, this is what we're having. *It was a culture shock. Angie then came in and said, 'You've got a problem – Mick's just packed his suitcase and he's at Beckenham station now. He's going home.'*

Mick had told her, 'You've won't get me on stage wearing that! I've got friends!' [Laughs] *David said to me, 'Follow him! Say whatever you've got to say, you've got to get him back. You've got to explain it.' So, I had to walk down to the station and sit with Mick for about half an hour. I managed to convince him in the end.*

We knew we were different, but I did think, 'Is this too far? Will they get this?' You had the feeling that either it'd really take off or that you were going to get rotten tomatoes. You didn't know whether it was going to be the start of your career or the end of it!

I guess it was brave. But it was the music that was the most important thing, and we understood that if we stood there in denims and a tie-dye T-shirt playing 'Starman', it wouldn't be as effective. So, everything we did, no matter how glamorous it got, was always to push the music forward, to make it more communicative to an audience so that they could get more involved, and so it would have a greater effect than being just stood there in jeans.[4]

NATIONWIDE, BBC TV

DAVID BOWIE SPECIAL

Sometimes, the BBC could be a culturally daring organisation which championed the new despite the risk of ridicule and to ratings. At other times, it could be, well ... the BBC, the old BBC, whose old-school superiority seemed permanently stuck in some distant decade. This was one of those times.

Nationwide, one of the leading current affairs programmes of its day, decided to do a special on Bowie; the presenter of it was Bernard Falk, a hardened news journalist with a sharp turn of phrase – Falk had once served time in jail for protecting his sources. But in this special feature, he was so keen to show how 'above it all' he was that he rarely passed up an opportunity for a snide remark. His comeuppance was served from the hands of a disdainful young female fan.

Falk began his report by describing Bowie as a freak with a pasty complexion and skinny legs (Lulu once eulogised about Bowie's thighs as 'muscly and powerful', and she certainly got a close look), before he turned his patronising glare to the attendant teenagers.

Why Falk felt the need to demean Bowie and his fans was especially odd given Falk's own antecedence: he himself had been a rock'n'roller who had even played the legendary Cavern Club with his band, Tony Snow and the Blizzards, coincidentally featuring another *Nationwide* stalwart, Richard Stilgoe. Falk later renamed the band The

Bohemians. Despite now meeting a *genuine* bohemian, Falk seemed blissfully unaware that his subject might be anything other than a brief teeny-bop sensation. By acting as if he had seen it all, Falk saw almost nothing at all.

Bowie took the disdain with charm and good grace, allowing the camera to access all areas, while knowing that he was being set up for a send-up.

'The BBC did one of their traditional, "Good heavens, whatever next?"-type reports at Bournemouth,' said Bowie years later. 'Lots of confusing questioning and following me swanning around backstage, putting silly clothes on. It was all too funny.'5

But when Falk bothered to engage with his subject, the results were revealing.

'I like startling people,' Bowie tells him.

'Startling?' Falk replies, prompting Bowie to talk at length about his love of playing characters.

'Like an actor,' says Falk, hitting the nail on the head.

'Yes, I'm an actor,' agrees Bowie.

Despite the frequent condescension, this is a terrific mini-documentary. A teatime news programme had managed to catch the Ziggy Stardust phenomenon at its peak. The desperate fans, the electric performances, the make-up, the tatty, cramped dressing rooms in decrepit Victorian theatres, and Bowie himself, are all here in colourful close-up.

Within a month, Bowie had finished off Ziggy. Falk may have believed he had simply caught another manufactured flash in the pan on the verge of becoming last month's thing. Instead, he captured a priceless slice of rock history.

<Shots of Bowie getting ready backstage.>

BERNARD FALK: [*Voiceover*] A superstar of the beat age prepares to meet his public. David Bowie spends two hours before a show caressing his body with paint. Bowie is a skinny lad with a pasty complexion and ochre-dyed hair in a Teddy-boy style of 20 years ago. Yet, with a dash of make-up, he is transforming himself into an object that is worshipped by millions of girls. Outside the Winter Gardens of Bournemouth, some of those fans are arriving to pay homage to a man who has become the high priest of pop.

> *<The camera focuses on a young girl crying who came early and waited for Bowie but still managed to miss him. Another two girls then bounce into shot, absolutely thrilled at having encountered their hero, blissfully unaware of the other girl's unhappiness. They shout: 'I kissed him! I kissed his hand!' They then see the distraught figure crying and try to console her, if only briefly.>*

HAPPY GIRL: [*Sympathetically*] Oh, don't worry. [*Delightedly*] I kissed his hand!

BF: He's got thin, little legs.

UNHAPPY GIRL: He's got lovely legs!

> *<Backstage shots of Bowie getting dressed and having his nails painted.>*

BF: An ex-art student from Brixton, whose father worked for Dr Barnardo's Homes, has turned himself into a bizarre, self-constructed freak.

DB: Impromptu, isn't it?

BF: It is a sign of our times that a man with a painted face and carefully adjusted lipstick should ensure adoration of girls aged between 14 and 20.

BF: Do you get nervous?

DB: Do I get nervous? You're joking. Yeah!

> *<Falk speaks to a small huddle of young fans waiting in a corridor outside Bowie's hotel room.>*

BF: What would it mean to you to be able to go through that door?

FEMALE FAN: I'd give anything to go in there – I really would.

BF: He's just another fellow, you know.

MALE FAN: Well, no, he's not. Nobody else … could produce that music. He's a fantastic person.

BF: Isn't it a bit degrading standing outside the door when he is inside?

FANS: [*In unison*] No!

BF: Why? It's degrading for me standing outside here.

FEMALE FAN: [*Annoyed*] Why don't you go in then?!

BF: Don't you find … I mean, why do you stand for it?

FEMALE FAN: [*Contemptuously*] Why do you think?!

> *<Footage of David Bowie prepares to take the stage in May of 1973. His 1973* Ziggy Stardust *tour promoted the albums* The Rise and Fall of Ziggy Stardust and The Spiders from Mars *and* Aladdin Sane. *The setlist from this tour prominently featured songs from these two albums, among others.>*

BF: [*Voiceover*] In reality, he's more of a showman than a freak. Hollywood razzmatazz has come to the world of beat.

<Falk speaks to Bowie backstage.>

DB: Most of the reasons that I do what I do is because I just like startling people.

BF: Startling?

DB: Yeah, it's something to do. [*Laughs*] England has a marvellous habit of being able to dissipate everything through this marvellous media, and long hair quickly got dissipated. I used to be able to stop traffic quite easily by just walking down the street, no more than that, just because I had long hair. This is my life really, writing or performing. There's not much else I want. It's the biggest kick I know. I know there's drugs, and you get a different kind of buzz off those, but stage is something else, it's partaking of people. I'm very much a character when I go on stage, I feel.

BF: Like an actor?

DB: Yeah, I believe in my part all the way down the line. Right the way down. But I do play it for all it's worth because that's the way I do my stage thing. That's part of what Bowie's supposedly all about. I'm an actor.

<Footage of Bowie leaving performance venue.>

BF: [*Voiceover*] It's worth wondering, though, what the beat age will spawn next, when someone like David Bowie isn't even freakish enough to shock us anymore.

CRACKED ACTOR, BBC TV

A DOCUMENTARY BY ALAN YENTOB FOR OMNIBUS

This fly-on-the-wall documentary, one of the first of its kind, not only kick-started the career of arts doyen Alan Yentob, it also created a new type of arts show. But what started out as a fly-on-the-wall feature quickly became a 'fly-in-my-milk' riddle. Bowie gazed down at the struggling insect in his milk carton as he contemplated the impact of America on his life. 'He's an alien body like me,' Bowie says of the perhaps real, perhaps imagined fly, 'soaking up' a new world. A stranger in a strange land. But the metaphor is even more apposite than Bowie intended. The fly in the carton is not, of course, 'soaking up' the milk, it's trapped in the stuff and is drowning. Unless it finds a way out, it'll die. Los Angeles would, indeed, eventually overwhelm Bowie. He would overdose several times and, only by good fortune, would he still be alive a year later to escape the carton's confines and make it to Berlin.

The singer is filmed in a frenzy of creativity during his 1974 *Diamond Dogs* tour of America, which would rip up the live performance rule book. Madonna credits the tour for awakening her to the importance of theatricality. Even Michael Jackson, not someone you might expect to be overly influenced by Bowie, went to all the singer's LA shows and quizzed Bowie afterwards on everything, from the set designs to choreography. Throw in some astonishingly frank footage of

Bowie's paranoia and sniffling, more than hinting at his cocaine addiction, and add Britain's most talented arts film director, and you have not just a great film made about a rock star, but also one of the most intimately revealing and influential arts documentaries ever made.

Cameron Crowe, a *Rolling Stone* reporter who would go on to become an Oscar-winning director, described Bowie as 'The most generous and exciting interview subject that I was ever allowed time with.'[6] Bowie was to gain a reputation as being difficult and evasive, but the evidence here points to the contrary; not only are his answers humorous, enlightening and original, they also contain an honesty that is disarming and unexpected.

This is also the documentary that launched Bowie's acting career. In what was surely the most obvious casting choice in movie history, Nic Roeg picked Bowie to play his alien in *The Man Who Fell to Earth* after watching *Cracked Actor*. Roeg loved the singer's skeletal look, different-coloured eyes and orange-flecked hair, not to mention the fact that Bowie had already auditioned for over a year by playing a space alien on stage. But what swung it for Roeg was something more subtle. 'I noticed the artificial voice,' the director said. 'It was English, but you couldn't tell exactly where it was from.'[7]

Much has been made of Bowie's frail mental health in LA, from his paranoia and hallucinations to an obsession with dark forces. Physically, too, Bowie was looking unwell; his thin frame had turned cadaverous, and his skin would soon take on the yellow hue of the wax figures in the desert museum he would laugh at in this documentary. Jaundice is a symptom of both anorexia and heavy cocaine use, a result of liver damage. It would be liver cancer that would eventually kill Bowie. So, perhaps after all, the darker meaning of Bowie's metaphor was correct: the milk – Los Angeles, the drugs, this whole period of his life – would eventually get its fly.

<Footage of Bowie being interviewed on CBS News by reporter Wayne Satz.>

WAYNE SATZ: I just wonder if you get tired of being outrageous?

DAVID BOWIE: I don't think I'm outrageous at all.

WS: At all?

DB: No.

WS: Do you describe yourself as ordinary? What adjective would you use?

DB: Um … ah … um … David Bowie.

WS: Aha. Well, I'm reluctant to make the judgement about what category you fit into.

DB: Good. Good.

WS: Oh no, I wouldn't be that pretentious, but maybe you have a feeling yourself?

DB: No, I'm really very old-fashioned. I like moving from one area of writing or performing to another … to keep me excited, to keep me interested, to keep the people who come to see me or buy records interested and excited as well.

<Footage of Wayne Satz concluding his report by telling viewers, 'If you didn't understand that, don't feel badly, because I certainly didn't. David, I know you're watching tonight with the BBC film crew, and it's wonderful to have your old-fashioned entertainment around until The Beatles get back together, but it sure would be nice to talk to somebody who's not being evasive and discussing riddles.'>

<Footage of Bowie having a plaster cast taken of his face and then performing onstage as Ziggy.>

ALAN YENTOB: [Voiceover] And then, at the height of his fame, in front of thousands of screaming fans, David Bowie killed him off … Two years ago, he came to America and buried Ziggy somewhere between New York and Hollywood.

<Bowie is filmed in the back of a limo driving through the desert of the American southwest. Aretha Franklin's '(You Make Me Feel Like) A Natural Woman' is playing in the car. Bowie is having fun by singing along to the backing vocals in an exaggerated fashion. He is drinking from a large carton of milk.>

AY: Since you've been in America you seem to have picked up on a lot of the idioms and themes of American music and American culture. How's that happened?

DB: There's a fly floating around in my milk and he's … he's a foreign body in it, you see, and he's getting a lot of milk. [Laughs] … That's kind of how I felt – a foreign body and I couldn't help but soak it up, you know. I hated it when I first came here, I couldn't see any of it.

<Distracted, Bowie looks out of the car window.>

DB: Look, a wax museum! How do you have a bleedin' wax museum out in the desert? You'd think it would melt, wouldn't you? [Laughs]

AY: What made all of this important to you? I mean, with your background, why were you intrigued by all of this?

DB: Um … it filled a vast expanse of my imagination. I was always pretty imaginative and the imagination can dry up wherever you're living in England, often, if there's nothing to keep it going. It just supplied a need in me … America became a myth-land for me. I think every kid goes through it eventually, but I just got on to it earlier.

> *<The audience arrive for his LA concert. Among them is Elizabeth Taylor. Bowie performs 'Cracked Actor' on stage, draped in a cape, holding a skull which he vigorously kisses. After the show, he is shown in the backseat of his limo. A police siren wails nearby.>*

DB: I hope we're not stopped. Is there anything behind us? [*Sniffs noticeably*]

OFF-CAMERA FEMALE: No.

DB: There's an underlying unease here, definitely. You can feel it in every avenue, but it's very calm. And it's a kind of superficial calmness that they've developed to underplay the fact that it's … there's a lot of high pressure here as it's a very big entertainment industry area. And you get this feeling of unease with everybody. The first time that it really came home to me what a kind of strange fascination it has, is I came in on the train … on the earthquake, and the earthquake was actually taking place when the train came in. And the hotel that we were in … just tremored every few minutes. I mean, it was just a revolting feeling. And ever since then I've always been very aware of how dubious a position it is to stay here for any length of time. [*Laughs*]

> *<Bowie is filmed at a table using scissors to cut up handwritten words and phrases.>*

DB: This is the way I do cut-ups. I don't know if it's like the way Brion Gysin does his or Burroughs does his, I don't know. But this is the way I do it. I've used this method only on a couple of actual songs. What I've used it for, more than anything else, is igniting anything that might be in my imagination, and you can often come up with very interesting attitudes to look into. I tried doing it with diaries and things, and I was finding out amazing things about me and what I'd done and where I was going. And a lot of the things that I'd done, it seemed that it would predict things about the future or tell me a lot about the past. It's really quite an astonishing thing. I suppose it's a very western tarot, I don't know. Anyway, let's see what happens.

<Bowie, dressed in a 'Ghouster' suit with shoulder pads, sings 'Moonage Daydream' on stage.>

DB: I never wanted to be a rock'n'roll star. [*Adopts a Cockney accent*] 'I never, honest guv, I wasn't even there.' But I was, you see, I was there. That's what happened. No … no, it excited me just because it was there, that was enough. I mean, personally, I was playing saxophone and I was trying to make up my mind whether I wanted to play rock'n'roll or jazz and as I wasn't very good at jazz and I could fake it pretty well on rock'n'roll, so I played rock'n'roll. And I found I enjoyed writing. The only thing I was ever really good at at school was composition. Not grammatically, I was always terrible on grammar, but I could always write better stories than anybody else.

<Bowie walks around an empty gas station as the limo is filled up. We hear 'Aladdin Sane'.>

DB: It was my initial fascination with mime and expressing things with facial movements and body-talk rather than articulating things.

I mean, I'd done as much articulating as I'd felt was necessary with the actual songs, and if I was going to present them in more than a single dimension, I mean, if I was going to present them visually, then I wanted my body or my muscles to play an active part in the performance. It's funny that the same, very similar masks to the kabuki schtick were used with the English mummers' theatre. It's very strange that they should come up with very similar designs for faces. I don't know what the link would have been, but there must have been some link.

> *<In a hotel room, Bowie unclips a large trunk and picks up a vinyl black jumpsuit with white stripes, whose legs balloon out to either side, one of his most famous Kansai Yamamoto costumes.>*

DB: That is kind of from the *Aladdin Sane* album. Aladdin Sane was a schizophrenic. That's counted for lots of the … why there were so many costume changes, because he had so many personalities that each, as far as I was concerned, each costume change was a different facet of personality. This is, likewise, another Japanese costume. [*Holds up a silk kimono-like outfit*] These are all Japanese … most of this stuff is Japanese, most of my clothes are Japanese. I've always been fond of kabuki-style clothes. That's another Aladdin Sane thing. [*Picks up one of his costumes with a lightning bolt on*] I found a lightning bolt really represented him. This was the first Japanese costume that I got. Originally worn by a woodland creature. That's why it has funny little animals on it. It says in there, 'Yamamoto Kansai, dry cleaning only'. [*Laughs*]

> *<Bowie puts on his own eye make-up backstage.>*

DB: More than anything else I saw that a lot of my songs were very illustrative and picturesque, and I felt there were other ways of performing them onstage. I was never very confident of my voice, you see, as a singer. So, I thought, rather than just sing them, which would probably bore the pants off everybody, I would like to kind of portray the songs rather than just sing them. That's really how it started … wanting to portray the material I was writing. I always found that my material … I felt that it was more three-dimensional. I wanted to give it dimension. I wanted to give it some other dimension other than that of just being a song. [*Asks person off camera*] What time is it?

OFF-CAMERA MALE: It's eight o'clock on the nose.

DB: Right. Did anybody say how long I've got?

OFF-CAMERA MALE: They said five minutes, ten minutes ago. [*Laughs*]

DB: Did they? It's a quarter-past-eight start. [*Pretends to fall asleep*]

> <*Bowie performs 'Time' on stage. He is then filmed sitting on a couch, perhaps back at the hotel, as he answers Yentob's questions.*>

AY: You saw for a long period, or for certainly over the last couple of years, a lot of kids sort of aping you almost, or looking very like you, so that they would dress up and put things on very similar to you.

DB: Yeah.

AY: How did you feel about that?

DB: Well, a lot of it came about starting off like that, but over the last year or so it's changing, in as much that they're finding out things maybe nothing to do with me but the idea of finding another character within themselves. I mean, if I've been at all responsible for people finding more characters in themselves than they originally thought they had, then I'm pleased, because that's something I feel very strongly about, that one isn't totally what one has been conditioned to think one is, that there are many facets of the personality which a lot of us have trouble finding and some of us do find too quickly.

DB: Do you know that feeling you get in a car when somebody's accelerating very fast and you're not driving? And you get that 'Uh' thing in your chest when you're being forced backwards and you think 'Uh', and you're not sure whether you like it or not? It's that kind of feeling. That's what success was like. The first thrust of being totally unknown to being what seemed to be very quickly known. It was very frightening for me, and coping with it was something that I tried to do. And that's what happened. That was me coping. Some of those albums were me coping, taking it all very seriously, I was.

AY: Wasn't it a rather dangerous thing to do, to play the roles?

DB: Well, I didn't know. When you're that mixed up – and I've been mixed up, man. [*Laughs*] I mean, really it was … one doesn't know. One half of me is putting a concept forward and the other half is trying to sort out my own emotions. And a lot of my space creations are, in fact, facets of me I have now since discovered. [*Laughs*] But I wouldn't even admit that to myself at the time. That I would put everything … just make everything a little kind of upfront personification of how I felt about things. Ziggy would be something and it would relate to me now, I find. And Major Tom in 'Space Oddity' was something, Aladdin Sane. They were all facets of me, and I wasn't really … I got lost at one point. I couldn't decide whether I was writing the characters or whether the characters were writing me. Or, whether we were all one and the same.

AY: Would you say that Ziggy was a monster?

DB: Mmm. [*Nods*] Oh, he certainly was. When I first wrote Ziggy …
I mean, it was just an experiment. It was an exercise for me, and he
really grew sort of out of proportion, I must admit. Got much bigger
than I thought Ziggy was going to be. I didn't ever see Ziggy as big.
Ziggy just overshadowed everything.

<Bowie sings 'Ziggy Stardust' on stage.>

AY: How much of Ziggy's death had to do with his own personality
or with the circumstances in which he existed?

DB: Yeah, it was … really it was his own personality being unable
to cope with the circumstances he found himself in, which is being
an almighty prophet-like superstar rocker who found he didn't know
what to do with it once he got it. Which is … it's an archetype really,
it's the definitive rock'n'roll star. It often happens and I was just
trying to document it as such.

<Bowie sings 'My Death' followed by 'Rock 'n' Roll Suicide' on stage.>

DB: Yes, I had a kind of … a kind of strange, psychosomatic death-
wish thing, I think. But that's because I was so lost in Ziggy, I think,
again. It was all the schizophrenia.

<Bowie is tied up on stage as he sings 'Diamond Dogs'.>

AY: It did look as if it was the ghost of Ziggy Stardust you were
tying up?

DB: Yes, exactly. That's what happened. It was trying to get rid of

the damn character that was kind of following me around. And …
hopefully … you see, I'm very … I'm very happy with Ziggy, I think
he was a very successful character and I think I played him very well.
But I … I'm glad I'm me now. [*Laughs*] 'I'm glad I'm me now.' My
God, I can trot 'em out!

> <*In a studio, Bowie sings vocals to a soul song with Luther Vandross and Ava Cherry.*>

AY: [*Voiceover*] So, David Bowie becomes a soul singer.

> <*Bowie performs 'John, I'm Only Dancing' on stage.*>

DAVID BOWIE, BBC RADIO

A FOUR-PART DOCUMENTARY BY STUART GRUNDY

Who, or perhaps what, was David Bowie? That question weaves itself through this lengthy radio documentary, which contains new interviews with Bowie and his closest collaborators. Bowie says he considered himself a short-story writer; producer Tony Visconti says the records were simply a means for Bowie to get into movies, while drummer Woody Woodmansey saw the man in front of him not as a singer but as an actor. Elsewhere, Bowie talks about being a frustrated painter, while Grundy delves into Bowie's role as a Svengali to Lou Reed, Iggy Pop, Mott the Hoople and others. One thing Bowie insists he is not is a musician, let alone a rock star. 'Rock'n'roll is quite fun and everything, but I'm only using it as a medium,' he says.

While most singers of his age (29 at this time) seemed to have given up or given in, Bowie still appears to be on the threshold of something new. Here, he is on the verge of heading off to Germany and a new world of sound and experimentation, to create yet another version of himself. Touchingly, Bowie seems to have no idea at all that in a few months he'll be jetting off to a new land and life. But what he does have is the key to his next album. 'There's no experimentation when I go in the studio,' he says. 'But the next album, I'm going to open myself up to experimentation and we'll see what happens.' *Low* will have no grand theme, there'll be no overriding, character-driven personality, and lyrics

47

will take a backseat. This will be the first time he will overtly use the studio itself as an instrument.

As for the question at the heart of this documentary, Bowie ends by saying, 'I think it's still very hard for anybody to pin down David Bowie, which I think is lovely. It's exactly what I wanted.'

PART 1: LOVE YOU TILL TUESDAY

> *<The documentary starts in 1965 with a struggling Davy Jones and one*
> *of Bowie's first champions, producer Tony Hatch.>*

TONY HATCH: He really must have been the first of the singer-songwriters … Bowie was essentially a singer-songwriter-creator right from the beginning. Even if we used studio musicians, he would still have all the ideas and I'd probably just put them down on paper and give them to the musicians … There was no way I would have got a hit with him because he simply wasn't ready. I believe that for every great artist that happens, they have a time … But I believe also I was a stepping stone on the way for him, and that makes me proud.

KEN PITT, Bowie's manager: I went to the Marquee … and I suddenly realised that this was someone I had been looking for, for a long time. I have a great interest in theatre and film, and I always wanted to manage somebody who I could help build up and who would eventually be something more than what I've always called a 'guitar cowboy'. Just by watching, you could tell there was something magical going on – just a movement of a hand, or the way he tilted his head – that was something I'd never seen in any other pop singer.

DAVID BOWIE: I never knew, really, if I wanted to be a short-story writer. A singer really was the last thing I wanted to be. I knew I wanted to write words down in some kind of either poem form or prose form, and I wrote them as little stories. It seemed quite easy to set them to music, so they became songs. I guess if I hadn't had any musical inspiration of any kind, I would have been a straight writer; I would have written novels, I think.

TONY HALL, Decca Records promotion head: I must say, I did flip because this guy had such a different sound, a different approach ... People knew this guy just had something different to offer.

DB: I don't think I've ever produced an album like that [his first LP, released in June 1967]. I contribute an awful lot of the ideas and I'm a bit of, [*adopts a Yorkshire accent*] 'Well, if I hear it, I know what I like.' Over the last couple of years, I've got quite technical, and I know what things do. But up until *Diamond Dogs* and including *Diamond Dogs*, I didn't have a clue what anything did on a board. But the sound concept was very much mine, all the time. The only one I've been puzzled with was *Space Oddity*. It's very hard to know, actually, how much anybody sort of ... I think it was a conglomerate production between Gus [Dudgeon], myself and – Gus is really very good, Gus is an excellent producer, he turned out to be really good – and Paul Buckmaster, of course. I think Paul was a very important part of that period. Paul is the one who took me out of the story-writing thing and introduced me to sound and the visual aspects of songs.

LOVE YOU TILL TUESDAY

DB: It got some air play, as we say in the biz, but I didn't get any people buying me and I wasn't asked to perform, so I suppose in that respect, it was a bit of a failure. But the idea of writing short stories, I think that was quite novel at the time, excuse the pun. [*Laughs*] It set me up. I was quite satisfied with the way things were going. I mean, I hadn't found any voice style and I hadn't found any way to perform. I was very much in the Tony Newley thing, mainly because I came from London and it seemed more natural. It was much a combination of Tony Newley and Syd Barrett, who were both, I thought, A1 English artists in their own things.

KP: David thought he would change his tactics, and he said, 'I'm going to write a lot of rubbish – this way we will get on the charts.' But all the new songs were turned down and Bowie left Decca … We just couldn't get a recording contract … He used to get discouraged … I've known him to break down in tears at some of the rejections he got. Not through big-headedness but just sheer frustration, 'What do I have to do?'

DB: I was in a mixed media [*Laughs*] group, which means that one of us could dance, another one could sing and one had some rotten poetry, and we put it all together and went underground. It was called Feathers. And the girl was Hermione Farthingale, who I fell in love with. I'm glad I fell in love because it gave rise to lots of songs. The guy was Hutch [John Hutchinson] on guitar. I don't know what Hutch is doing anymore. And it was fairly successful. It was very influenced by Lindsay Kemp and the mime company.

• • •

DB: Most of the time it was earning a few pennies at the Roundhouse. I mean it was fun, it was very Notting Hill Gate, we just lived on what we could get. And we all lived in one room in some place in – where was it, now? Oh, yeah, we found a classy area somewhere in Chelsea. We had somebody's room. We borrowed a room off a rich friend of ours, a patron, who helped us out with costumes and stuff. Hermione and I had a room there, and Hutch had a room with some friends in Notting Hill Gate.

<Grundy describes how producer Tony Visconti came into the picture.>

DB: I met him [Visconti] up in the offices of Denny Cordell. Denny was sort of a friend, and he was producing a few artists. Tony had been brought over to England to do the string arrangements for

Denny Laine and his electric string band, and I met him while he was working in that capacity, and he said, 'Hey, I've started doing some producing.' He said that Denny had given him some jobs to do, like writing some more string parts for Move and Joe Cocker. And we got together and we became friends first. We didn't talk much about music. I was still wondering if I had found God as a Buddhist, or whether I wanted to be a rock'n'roll star. So, we had a lot to talk about … East and West, and Tony was, [*Laughs and adopts a northern accent*] well into the Tibetan thing, you know. So, we used to spend crazy evenings, a lot of them with Buckmaster as well – Paul. And out of that, somewhere along the line, Tony said, 'Listen, you've got some funny little songs, why don't I record them?' And I said, 'Yeah, that'd be great.' And then I played him 'Space Oddity' and he said, 'No, I'm not doing that, it's terrible.' [*Laughs*] And so I said, 'Oh well, do you mind if I go and ask someone else to do it with me?' And he said sure, so we did that. And then I did the rest of the album with Tony, which I think hurt Gus [Dudgeon, producer] at the time. Though I didn't mean … sorry Gus, I didn't mean to do that, but I was friends with Tony, you see, and I didn't know you very well. You were petty bourgeois, you see! You had an apartment! [*Laughs*] If things had gone another way, I might have stayed with Gus. I might have been Elton John, Mum!

> <*Grundy describes how Bowie frittered away the opportunity 'Space Oddity' had given him. Bowie's discipline waned, as he shot off in all directions again: miming, meditating, making music and trying not to miss a moment.*>

DB: All this wild, hectic experience was squeezed into two or three years. [19]71 is when I got down to seriously writing and trying not to diversify too much. I mean, I was just diversifying all over the place. I would try to get involved in anything that I felt was a useful tool for an artistic medium, from writing songs to putting on arts-lab shows and street theatre. I was trying to be a one-man revolution. [*Laughs*]

PART 2: CHANGES

DB: When I had that *Space Oddity* record out, I was still a little Cockney Dylan, and I was going out into ballrooms and playing to pretty rock'n'roll audiences and the outcome was not what I expected. I didn't expect any outcome, really, but what I got was cigarettes and things. It wasn't nice. [*Adopts an upset tone and laughs*] It wasn't like they said it was in the papers! So, I stopped doing it. I just gave up for a bit.

STUART GRUNDY: [*Voiceover*] Bowie releases another album. Again, it's a flop. He begins to distance himself from manager Ken Pitt and releases 'The Prettiest Star', another flop.

DB: I did that ['The Prettiest Star'] with old Boley. Marc [Bolan] was just going through the stumbling of learning to play lead guitar, and I liked some of the mistakes he was making. And I asked him if he'd come along and play lead guitar on it. I like guitarists who make a lot of mistakes, and Marc was making a lot of mistakes [*Laughs*] in those days, and he produced a beautiful solo and we lost the tapes. It only came out the once. It was my first slipped disc. [*Laughs*] It came out after 'Space Oddity'. But the tapes disappeared, the master tapes.

SG: [*Voiceover*] By now, Angie Bowie has come on the scene, and Visconti has joined them at Haddon Hall (a Victorian villa in Beckenham) along with a band from Hull called The Rats. The have their first gig at the BBC for John Peel.

DB: We rehearsed in the morning and did the show very badly. And then a couple of weeks later, we started working as a band called Hype and we did the Roundhouse. Oooh, we *bombed* at the Roundhouse. Marc Bolan was the only person who clapped. He stood in the front with … he'd bought one of those [*Laughs*] funny little plastic … like Caesar's, the Romans', chest plates with elastic bands – he'd got it from Woolworths – and a funny helmet and all his Syd Barrett hair coming out, and he stood at the front and clapped. And quite rightly so. We were all wearing Dan Dare outfits and Superman stuff. I don't know what we were doing there. We were right out of it. It was all *Man Who Sold the World* stuff. Sound-wise, it fitted in with the Roundhouse, but visually, of course, it was right up the wall.

<Grundy describes Bowie as fickle, and Bowie agrees.>

DB: Really, it's an integral part of what I do now, but it's honed itself a little and it's a little more sophisticated, I guess. And a bit more mature, but I've still got that same erratic, faddy thing about me; I mean, I still get turned on by something only for a couple of weeks and I drop it. I've forgotten about it a couple of weeks later. I went crazy over Man Ray photographs, at one time, black-and-white photographs. That lasted about a month. For me, it was the only thing. And I threw everything away. I started taking Man Ray pictures and then I changed my mind, and I always supported myself with a reason why I changed my mind. But now I realise that I just change my mind a lot. I always tried to give it a reason before, and I didn't realise that I'm just by nature a very flighty person. I get turned off and on things all the time, very quickly. And having accepted that, it's a lot easier to live with it. And everybody laughs. The band know what I'm like, 'Oh Bowie's on a new kick this week. Oh, he's always got something. Hey, this is great.' But I know I'm not going to have a sustained interest with it, except with people; there's people that mean a lot to me.

SG: [*Voiceover*] Bowie was going through a lengthy period of re-evaluation. Was he coming to any conclusions, though?

DB: I thought, 'Well, here I am. I'm a bit mixed up creatively. I've got all these things going on I like doing at once, on stage, or whatever. I'm not quite sure if I'm a mime, or a songwriter or a singer, or do I want to go back to painting again. Why am I doing any of these things anyway?' And I realised it was because I wanted to be well known, basically. [*Laughs*] And I wanted to be thought of someone who was very much a trendy person rather than a trend. I didn't want to be a trend, I wanted to be the instigator of new ideas. I wanted to turn people on to new things and new perspectives. I always wanted to be that catalytic kind of thing. And so, I had to govern everything around that. And I just poured myself in and decided that to use the easiest medium to start off with, which was rock'n'roll, and then add bits and pieces to it over the years, so that, really, by the end of it, I was my own medium. I mean that'll happen, hopefully, one day. That's why I do it all, to become a medium. [*Laughs*]

SG: [*Voiceover*] *The Man Who Sold the World* was being created in the early months of 1971. It was destined to be the least successful of all his records from a sales point of view.

DB: It was nightmare, that album. I hated the actual process of making it. I'd never done an album with that kind of professionalism, and that scared me a lot. I felt it invalid somehow. I wished we were doing it on four-track at the time and we were on eight tracks, [*Laughs*] and it all seemed too glossy. Also, the subject matter was very telling for me. It was all family problems and analogies put into science-fiction form.

SG: [*Voiceover*] It seemed a more mature exploration of the moods and themes of earlier years, when he first encountered the German philosophers.

DB: I was still going through the thing where I was pretending I was Nietzsche. [*Laughs*] My Nietzschean effort. A lot of them come out of trying to simplify books that I'd read for myself, and try to understand them and put them in … it was probably [*Thus Spoke*] *Zarathustra* that I'd read, or *Beyond Good and Evil*, and I tried to translate it into my own terms to understand it, and so 'Supermen' came out of that. It was pre-fascist. It wasn't a fascist song, but it was a very much a German Romantic thing.

SG: [*Voiceover*] Once the album had been made, the group broke up. Tony Visconti, too, had had enough and decided to concentrate on Marc Bolan. But Bowie had a surprise up his voluminous sleeve for all of them, though. When the album came out, its cover featured him, back and front, long-haired and wearing a dress.

DB: Well, that was a stab at being a Pre-Raphaelite. [*Laughs*] That was my [Dante] Gabriel Rossetti look. But it wasn't worth telling anybody that, so I said it was drag. [*Laughs*]

TONY VISCONTI: He seemed perfectly at ease and almost a look of relief on his face that he was doing all this. It's more being outrageous than being bisexual. He always wanted to be outrageous, and in fact he invited a lot of outrageous-looking people to our flat, which was another reason why we left, because I couldn't put up with [*Laughs*] a constant parade of freaks coming in and out of our house. But as soon as someone would leave … David would rush to the loo and get a brush and start combing his hair in that style to see how it would look on him. He was definitely searching for an image in those days.

SG: [*Voiceover*] All David needed was for somebody to come along and point him in a more positive direction.

DB: Somebody did come along and grab me by the empty wallet and said, 'I'm Tony Defries and I'm going to make you a star.' [*Laughs loudly*] I said, 'Oh yeah?' And he did! So they say. I've read about it. [*Laughs*] Yeah, that's when Tony Defries entered my life … and me wallet. [*Laughs*]

SG: [*Voiceover*] Tony Defries was just what Bowie needed: a manager with big ideas and an uncomplicated attitude towards success. With record deals renegotiated, Bowie was quickly into the new album, one which reflected a new-found confidence and was to break a two-year run of failure. Mick and Woody came down from Hull again, and brought with them Trevor Bolder. Things were underway at last.

DB: A very optimistic album that was, *Hunky Dory*. I'd just moved to Haddon Hall, in the borough of Beckenham. Angie was with me, and I collected all my friends and, I think, I'd just got back from America. Tony Defries had appeared on the scene and everything seemed all systems go after the struggle of *The Man Who Sold the World*. *Hunky Dory* was the album that said, 'Yes, alright, I understand what I've got to do now.'

CHANGES

SG: [*Voiceover*] 'Changes', one of the most significant of Bowie's songs. It remains the first true revelation of his very nature: the butterfly at his best, acknowledging the conflictions within himself.

DB: That's the kind of song where I was putting it all together in its different parts and I realised I was a sack of things.

SG: [*Voiceover*] Another of the songs on that album was originally released by Peter Noone, 'Oh! You Pretty Things'. Peter's version was rather lightweight compared to the one which ended up on *Hunky Dory*.

DB: 'A hand coming through the crack in the sky' is more what it's about than 'pretty things'. It's the more down-to-earth me looking at the poseur, David Bowie. A lot of the songs do deal with some kind of schizophrenia or alternating ID problems, and 'Pretty Things' was one of them. The crack in the sky, according to Jung, to see cracks in the sky is not really [*Laughs*] quite on. The sky, for me, represented something solid that could be cracked. I still had the dome over the world, which again I found out was just my own repressions. Hmm, yeah. I haven't been to an analyst, no. My parents went, and my brothers and sisters and whatever, aunts and uncles and cousins, and they did that and they ended up in a much worse state, so I stayed away. I thought I'd write my problems out, really.

OH! YOU PRETTY THINGS

SG: [*Voiceover*] What with insanity, extraterrestrial strangers come to stay and everything else on *Hunky Dory*, you'd think that Bowie had played all his cards. But his biggest was yet to come. Two or three weeks after the album, he casually mentioned to a reporter he was bisexual. Always had been. It earned him huge headlines.

DB: Yeah, [*Laughs*] oh yeah. [*Adopts a Yorkshire accent*] That went down very well, didn't it! It was a bit of a throwaway. But I stuck to my guns. [*Laughs*]

KP: What people don't know is that one of the first major interviews David gave was to a gay magazine called *Jeremy*. In those days, you didn't do such a thing … David was the first.

DB: *Jeremy* magazine, good God, yeah. There were about three copies out, then it closed down. I remember Jeremy. Yeah, I did interviews with him. So, it was an old statement by the time it was printed. Yes, it was … I think the one thing about that statement was at least it was a tag that people could identify me with. It gave me a category, anyway. So, I suppose it helped me in that aspect. Unfortunate … [*Laughs and adopts an upper-class female Scottish-type accent*] because there's so much more to me than that! No, I think it was … in time, it just … God knows how that all happened … I really don't know. I know when I got to America it meant a lot more, it was a much heavier statement over there, it became radical and very political, in a way, because they were going through the gay lib thing. For the first couple of years, I had a heavy battle because it was hard to tell people that if that whole bisexuality thing was a part of me, it wasn't necessarily part of the work I did, and that because I wore funny clothes on stage didn't mean I was into drag, that they weren't drag clothes. But Americans [*Adopts an amused tone*] don't appreciate the subtleties of dress as they do in Europe. I mean Europe, if you wear some funny clothes, then it's seen as being part of the character you're playing, but in America, especially at that time, if you wore anything that wasn't jeans, it was drag. That was the hardest problem I had in the States, trying to convince people that because I was bisexual, it didn't mean that everything I wrote about or did meant that it was all gay, but that that bisexual thing was part of my private life and none of their business. [*Laughs*] That the songs and the albums and the stage performances were what I was all about. But it took a long time. Eventually, I mean, that was the biggest obstacle I had, was getting away from being put up there as some kind of token gay performer.

RICK WAKEMAN, keyboardist: I remember coming away from this [playing on *Hunky Dory*] raving about it. It had to be one of the hugest albums of all time. It had to be. There just wasn't even a weakness on it.

SG: [*Voiceover*] 'Life on Mars?' was the impatient, bored finger-drumming Bowie waiting for something to happen, but still a little unsure of who or what he was.

DB: I couldn't come through at all. I didn't know who to be when I got out there. That was the big struggle … I was wondering whether I should try to be me or, if I couldn't cope with that, then make up some people and would I be them easier? And it was much easier to be somebody else, so I was somebody else and then it worked better. So, therefore, I must have been an actor, I thought. Well, I'll be an actor. I'll say I'm an actor, and that gives me reason for changing. And so, I said I was an actor and then I came up with all these different guises and that seems to be how it evolved. And now I seem to be finding it much easier to be nearer some kind of me. But I wonder, I don't know. I don't think so. Maybe I'm still acting up there.

SG: [*Voiceover*] Back in 1972 it was the gay tag he was trying, at least in part, to shed, that accelerated him into adopting another role. One that he created and defined.

DB: I wanted to be anybody but me, I think. And that's how Ziggy got started, you see. So, I thought, well if I don't like being David Jones, then we'll think of somebody else to be for a bit. And we came up with Ziggy.

PART 3: THE JEAN GENIE

SG: [*Voiceover*] Within six months of his *Hunky Dory* album coming out, David Bowie had another album, *Ziggy Stardust*. Bowie's imagination, once sidetracked, now homed in on a successful trail. One of his motive forces, so perfectly expressed in 'Life on Mars?', was boredom.

DB: I never get bored to a point where there's nowhere else to turn. I'm very good at being my own salvation. I can always pick up on something else that'll keep me interested. But it does make for some rapid, quick changes, and that keeps it all alive for me.

SG: [*Voiceover*] Ziggy Stardust, the archetypal rock'n'roller, a perfect skin for the actor Bowie to take refuge under.

DB: That's where the thing about poseur comes from in the English rock'n'roll … that it's the artist's stance. In America they really are rock'n'rollers, they come straight out of factories and play guitars. But in England, you just tamper around with rock'n'roll and use it for something. I guess I was one of the first to come out and say, 'Yeah, I'm using rock'n'roll, but it's not my life,' like it is to an American rock'n'roller. Rock'n'roll is quite fun and everything. But I'm only using it as a medium. I think that's just a typical attitude of the English rock'n'roller, but I actually voiced it. I don't think it had been really voiced before then, that rock'n'roll is used by the English, not by the musicians – none of us are really musicians, we are all old ex-painters and beatniks and things.

TREVOR BOLDER, bassist: Then he started dragging us downstairs to a girl, Zoe, to try costumes on. [*Laughs*] It slowly worked into a band with costumes … if he'd pushed it at us, I think we might have pulled away.

DB: It was Ziggy Stardust and The Spiders from Mars and somehow, along the lines, The Spiders got attached to David Bowie. So, then the confusion set in about who was Ziggy and who was David Bowie, and even I didn't quite understand how all that happened. Suddenly, I had a band called The Spiders and I was willing to go with it because it worked on stage and I liked the ambiguity of not being quite able to separate personas. Much like Nic Roeg's film, *The Man Who Fell To Earth*, it's the ominous sort of enigma of split personality and which side is which. And having half the creation – The Spiders, who were a figment of the imagination – actually working with a real character, David Bowie, on stage, that poses a serious sort of head problem.

SG: [*Voiceover*] Oh, complications again! All we can safely assume is that The Spiders knew who they were.

DB: They played the part perfectly. I actually sort of picked them for that. They were, at the time, the number one spacey punk-rock band. They were absolutely archetypes, all of them. Everyone was absolutely right … right out of a cartoon book. But I couldn't sort of encourage them to change their roles because they weren't natural-born actors. But that's fine; they were great musicians.

SG: [*Voiceover*] Just how much of David Bowie went on stage?

DB: There's no comparison between David Bowie on stage and David Bowie off. They're hopelessly different. It's a good release valve, safety valve, for me. I'm quite a cold-emotion sort of figure on stage, but there's always that little last saving grace somewhere that I can … I don't know what it is. Is it a nagging fear that one's not being accepted? And I become sort of vaudevillian, and then I'm back to this sort of shop dummy, mannequin, strange white light, supermarket thing again. The perfect consumer's product. It's give and take. [*Laughs*]

SG: [*Voiceover*] Was he then living out his fantasies on stage?

DB: On stage, I don't like the idea of living at all. I can't stand that concept. You can't go on stage and live, it's absolutely false, all the way. That's what I like about it. I can't stand the premise of going on in jeans and being real; that's impossible. There's not one man that can actually believe that he's giving them life, going up there with a pair of jeans on and a guitar and looking as real as he can be in front of 18,000 people, I mean, it's not normal. [*Laughs*]

SG: [*Voiceover*] Normal, an adjective that doesn't normally spring to mind when talking of David Bowie. The Bowie who claimed he never wanted to shock, excite or necessarily move his audience in any particular direction.

DB: I don't think I want anything. I think what I do is come up with all these sort of crazy ideas and I put them on and there is always an effect. But I've never calculated the effect, I've calculated the performance, and I've usually governed the feeling that's going to come out. I know why I'm doing it and what point it is supposed to be making. I know the point I'm making when I go on stage but I can never quite tell what the effect is going to be. It's not a calculated show to pull a particular effect out, because it really doesn't happen like that for me. A lot of people think it is, but when they've seen a few shows, they realised it isn't. I just go on with a particular statement and it causes an effect, and the effect changes drastically from area to area.

<*Grundy then talks about how Bowie saved Mott the Hoople, who had just broken up, by offering them a sure-fire hit.*>

PETE OVEREND WATTS, founder of Mott the Hoople: The next thing we heard is that he wanted us to come and see him and his manager and that they had a song for us, which turned out to be 'All the Young Dudes'. It was incredible. It was like a fairy godmother situation, in that they just came in and took over completely, because by that time we were completely baffled and bewildered. We didn't know what we were doing. We were in so much debt, in so much trouble with lost audiences, loss of faith with our old record company, that we were in no state to do anything for ourselves. We couldn't believe that anybody would give 'All the Young Dudes' away, because David at that time hadn't had a chart hit since 'Space Oddity'. He was beginning to break, but he still wasn't a big name, and that he was giving us 'All the Young Dudes', which is like an anthem of the seventies, really, we were just flabbergasted. We went away from the meeting saying, 'What's his angle? Why's he giving us this song? What do they want with us?'

SG: [*Voiceover*] The single got into the Top 3. Some crisis of identity had been created, though, and it was something that Bowie was aware of, too.

DB: It was my statement of what Mott the Hoople were about. That was always my problem, that when I took an artist in a studio, that I would inflict my definition of the artist on the artist. And that's why I stepped out of producing people for a bit, because I realised that, in a way, I was corrupting what they were trying to do. I did that with Mott. I mean, it might have helped them commercially and all that, but it was not the Mott the Hoople that Mott the Hoople thought they were. And again, having created an identity, my identity of what they were all about, they were stuck with a dilemma about, 'Well, we can't quite understand what we are anymore.'

<Grundy digresses to talk about how Bowie, according to his bandmates, was a natural actor.>

WW: His basic thing is … he loves acting. I mean, he used to put on shows in the front room. He'd come in dressed as an old woman. His face was an old woman's. Without that much make-up, he totally got into an old woman's thing. I mean, it was scary. It's so convincing. He was an old woman.

SG: [*Voiceover*] By the time that the American tour was over, March 1973, Ziggy had outgrown his skin. But what of The Spiders? Had they, like Bowie, understood and seen themselves as purely leasehold Spiders?

DB: No, never. I don't think at any time. But I didn't expect them to. [*Laughs*] And that's fair enough. It certainly wasn't through lack of intelligence or anything, it was because they weren't writing the stuff. They just knew that they were in a band called The Spiders, and that there was this thing that I'd written called *Ziggy Stardust and The Spiders*, so they were sort of playing the part; but for them, they really were The Spiders. It must have been very anticlimactic when I said, 'Well that show's all over now. You can call yourselves The Spiders, but really it's all dead because I'm now Aladdin Sane.' I could see it happening to them, 'Well, what, what are we supposed to be now?' And I didn't know what to tell them, [*Laughs*] frankly. I mean, it had to end, The Spiders really had to end because I didn't know how to get them to understand how I deal with the changes of persona, and they couldn't handle that.

SG: [*Voiceover*] So, who, or what, was Aladdin Sane?

DB: That's Ziggy Stardust meets 'Fame'. *Ziggy Stardust*, the album, was an objective point of view, and *Aladdin Sane* was himself talking about being a star and hitting America. Because I'd had that first experience of America, I had plenty of material for it, so it was a subjective Ziggy talking, showing the break-up.

SG: [*Voiceover*] Bowie's instructions to pianist Mike Garson were to play crazy, create the feeling of insanity. And that's what he did.

DB: That was again running back to the old avant-garde, the old, prepared piano. Again, that's right out of the sixties. But not now, of course, it sounds part of the new genre.

SG: [*Voiceover*] That theme again – insanity.

DB: It's been part of the family, really. [*Laughs*] All the family is nuts, they're all pretty crazy. I don't know if they still are. I've not seen any for a year. There's quite an amount of insanity in any family, I think we just got more than our share. But it's better to recognise the angels and devils in oneself, I think. And that prevents true insanity. I mean, I'm no more insane than the next man, but I keep making myself aware of how flighty I am, what a grasshopper I am, and how my moods change such a lot, so drastically. And even my persona, privately, changes a lot – one minute I can be quite verbose and articulate, and the next minute I feel like a stumbling philistine, I can't express anything, and I can't even think the same way, and points of view change all the time. I think as long as you keep recognising it and kind of stand outside whoever's taking over at the time and the other one stands outside and has a look.

WW: The stage thing, the rock thing, always seemed, like he admits, like an actor. It totally was that. You could pick it up on stage behind him. He'd be stood on a speaker at the front and you could practically hear his brain ticking, 'What would a famous rock star do now?' And click, he had the right thing. And he had the fantastic ability to move his body, do with his body, whatever he wanted when he was on stage. He would do the rock poses, but better than anyone else had done them before.

SG: [*Voiceover*] In retrospect, Bowie doesn't consider the album [*Aladdin Sane*] one of his best.

DB: One painting isn't the painter's life. And often a painter will do lots of paintings and he is only satisfied with a couple in his entire career, and I think that applies to me, definitely. I'm only happy with a couple of albums. Occasionally, I'll strike something that's very good. But you can't set out and do a painting and say, 'This is it,' and it is it. You just hope and try, and if it doesn't work out, you have to put it to one side and do another one. I think that's an important thing to remember about a number of British rock albums – that it doesn't matter if they're not all good. They can't all be good because there's only one that's going to come up every 10 albums or so that's going to be meaningful.

TB: He travelled separate from the band. He used to travel in a limousine, whereas we'd travel on the coach. We only used to see him on the night just before the gig, and then afterwards we would maybe see him now and again in the hotel. So, we never used to get to talk to him. It slowly broke down. We never bothered with each other. I suppose we were all happy going out on the road enjoying ourselves. In the end he decided to split it up, and that was it.

TONY VISCONTI: He was doing this [Ziggy Stardust] as a vehicle to get somewhere out of frustration. It was always very important for David to become very successful, because at the back of his mind he always wanted to do the things he's getting into now, movies and all that. I quite honestly think that Ziggy was a vehicle to get to the position where he is now. And if he didn't get to this position, I truly think he would have gone insane, because he was a difficult person to be around those days; he wouldn't ever stop and sit still, either writing a song or sketching or having these people over the house – his mind was totally occupied.

<Grundy talks about Pin-Ups, *the covers album which followed* Aladdin Sane.>

DB: It was really to give The Spiders something to do. I didn't [*Laughs*] quite know how to put them into the next thing, so I thought we'd just go in the studio and play a few old favourites to keep their interest up more than anything else. That was an insiders' album; that was for me to keep the band together or to break it up, one of the two. I thought something like that might do it, to give them something without any concept and see if they really enjoyed doing that, and they did, you see. And they decided they wanted to work more like that, and I said, 'No, I'm going back to big, heavy melodrama. [*Adopts a German accent*] And you don't fit into my scheme of things.' [*Laughs*] I finished it. [*Adopts an upper-class accent*] A cruel and cutting blow. But it had to be done, [*Sarcastically*] sometimes you've got to be cruel to be kind. [*Laughs*]

PART 4: REBEL REBEL

SG: [*Voiceover*] With the end of The Spiders, Bowie will, from now on, employ musicians on a project-by-project basis.

DB: The nicest thing about that particular kind of working is that they don't feel they're my band. I mean, they work with me and that's as far as it goes, which is the nicest thing. When we finish a tour, they go immediately and do other things with other people and other bands. They don't look to me to supply them with ideas and whatever. They come in and they work and work well, and want to work with me, but they'd hate to feel that they were tied to me. Maybe if The Spiders had worked with me in that capacity, I think we may well have been together still. But they felt too tight, and they were really looking to me to supply them with new identities and I said, 'But no, there isn't a band in the next concept.' The next concept is Aladdin Sane on his own and then, having done that, I wanted to write about the cities that Ziggy comes from, like the *Diamond Dogs* thing, and there isn't a band in that.

DB: It [The Spiders] might have stagnated. It would have stagnated, I know, because Mick and I weren't seeing eye-to-eye towards the end. I wanted to get more illegitimate and he wanted to get more legitimate rock'n'roll, which of course is exactly what he has done now working with Dylan, whatever – you couldn't get more reactionary than that. 'Michael, [*Adopts a parental tone*] get away from there, what're you doing?' [*Laughs*] I wanted not to become that establishment. I still wanted to be able to be treated still more as a clown, or thought of as somebody who plays with rock'n'roll and doesn't take it seriously.

SG: [*Voiceover*] How do the creative juices of Bowie flow?

DB: I spend most of the time just thinking about the concept and shape and size and texture of a thing rather than the actual writing of it. But I think that's as an important a part of creative work as actually doing anything, like putting it down on paper or a tape or whatnot. I think thinking. I spend a lot of time thinking. That tires me out. Then I have a sleep. Then I go and get drunk, and I go and do things that I can think about the next day. [*Laughs*] And somewhere along the line, they get transferred into actual physical matter, like an album or a photograph or a painting or something.

SG: [*Voiceover*] The actual studio time involved can be very short.

DB: I can knock an album out in a week, complete, mixed and everything. As soon as I go in, I know exactly what I'm doing. There's no experimentation when I go in the studio. There hasn't been anyway, up until now, but the next album I think I'm going to open myself up to sort of leeway of experimentation and we'll see what happens. I don't know what'll happen. I've never worked like that before. I've always been very tight and very calculating about that, but that's because I was a draughtsman and a commercial artist, I guess, so it comes out of a concept. The concept's born up there and you think about that a lot, and you just slam into it and you know exactly what it's going to look like before you start, and that's how the albums came round. The guys I'm working with often have trouble keeping up with me because I work very quickly. They are often dissatisfied with their own takes and things, and I'll say, 'No, that's the one I want', and move straight on … 'Moving right along now!' As long as it has some integral quality of disharmony about it, it's on.

SG: [*Voiceover*] Bowie had written and produced a hit for Lou, 'Walk on the Wild Side'.

DB: We tried to produce Lou, which was a bad mistake. But, I suppose, commercially it did well for him, and I guess because of that he probably holds it against me. [*Laughs*] But Lou's like that. Oh, he is, [*Adopts a northern accent*] he is stubborn. [*Laughs*] Yeah, we tried to do a number on Lou because I wanted to have a lot of my attitude toward Lou Reed on the album. Lou, of course, just revolted and went straight back to what he used to, for a bit. And that Lulu thing. [*Laughs*] I was amazed. To give her a song about finding angels and devils in yourself, [*Laughs*] it was sort of a naughty thing to do, but it seemed right at the time. And again, it was hard for Lulu to do anything after that with the particular thing that I gave her. She started dressing up in these funny suits, looking like a boy and everything. [*Laughs*] Again, she was trying to get lost in my identity of her. So, when I'd done Lulu, I thought I'd better stop doing this because I felt somewhat like a Svengali. It's very easy for me to do that, to fall into that role. It's a director's job. I was, again, giving vent to my cinematic pretensions and creating little pastiche filmlet [sic] things for people and casting them in roles and directing the whole thing, and then forgetting to tell them it was a film. So, they wanted the next day's shooting and I didn't have any more scripts.

SG: [*Voiceover*] Perhaps one day we may see Bowie in the role of film director. Back to *Diamond Dogs* and the 1974 American tour which resulted from it.

DB: I started thinking about how hard it is for musicians to take a part in rock theatre, and that's when I tried to lose musicians on the *Diamond Dogs* show. That failed abysmally [*Laughs*] because everybody complained, 'We don't like playing behind these bleedin' screens!' I said, 'You've got to because I haven't got any parts for you! I don't want people to see you playing because it doesn't look like a street if there's a bass amp stuck in the middle.' But it was very hard to convince them about that. [*Laughs*] So, they all left me! And the show gradually fell apart, which it should have done because it was about a decaying city so it was quite apropos that it should fall down in the middle of the tour. It really did become the *Diamond Dogs* city.

SG: [*Voiceover*] In the middle of the tour, there was a break for four weeks, and that's when work on the *Young Americans* album began.

DB: That's when I became B.B. King, [*Laughs*] a sort of R'n'B thing, because I was left to meddle around a bit not having a concept to work on so I thought, 'Well, I'll be the radio.' So, I recorded the radio for a few weeks and listened to some soul things and did the *Young Americans* album, which was the radio, really. *Young Americans* was American radio. If anybody 10 years ago had said that was a R'n'B album, it would have been a laughing stock because it's not, it has nothing to do with R'n'B; it's perfect synthetic radio stuff, the stuff of radio.

SG: [*Voiceover*] 'Fame' was an American Number 1, his greatest single success. The album was a major seller as well. There were more changes to come. David and his manager, Tony Defries, parted company. Now, David manages himself.

DB: I'm much more laidback about business and how much people should pay me for doing a job. That's all it is. That's all management is. You look at yourself and decide how much you are worth. So, I've got used to putting a price on myself, which is a really odd thing to have to do, but it's quite fun, actually.

SG: [*Voiceover*] Bowie's first major screen part was to come. Filmed in New Mexico last summer, Nicolas Roeg's film, *The Man Who Fell to Earth*, features Bowie as a visitor from another planet. For those who know him well, there's a lot of Bowie in Thomas Newton. Even so, the part was a complete change for him.

DB: The film is the first thing that I'd been given where I didn't have to play a rock'n'roll star, for a start. I wasn't required to sing. The only thing they asked me to do was write some music, which I got out of doing because I didn't want my music attached to the film either. I didn't want it to sell on a soundtrack, I wanted it to be considered as a serious attempt at acting – or non-acting, as the character has no idea of expression, no humour whatsoever, so I had to play him very, very straight. And some days my face ached through not being able to use it. Everything had to be absolutely expressionless, and I wasn't to put ennui or innuendo in any of the statements I made. It was very much like that. It was painful to do that way. Three months of being totally *The Iceman Cometh*. It was absolutely that. But I realised when I'd done the film and seen some of the rushes on video, how effective it is putting that non-acting role into … surrounded by people who were totally caught up in their own emotions like Candy Clark is, an overabundance of emotion. And to put someone with that little emotion in them produces a very poignant situation.

SG: [*Voiceover*] How did his notoriously butterfly nature put up with the discipline of filming?

DB: The flitting that I do [*Laughs*] in what I do only comes in the creation of something. Once I settle down to do it, I take the concept through to its logical conclusion and I'm right behind it. I don't fall out of love with things in the middle of them. If I'm serious about them, I'll do them. But once I've done them, I don't want to have to look at them anymore or have anything to do with it because I usually drain myself off into that particular thing.

SG: [*Voiceover*] Filming was completed in autumn 1975. What then?

DB: And then I thought I'd better settle down to doing some work then. [*Laughs*] Oh, I'm going back to Europe, so I'll write a European album, *Station to Station*, which is my salute to the East from the West, America. It's really European. It really is, isn't it? [*Laughs*] I'm going to have to listen to it again. Of course, not all of it, but there's lots of it that owe a lot to the French and German rock scene. Things like 'Word on a Wing' and the opening track, 'Station to Station', is quite German. And 'Word on a Wing' is a very Germanic, Romantic statement. It's back to me German umlauts again. 'TVC 15', I guess, that's a bit of a hotchpotch, sort of influenced by the film or the television sets.

SG: [*Voiceover*] There's a growing feeling among his friends and associates that David is beginning to lose his interest in music and is now recording and touring simply to finance his interest in films.

DB: I want to work with directors that I admire, just to see how they do it, and how they got where they are, artistically, how they arrived at their conclusions. And steal a little bit from each in technique, how to handle crews and things like that. That's a problem that one doesn't think about before you go and do a film – how you handle a great 50-, 60-strong film crew. Film crews are different to rock'n'roll road crews. So, I sit back and be very Capricorn and just watch everything and learn how to do it. And then I'll go and do it better. [*Laughs*]

SG: [*Voiceover*] Bowie is quite critical of his own work, dismissing the greater part of it in a few words. What, then, was really worthwhile?

DB: The ones that I think that were quite worthy of something were *Diamond Dogs* and *Ziggy Stardust*. *Ziggy Stardust* is probably my definitive album, as I've been told. And *Diamond Dogs* is a very important album. I thought that's the nearest that I've done to a cinematic experience. For me, personally, it was my Fritz Lang statement. It was my *Metropolis* [Fritz Lang film] in a sound form. I think *Station to Station* is interesting; it's not important but it's interesting, because it seems to indicate some return to an earlier style of recording and writing for me. So, I'm quite excited about the next one, I can't wait to see what it's going to be like. I expect it'll be quite … interesting. [*Laughs*] I don't know if it'll be important, though. I think time tells that. It's always like painting to me, all of this – even a stage performance is the same, but recording especially is just like doing a painting; you start off with a blank bit of canvas and you start work on it, and sometimes it comes off and sometimes it doesn't. There's no difference between that and painting. There really isn't.

SG: [*Voiceover*] At the point at which your average rock star, a definition which he's always disclaimed, has either gone or is on his way out, Bowie always seems to be just on the threshold of his career. Had he any understanding or reason for this phenomenon?

DB: I'm very quick, for me, to own up to Ziggy Stardust was my statement. But I've always thought that in rock, that you can only say one thing in rock'n'roll, really, and everything else is just an expansion of that original statement. It certainly seems like that with the stuff that I've done. Some of it does qualify the original statement. And it's the whole period … this was my rock'n'roll period. Rather than dividing the rock period up into bits, it's just looking at the whole rock period and saying, 'That was my rock period', and it dealt with this particular attitude: rock'n'roll is the decision of being establishment or non-establishment, that's the problem that rock'n'roll poses … to be or not to be a rebel, is really what it says and always has said.

• • •

DB: I think it's still very hard for anybody to pin down David Bowie, which I think is lovely. That's very cute and is exactly what I wanted.

STUART GRUNDY, BBC RADIO

INTERVIEWER: STUART GRUNDY

A rock star at the height of his fame dropping out of the limelight for the then relative backwoods of Germany was unheard of at the time.

Here, Bowie gives various reasons for the move to Berlin, the main one appearing to be 'one particular incident, which I don't really want to go into now'. An overdose, perhaps, of which he reportedly had several? He adds that he needed to get away from LA and its people, was searching for a new way to live and write, needed to escape rock music, and aimed to get back on the road to live a more Jack Kerouac-type lifestyle. He also hints at incipient schizophrenia when he says he needed to lock his different personalities in a wardrobe. The lure of ground-breaking German bands like Kraftwerk, the chance to live more quietly, and the image of bohemian Berlin also all played their part.

Low and *Heroes* are now regarded as seminal classics. But it wasn't always so. Grundy wasn't afraid to say what many perplexed fans at the time were saying: too many instrumentals, too many impenetrable lyrics, too much Brian Eno. Bowie apologises good-naturedly before explaining that he was bored with a standard songwriting approach and was looking to create a new musical language.

Bowie also talked about his acting career and his plans to play the expressionist painter, Egon Schiele, in a film directed by Clive Donner, who made *The Caretaker* and *What's New Pussycat?* For whatever reason, the film never got off the ground. Instead, Bowie would opt for a film so bad he later described it as 'my 32 Elvis movies rolled into one'.

STUART GRUNDY: Once upon a time there was David Bowie and then there was the band.

DAVID BOWIE: Yeah.

SG: Have you tired, perhaps, of carrying all the responsibility on your shoulders, or is this just a natural progression?

DB: Yes, I think it's a natural progression in as much that I needed somebody to work with, to relate to, if I was going to discover for myself how I was going to write in the future. I needed some help. I couldn't do it myself, because I couldn't look at myself properly at the time. And I think I was very fortunate in deciding on such an empathetic git as Eno to work with, who is an absolutely wonderful man, terrific. The funniest thing really is that for every hour we recorded in the studio – he has an incredible sense of humour. I don't know whether you know Eno at all? – Fripp and Eno and I spent about 40 minutes out of every 60 laughing. It's just incredibly surrealistic humour that Brian can come up with and, indeed, Fripp. Fripp has that much more [*Adopts a West Country accent*] down-to-earth type of humour. [*Laughs*]

SG: Let me ask you about the lyrics, because it seems to me that your lyrics nowadays are becoming more obscure, unfathomable than they used to be.

DB: Yes, they are, aren't they? Well, there is a logic [*Laughs*] behind that, if only I could think of it. No, what I did is that I'm working very much in fragment lyrics, even more than I ever did. It started with *Diamond Dogs*, there are a couple of tracks on there that were written with a lot of inspiration due to Burroughs's work, William Burroughs. And I've really taken the plunge on this last album, I suppose. It's arrived at by putting together three or four statements at variance with each other, sometimes completely unrelated statements, and from those, say, arbitrary three statements, one arrives at a fourth piece of information from the rearrangement of what is involved. Now that sounds like an awful easy thing to do. Well, it is. I think everybody should do it.

SG: I remember you telling me something before about writing things down on bits of paper and rearranging them. Is this what you literally do?

DB: Yes, it's the cut-up technique. It was a very popular writing form in the sixties. I mean, it's sort of quite reactionary, really. I also like the spontaneous writing, just writing for the sake of it and then rereading it and seeing what came out. You see, you must understand, it all sounds incredibly indulgent, and indeed it is because what I'm trying to do is mould the traditional methods of rock'n'roll with newer processes. I mean, it is a re-evaluation, and it is trying to find a new form of language … musically … or artistically, I guess, because I'm not a musician … but artistically.

SG: But it does make the lyrics less accessible.

DB: On a surface level. But you see I think that they are very accessible on a subconscious and emotional level. That was the point of cut-up writing, is that it didn't relate to linear thought at all; it worked very much on the spontaneous and immediate images that one gets in one's mind, especially when one is driving, there are incredibly fast shapes and forms. And it can relate very strongly on that level.

SOUND AND VISION

DB: There's one bohemian half of me which says, 'I wish they'd never buy another one and then I could go back and be a painter,' and the other part says, 'Well, who's going to gratify your ego, then?' And the other one says, 'Well, I'll be a successful painter!' [*Laughs*]

SG: Well, that really prompts a question I was going to ask right at the end, [*DB laughs*] and I'll ask it now. I really wanted to know if at any time in your career you'd ever had to ask yourself the question, 'What the bloody hell am I doing, how did I get into this? I wish I could get out and be an ordinary person.'

DB: Oh God, yes. In Los Angeles, I was talking to myself and receiving the most idiotic replies all the time. I'd quite cut down the middle then. Some particular incident, which I really don't want to go into now, brought me back down to earth with a bump. That's when I sort of decided to get out of, that area of rock'n'roll that I always used to despise and found that I'd got myself involved in without really seeing that I was getting involved in it. And sort of dropped out again, to use an old term, and get back on my old Kerouac road, and just travel again. Just to help me re-evaluate, as I say. And so, along with that, being a personal problem, it applied to my work, as it must do, because with me the way I live is also what very much produces my work, so I have to keep examining my life to make sure that I'm in constant change and not getting too bloated with philosophic opulence. Keep throwing bits and pieces away. To change countries is one way of doing that.

SG: Well, let me change tack. If I were to have one criticism of the Bowie of today, the Bowie on *Low* and *Heroes*, I'd say we don't seem to be getting as much of your vocals as we used to do. In fact, almost the whole of the second side of *Heroes* is instrumental. I think that's a very great pity.

DB: Um … what can I say? I've only written that many songs and the rest of it was instrumental. I … yes, I … um … I, I'm sorry. [*Laughs*]

SG: But you're obviously very happy with the sound of them, I think you were saying that earlier.

DB: I'm happy with the album, and I'm also happy with life in general, actually. I'm very content, at the moment. I hope it goes on like this. It'd be super.

V-2 SCHNEIDER

DB: Yeah, there's a communication prospect with them when we approach any album, which is one knows that one has already defined one's area with them. We don't have to talk very much before we start playing anything.

SG: You mean you've developed your own language or communication system?

DB: Yes. Definitely. Definitely. A bit like bats. [*Both laugh*]

SG: With these last two albums, you've certainly settled down into what is a more stable situation, I think. Does that mean you are no longer the chameleon, or did you tire of creating new faces, new images for yourself?

DB: Yes, I did tire of it. They were starting to get me down, in the States especially, I had all these people … I'll tell you a funny story about that. When I left Los Angeles, the way I psychologically rid myself of all those people for a bit was to open a wardrobe door and to push them in, mentally, and then I locked the wardrobe door and I've still got the key, which I think is hedging one's bet, really. [*Laughs*] I mean, if I'd gone all the way I should have thrown the key away, but I didn't.

SG: Does that mean that when you came over to Europe that you'd really had quite enough of LA and its people?

DB: Not only LA and its people, but my approach to writing. I was tiring of the method that I was writing in. I wanted to develop a new language, so I knew my next move was to have to do that.

SG: Well, I said I wanted to talk about the last two albums. My feeling about *Low* was, and you've already talked about Eno, that there was as much Eno on that album as there was David Bowie. Is that a good thing, David?

DB: Um … I think there was an awful lot of Eno influence on the album. I think that is, fairly, to be expected. When one works with somebody that one admires, one tends to move more in their areas and give them wider berth for showing you something new. And I think that was fairly evident on *Low*, although proportionate amount of work done was about equal. It was a collaboration, no doubt about that. I would be wary of committing myself to saying that it was one-sided on either part. This new album is an even more successful blending of what we are doing, I think. Not quite so obviously this or that. It's a highly successful collaboration, the new one. And with the addition of Fripp as middleman, I think that helps an awful lot, as well.

BEAUTY AND THE BEAST

SG: You've produced a couple of albums with Iggy, and my feeling is that he is becoming very Bowie-esque.

DB: [*Pauses*] Well, you know, I think there was probably a little bit too much of me than was necessary on *Idiot*, but I think that was more because Iggy was still feeling his way again after a considerable absence from things. But I would tend to disagree. I think 'Lust for Life' is far more like the old Iggy than anything he has done for a long time. And he really is very much his own boss, you know.

I think that he's been able to shake my phantom off fairly quickly, considering, which I know is unfortunate, but every time I get involved with an artist that always tends to be one of the criticisms levelled at anything that comes as a result of our working together. But I think Iggy's going to get even stronger in the future.

SG: So, you do think you've avoided most of the inherent dangers in that sort of professional relationship?

DB: I don't know. I hope so, for his sake. And he seems very happy with things as they are. He fully intends to do another album with me, so I can't see that we've gone very wrong as far as he's concerned, and it's him that it's all about, so it's most important that he feels at ease with the situation.

SG: Okay, well the producer has just been giving us the wind-up here, so let me just ask you a couple of quick questions. You seem to have been spending a bit of time over here recently, at least if one looks at the press, we've seen your photograph on various occasions, have you …

DB: That's misleading, actually. I've been over here quite a bit, yes, but I've also been in the Far East a lot. But I fly a lot, you see, now, and so it makes it seem as though I'm over here a lot as I keep popping in and out. But I often try to get back to Japan as much as possible because I haven't finished looking around there.

SG: Is that going to be your next base, do you think?

DB: [*Laughs*] Ha-ha. Funny you should ask that. It might well be.

SG: Okay, just one more question. If we could look at your diary for the next few months, what's planned for you?

DB: Well, a rather obvious answer: I'm going to travel. I'm doing nothing but travelling up until at least December. A few countries

I want to go to … Israel, South America and Africa is what I intend to do.

SG: And what about the tour?

DB: Sometime next year, depending on the film that I'm doing.

SG: And the film you're doing, is this something of your own creation?

DB: No, it was brought to my attention by Clive Donner. It's a period of the life of an expressionist painter called Egon Schiele. It's around the period 1900, 1918 and takes place in Vienna and Paris, and it's a sort of intimate portrait of his relationship with his model. Not too intimate. [*Adopts a 'shocked' tone*] It's not sensationalist. Just good cuisine, good food, that kind of thing.

SG: Okay, we look forward to it and we look forward to the tour as well. Thanks, David.

DB: Pleasure. Bye-bye.

REPORTING SCOTLAND, BBC TV

INTERVIEWER: FIDELMA COOK

Bowie was cool in terms of image, but also cool in terms of being calm and collected. So cool, in fact, that he would happily be interviewed on his way from the dressing room to the stage.

It's hard to imagine many other singers being easy-going enough to chat to reporters on that nerve-wracking final walk to face the audience. But Bowie wasn't bothered. Here he is, dressed in a kimono, chatting to Fidelma Cook of BBC Scotland as he heads along the corridor towards the stage of the Apollo.

As for the interview, the subject was the future of the Apollo itself. Glasgow's main music venue, which had a capacity of 4,500 but would often pack in 6,000, was on the verge of being turned into a bingo hall. Various musicians had joined a chorus of disapproval, including Bob Geldof who, never short of a sharp phrase, was quoted as saying, 'Fuck bingo, long live rock.'[8]

One of the special features of the Apollo was 'the bouncy balcony', which would indeed bounce if those on it were daring enough to jump up and down in unison to the music. On seeing this unique phenomenon, some musicians became convinced the place was about to fall down. Others, like Francis Rossi, were more sanguine. The Status Quo frontman ordered the crowd to bounce even more wildly, as the band's lighting crew were also up there.

'A nice bunch of fellas,' Rossi told the crowd, 'but scared shitless of balconies.'[9]

As for people falling down, it seems that when Bowie had played there previously, it was Mick Ronson who went for a burton. According to the audience, the guitarist proudly stood atop one of his amps only to promptly fall off.

The campaign to save the Apollo worked, albeit briefly. It was shut down in 1985 and subsequently demolished.

FIDELMA COOK: Encouragement of the arts with a capital 'A' has been Glasgow's aim for the last few years. Heavily subsidised by government grants, the opera has taken its place in the city's cultural life, and football at Hampden is to be underwritten. But when it comes to catering for the kids from the sprawling council estates, culture develops a small 'c', and one councillor is already on record as saying their music loves are rubbish and give them a large field instead. Once the Apollo goes to the eyes-down, look-in brigade, there's little left in Scotland for the 15-to-20 age group. Mecca [the venue's landlords] find bingo more profitable, and theatre owners point to the cost of staging a tour like Bowie's as a reason for closures. But Bowie himself, cult hero to a generation that's grown up with the Apollo, considers Scotland a venue important enough to lose money on.

DAVID BOWIE: I started off here about 10 years ago, something like that, and it's always been a favourite of mine of the places that I've played in. This is the first real tour of England I've done in many years and I thought this would be a good chance to see people I used to work for once upon a time up here.

FC: So, you would agree with most artists who play here that a Glasgow audience is probably one of the best audiences you can get?

DB: It's an exceptionally exciting audience to work to, yeah.

FC: Why is that? What happens?

DB: They just seem very intoxicated with the idea of a theatrical show.

FC: You see, they were deprived of a certain amount of, certainly, rock music for a long time before the Apollo.

DB: I hear they are going to again, yeah.

FC: Well, this is it. How do you feel? Does your tour, or anybody's tours [of Scotland] stop?

DB: Mine wouldn't stop because I'd work in Scotland somewhere. I don't know where next time, but I'm always quite willing to bring my American show over to England. Because I can sort of make money around London, but doing these ones up here, it's really a question of really wanting to do them. But I don't know where I'd work if the Apollo went.

FC: This is it.

DB: Well, yeah, as far as I know.

FC: Have you played here before?

DB: Yes, yes, many times. But not for at least seven years, five years, about five years.

FC: I think it was Paul McCartney saying that the atmosphere in the Apollo itself is tremendous.

DB: It's electric. It is electric, yeah.

FC: Is there a possibility that you might finish touring altogether?

DB: Oh, I doubt it. No, whenever I need some funds to put into something, I'll have to go out on tour, and I'll do as I usually do. Some of them will be for money and some of them will be for wanting to do them.

FC: And if the Apollo goes, if there's anywhere else that they put up, you'll come to …?

DB: I'll ask my tour manager where else there is to work. We'd probably work something out.

FC: But it would be dreadful if you could never work Scotland again?

DB: Oh, of course, yes. I don't think that would be the case. I think I would work Scotland, but where, I don't know.

TONIGHT, BBC TV

INTERVIEWER: VALERIE SINGLETON

Bowie had just appeared in what proved to be the worst movie of his career. To his credit, he dutifully did the promotion rounds for *Just a Gigolo* when he could just as easily have pulled out. 'Everybody involved in that film, when they meet each other, they look away!' he would later say.

The one enticement was the promise that Marlene Dietrich was to be his co-star. But, unknown to Bowie, the German screen legend had insisted on filming her scenes in her Paris flat and refused to return to a city (Berlin) that held so painful memories. Bowie was genuinely upset; Dietrich was not just an original Berlin bohemian, but the prototype of androgyny in her top hat, tux and trousers. She had even personally stood up to Hitler. But instead of a heroic icon, Bowie got a piglet, which, for unexplained reasons, he was told to carry around on set and which, he said, 'kept shitting on me'.

Bowie could have chosen to walk out that first day. But when he arrived on set, he found a large cast and crew already busily at work. He knew that if he walked, they would all be fired. He stayed.

Bowie's sense of humour is once again on top form.

'Do you lack anything, David Bowie?' Valerie Singleton asks with furrowed brow and too much gravitas.

'Yes,' Bowie replies. 'A train ticket to Penge.'

'People tend to think of rock stars as "a bit thick",' Singleton adds. 'I presume there's more to you than that?'

'Oh no, I'm very thick.'

As for *Just a Gigolo*, did it sting his acting ego? Well, it certainly made him more choosy. It would be another five years before he acted again in a film.

VALERIE SINGLETON: [*Introduction*] When Bowie first became famous, his clothes, his hair, his make-up were purple and orange and designed to shock and, by shocking, to entertain. Latterly though, he's turned his attention to the cinema and with it a complete change of image. The proof of that is his latest film, Just a Gigolo, in which he stars with Marlene Dietrich. He plays the part of a young lieutenant at the end of the First World War coming to terms with the decadent Berlin of the twenties and the rising Nazi threat. He's in London this week promoting the film and, in it, Bowie looks much like the boy next door, a far cry from the teenage pop star who wallowed in the outrageous and was worshipped by millions.

• • •

VS: Yet another David Bowie. Is this the real one, this time?

DAVID BOWIE: Well, I think so, yes.

VS: Why did you change so often, what was the need for it? Was it just a gimmick?

DB: The point of it was … when I started writing songs, nobody would record them, so I had to do them myself. Being a Capricorn, I didn't want to expose myself to the public, so I developed a series of characters which fell in line with the material that I was writing.

VS: So, behind that, all the time, was a real David Bowie?

DB: At times, yes. I lost control a couple of times.

VS: So, did the roles that you played on stage kind of take you over sometimes into private life?

DB: Yes, yes.

VS: What about that period when you wore those outrageous, feminine clothes and the make-up?

DB: Feminine? [*Adopts a mock outraged tone*] Madame!

VS: They were! I thought 'David Bowie', and I immediately associate you with that.

DB: Yeah.

VS: That particular period, did that carry over into real life? Did you wear those kind of clothes in your home?

DB: I only used to wear that kind of stuff when I was about 17 or 18. By the time I'd reached the ripe old age of 20, 21, I'd got into high-heeled shoes and things. They came about through Japanese theatre more than anything else. I tried to put together kabuki and pantomime – over here, of course, it's mime, isn't it? – mime techniques to help enhance this character of Ziggy Stardust who was the be-all and end-all of rock'n'roll stars.

VS: A lot of people looking at some of those roles you played, I think would have been very shocked and found them very outrageous.

DB: Yeah.

VS: And, also, there's this tendency to think of rock stars, or pop stars more generally, as being a bit thick.

DB: Yes.

VS: I presume there's a lot more to you than that. Did it worry you that people had that kind of …

DB: No, I'm very thick. [*Laughs*]

VS: Are you?

DB: Yes, I became a rock star. I could have been a painter.

VS: But as a need, what, just to get something out of your system?

DB: No, no, no. I wanted to be some kind of artist. I wanted to prove myself in some field as an artist, and I didn't think I was a very good painter, so I went to music.

VS: You've had tremendous publicity over the years of your marriage to Angie, and you've admitted you are bisexual.

DB: Mmm. [*Nods*]

VS: Was that, in a way, publicity that you sought to help your career or did you think of that as a tremendous …

DB: Which?

VS: Well, the publicity you had about your relationship.

DB: No, that evolved, I think, because of the fact that I said many years ago that I was a bisexual. But that happened in the course of a conversation.

VS: But do your resent that kind of publicity? Do you think that is an intrusion on your privacy?

DB: No, it's not an intrusion of my privacy. I decline to read it. [*Laughs*] It's like television – you can switch it off if it's not interesting.

VS: You see, now you're looking exactly like the character you play in the film that you've just done, so I wondered whether you were slightly playing another role almost and, in a year or two, we're going to see another look?

DB: I had this shirt a few months before the film. [*Laughs*]

VS: So, you are not … this is really you? You are not still sort of playing the role of Paul in the film?

DB: One wonders. I was working with Nicolas Roeg in *The Man Who Fell to Earth* a couple of years ago, and he warned me that when one's finished a film, the role often carries over for many months after the film and that I should be prepared for that. I think that happened to me when I was performing the characters that I was performing in America and England, but I didn't have a director to tell me that they would carry over. So, they all built up and became a mass, conglomerate character.

VS: Why did you want to make this particular film, *Just a Gigolo*?

DB: [*Long pause*] Marlene Dietrich was dangled in front of me, for one thing. [*Swings his pinched fingers in front of his face in a dangling motion*] Also, I got on extremely well with David Hemmings and so between those two things, I think I was pulled into it.

VS: What was it like working with Marlene Dietrich?

DB: I wish I knew. I must ask somebody who did work with her.

VS: Why?

DB: Well, what happened … for the duration of the film, they were trying to get Marlene to come to Germany, but she wouldn't because, since a period in the fifties, she's been reluctant to go back because her views differed very much with what was happening in Germany during the war. So, she stayed in Paris and said, 'I will do my filming in Paris.' All the way through the film, she said this. I quite agreed with her. We talked to each other on the phone, and we decided it would be fine if I did my bit in Berlin and she did her bit in Paris and the two would gel together.

VS: You never actually met her?

DB: No.

VS: That's amazing.

DB: But I think it's quite nice in the context of the film because she's forever the observer, really, and knowing that, makes her even more of the observer … a mystical, wonderful Cocteau character, that she is.

VS: Well, let's have a look at you and Marlene Dietrich now in the film in this scene. This is where you actually do appear with her. She's playing the madame of a very select group of young beaus, the gigolos, and, attracted by this good-looking young man, she decides to recruit him.

   <*Footage of a scene from* Just a Gigolo.>

[*DB lights a cigarette*]

VS: Do you lack anything, David Bowie?

DB: [*Ignores question as he looks at Dietrich on the monitor*] Isn't she lovely?

VS: She's marvellous.

DB: I wish I'd met her a long time ago. [*Laughs*]

VS: She looks fantastic. I'm picking up the line she addressed to you in the film. Do you think you lack anything or do you have everything you want?

DB: Yes, a train ticket to Penge. I've got some friends out there and I promised I'd go and see them this week, but I haven't had the time to get down there yet.

VS: Are you going to give up music now and concentrate on acting? Is this a whole new direction?

DB: I'd like to expand my activities, as they say. No, I enjoy writing very much.

VS: Writing just music, or writing all sorts of writing?

DB: Funnily enough, I am studiously trying to write a book of short stories based on things that I've done, but writing music generally. Performance on stage – I think I've decided to cut it down to once every two years because I find it boring after 10 shows. It starts to become repetitious, every night the same thing.

VS: Will there be more acting, more films?

DB: Yes, there will. I'm heading towards directing, that's what I want to do.

VS: Are you?

DB: Yes, very much.

VS: That's a final hope, is it?

DB: No, I want to be a good painter again, is my really big dream.

VS: And are you painting at the moment?

DB: Yes, all the time.

VS: And writing and acting and still singing?

DB: Yes.

VS: Lots of things. Is there another film planned?

DB: I have a selection in front of me which I'm very proud of, and I'm going through them deciding which one I'm going to do. That's exciting.

VS: I look forward to seeing them. David Bowie, thank you very much for talking to me.

DB: Thank you very much.

FRIDAY NIGHT, SATURDAY MORNING, BBC TV

INTERVIEWER: TIM RICE

To go up on stage and sing your own songs takes courage. But to be a world-famous rock star who takes the lead role in a Broadway play requires a whole different level of bravery. Bowie said he might have backed out of *The Elephant Man* had the director given him more than two weeks warning. As it was, Bowie said, he was on stage before even getting a chance to have second thoughts.

'I was petrified,' he admitted. 'It was the most terrifying position I've ever put myself in.'

His courage paid off. The performance was loved by the public, and not just those who had come to see one of their favourite rock stars. It was also loved by the theatre critics who, as Tim Rice observes below, were a tough bunch to please. The knives would certainly have been out to cut a Rock God down to size. But the reviews were not polite or, for that matter, good – they were ecstatic.

'One of the greatest acting performances I have seen in years,' said *New York Post* critic Clive Barnes. 'He has made the most brilliant Broadway debut in recent memory.' The *New York Times* said his performance was 'splendid, ethereal and preternaturally wise', while the *Daily News* described it as 'piercing and haunted'.

Keith Richards unkindly said, 'I can't act. And neither can David Bowie.'[10] There are certainly films in which Bowie isn't great. But his performance here, large chunks of which can be viewed online, is truly moving. It also provides an example of where Bowie didn't take his own, now famous, advice about edging just out of your comfort zone. 'When you don't feel that your feet are quite touching the bottom,' he once said, 'you're just about in the right place to do something exciting.' Here, he didn't edge out – he jumped straight in at the deep end of acting's deepest pool.

TIM RICE: Well, here we are in the wonderfully warm suite of the Carlyle Hotel.

[*DAVID BOWIE wipes his forehead in agreement*]

TR: They're all warm, but this is one of the warmest. Thank you for sparing your time. Last night, I saw you on Broadway. First time I've seen you legitimately acting, or acting legitimate, as they call it here. Why have you done it? Obvious question.

DB: Perfunctory answer. Because somebody asked me if I would.

TR: Was it the play that attracted you or the idea?

DB: Not really. I saw the play … I missed it when it was in London at the Hampstead [Theatre, London]. But then Philip Anglim brought it over to New York and started it there. And I missed it on Broadway as well. I always wanted to go and see it when I'd heard about it because there was a book by Frank Edwards called *Strange People*, which came out when I was a teenager, which had all kinds of things like the 'Human Blowtorch', who was a young Black guy who walked into a Chicago hospital and said that he couldn't lie down on sheets because they used to burst into flame. He lay down on the bed and promptly set the pillow on fire. They held him for 24 hours but then he ran away in terror, and nobody ever knew what happened to him. It was full of those kind of stories, and one of them was John Merrick, the Elephant Man. That appealed to me ever since then, because I have a sort of eclectic thing about freaks and isolationists and alienated people, and I gather information on people like that – mentally, anyway. Then it became a play and that, of course, rekindled my interest in it. I went to see it on Broadway when it had already got smartened up, became a Broadway piece, and I was totally knocked out by it. It's a classic piece of Victorian melodramatic writing, with a slight socialist subtext, but it appealed to me strongly. I thought the structure was very good, but thought no more. And then Jack Hofsiss, the director, came to see me a couple of months later whilst I was back in New York yet again doing the *Scary Monsters* album, and asked me if I would consider taking over the role at the end of the year. And I was flabbergasted because I had never been asked to do anything that, sort of, supposedly legit. And I said I would adore to.

TR: And you began out of town?

DB: Yeah. They played safe and put me somewhere so I could die a quiet death. Denver. We did a week there and then three weeks in Chicago, and then they felt I was right for the big time.

TR: [*Laughs*] But, in fact, you didn't die a death …

DB: [*Sings*] 'Big time'. Bryan Ferry impersonation – you get everything on this show!

TR: In actual fact, it all went very well …

DB: Hello, Bryan. [*DB waves at the camera*]

TR: … the critics gave you a very kind reception.

DB: Yeah.

TR: Do you, after all the years of having had a pretty good run in the rock world, which is continuing, do you find getting praise from different sources …

DB: Well, it was a limp rather than run. Awkward at best, but …

TR: But you must be almost blasé at getting praise from rock papers – or, at least, the intelligent ones. Are you, in fact, much more thrilled by the audience response at Broadway? Is it a totally new excitement for you?

DB: Praise from rock papers has never been a gift given unto me.

TR: Or indeed to anybody.

DB: No, indeed. [*Laughs*]

TR: Well, say, the audience. I mean, there was a great ovation …

DB: Yeah, quite so. I've had a terrific audience that's been staunchly loyal in the main part to what I've done and the changes that I've taken, which have been quite, as you know, diverse, to say the least. There has been a knotty band that has stayed with me through all of that, and so I've tried never to feel self-satisfied with what I've been doing, which has prompted me to keep moving in different directions. But it certainly was an incredible fulfilment for me to do something so-called 'legitimate' and, in fact, to undergo that kind of discipline and find that I could withstand it and work within somebody else's very strict confines.

TR: Are you getting people saying, 'I enjoyed your performance, but I hadn't even heard of you before?' Is this possible?

DB: That element has crept into it, yeah. There have been some regular theatregoers who've come … well, they had heard of me, but in some either perverse fashion or some kind of really corrupted idea of what I was about, and I suppose they've got a different impression of me now. Little do they know. [*Laughs*]

TR: How long will you do the part for on Broadway?

DB: Two hours. [*Laughs*] Then I'll go to bed.

TR: How many two hours will you do!?

DB: I don't think I could personally go past Christmas. I know I'm tied up until Christmas.

TR: That's quite a run.

DB: So, it's a long run for somebody who is grasshopper-y by nature, as myself.

TR: And would you like to go back to stage on something else in due course?

DB: Not particularly, no. I've learnt an awful lot just in the few weeks I've been doing this. I hope I can explore the part even further. Good heavens, if I don't, then I'll be wasting a lot of time. I would like to be more adventurous with the part. I've been sticking very tightly to the way I first wanted to interpret the thing, whilst all this palaver has gone on about press and opening nights and whatever. Now things are relaxing more, I would like to stretch out into it more. There are certain avenues I'd like to follow that I haven't had the courage to do so yet, but now will probably take advantage.

TR: Now, simultaneously, you happen to have a brand-new album out, which has been a huge hit in England. Is it out in the States?

DB: It's just out for a week or so, yeah.

TR: The title of that is *Scary Monsters*. One might feel there is some link between that title and the fact that you play something that could be described as a scary monster in the play. Is that just a coincidence?

DB: Synchronicity!

TR: What does synchronicity mean? Coincidence?

DB: Exactly what you said. Kind of a coincidence. Well, let's go into the Jungian side of it! [*Pretends to read from a book*] No, it's something I was working on before the thing was cemented. It's quite likely that *The Elephant Man* did stay with me as a title, but I know just from my memory reference, it actually came from a Kellogg's Corn Flakes packet. [*TR laughs*] On the back they were giving away … it said 'Buy your packet of Kellogg's Corn Flakes and inside you will find scary monsters and superheroes.' So, presumably, you find supermen and Nosferatu in your mouth. And, as I was writing a New York album, it seemed the perfect collective title for the bits and pieces I was writing. So it was, yes, coincidental.

TR: Were you surprised by the huge success of the single in England?

DB: Frankly, yes, I was.

TR: Do you think your video had a lot to do with it?

DB: I don't know, I really don't know. I would tend to believe, I suppose that Major Tom, there's a comfortable feeling with him, being such an old figure of mine. He goes back to '68, '69, whenever it was. I guess that a lot of people have some kind of empathy with him because he became a little bouncy hero. I just wanted to bring him up to date a little bit and put him in a Victorian nursery rhyme atmosphere; even though it's not Victorian, it has that queasiness to that 'Ring a ring a roses, this is about the plague, we're all going to drop down dead, boom!', which is what I did with the piece.

TR: You directed that video yourself, didn't you?

DB: Yeah.

TR: Are you hoping to get into that direction?

DB: I think for the time being, it's quite likely that I would stay working with David Mamet, with whom I worked with on that one. We have a very good working relationship, and David allows me lots and lots of freedom to do very much what I want – the ways I want it edited. I storyboard it for him, show him exactly what frames I want done, how it should be done. Then he puts his input in as well and, especially on 'Ashes to Ashes', the combination has been very successful.

TR: That must be fairly expensive.

DB: That one was fairly expensive for me, yeah. Not compared to some of the other figures I've heard flying around for so-called major artists. It was quite a good budget.

TR: Who are your musical heroes these days?

DB: Musical heroes … that's hard. I know bits and pieces of work that I admire very much. At the moment, I'm impassioned by, and it's not too strong a word as I play them all the time, Philip Glass and Steve Reich. I like very mu … let me get it right … is it Buddha or Gandhi or something? I don't know his new work … that's quite likely. That's very rude of me. I was with him the other day and I didn't ask him what he'd been doing. Probably too busy talking about what I've been doing.

TR: Are there any of your, as it were, contemporaries … people who got going about the time you did, who you admire?

DB: Not really. I think we just remain friends. I think that's probably why we're friends, because we don't like each other's music. I know the people you're referring to. [*Both laugh*] We don't get on very well with each other's music so that doesn't crop up in our conversations, and I think that's probably why we end up knocking around with each other without any feelings of the peacock-y kind of thing.

TR: In your long and illustrious career, which has spanned 10, 12 years at the top, what are you most proud of to date?

DB: [*Clicks his tongue*]

TR: Keeping going?!

DB: Oh God, I can only give a flip answer to that. That really is
… you know, that's really hard. At the moment, this week, the fact
that I could do and sustain a role of that intensity on stage. But that
kind of pride is not a good thing to fall back on whilst you are still a
working artist. I think for me it's despairingly abysmal to ask me what
I'm proud of because it doesn't work like that. I can tell you what
I haven't liked that I've done more easily. I think it's a question of
re-evaluation all the time. The fact that I've never had to buy one of
my own records, I suppose.

TR: [*Laughs*]

DB: RCA has given me one. One!

TR: Well, David, thank you very much. It's been a great pleasure
meeting you.

DB: It's my pleasure, entirely.

TR: I've bought certainly more than one or two of your records.
I'm sure I shall buy some more.

DB: I'm flattered.

TR: Good luck with the rest of *The Elephant Man*'s run.

DB: Thank you.

ANDY PEEBLES, BBC RADIO

INTERVIEWER: ANDY PEEBLES

The day after the first half of this interview, Andy Peebles would talk to John Lennon. The DJ recalled that Bowie was so excited to discover this news that 'all he wanted to do was talk about The Beatles', and proceeded to bombard Peebles with questions about the Fab Four. Come Lennon's interview on Saturday, the ex-Beatle would be equally flattering, and talked about how he would like to make a record as good as *Heroes*. Two days later, on a Monday evening in December, just before 11pm, a deranged man would fire four bullets into Lennon's back.

Bowie was devastated. May Pang, Lennon's former girlfriend, went round to Bowie's apartment upon hearing the news to find the singer pacing up and down, repeatedly shouting, 'What the hell?! What the fuck is going on with the world?!'[11]

Lennon and Bowie had become friends one night in the mid-seventies at the Grammys. Backstage, Bowie had poured out his insecurities to the ex-Beatle about America not understanding him, before going on stage to present an award to Aretha Franklin, a singer whom he adored. As she grabbed the trophy, she said, 'I'm so happy, I could kiss David Bowie.' Clearly insecure about his sometimes other-worldly looks, Bowie dejectedly slunk backstage, only for Lennon to bound over in comical fashion to give him a theatrical hug and kiss, and say,

'See Dave, America loves ya!' 'We pretty much got on like a house on fire after that,' said Bowie.

The two recorded 'Fame' together, Bowie's first US Number 1, and hung out at each other's apartments. Bowie recalled watching an old VHS video shot in his apartment which happened to catch Lennon strumming hits of the day on acoustic guitar at the back of the room. When Lennon realised he was on camera, he shouted over, 'What the hell are you doing, Bowie? It's all so negative, your shit. All this *Diamond Dogs* mutant crap!' before bursting out laughing. 'I loved John,' said Bowie.[12]

Lennon was more than just a friend. As he was for generations to come, Lennon was a hero, too. Bowie's role in defining the seventies was a reaction to the sixties, the decade defined by the Beatles. But that didn't stop him worshipping Lennon, a man he would call 'my greatest mentor'. He covered some Beatles songs in his early days, and adored Lennon's painfully revelatory solo stuff. When a young *Sunday Times* reporter called Tina Brown, who would go on to become editor of *Vanity Fair* and *Newsweek*, finally tracked Bowie down after spending three months doggedly trailing him across America for an interview, he simply said to her, 'I don't know why you're interviewing me when you've got someone like Lennon. He's the last great original.' The respect was mutual. Yoko Ono said of Bowie that he was the only one of Lennon's friends who was John's equal in terms of talent and intellect.

All of this would explain how distraught Bowie was after the murder. But there was more. Details emerged that killer Mark Chapman had Bowie on his hit list. After a search through Chapman's possessions, police found Bowie's name ringed in black on a programme for *The Elephant Man*. Chapman's girlfriend would tell them that if her boyfriend had not found Lennon that night, he would have gone after Bowie. Chapman had already bought a ticket for the Tuesday night show.

The play's director, Jack Hofsiss, asked Bowie if he wanted to cancel the show. Bowie said no. Hofsiss asked if he wanted extra security. Again, Bowie declined.

So, the night after the murder of his friend, Bowie was on stage. Right in front of him were two empty seats. They had been reserved for John and Yoko. A few spaces further along was one other empty seat. This one had been reserved by Chapman. 'There were three empty seats in the front row,' said Bowie. 'I can't tell you how difficult that was, to go on. I almost didn't make it through that performance.'

This interview marks the end of another phase in Bowie's life. This phase is not to do with music but a whole attitude to life. In public, Bowie will now be in the company of a beefy minder. Privately, he will spend more time in his getaway chalet in Switzerland. He would even reportedly take self-defence lessons specifically tailored for celebrities. This is the period where Bowie develops a reputation as being sometimes aloof or increasingly difficult to contact, even for some of his old friends. In hindsight, it's easy to see just how vulnerable he must have felt.

ANDY PEEBLES: We came along on Friday night to see *The Elephant Man*, and I must say I was extremely impressed. I don't know whether I did the right or wrong thing by seeing the film first in London. Could I get your thoughts on the film and John Hurt's performance?

DAVID BOWIE: Fortunately, I can't give them to you because I've not seen it, and I probably won't see it until I finish my run at the moment on Broadway. I like John Hurt very much indeed. I think I probably would not want to see it, mainly because I wouldn't want to be influenced by anything he's doing.

AP: So, you're saying that's a deliberate tactic?

DB: And I also like David Lynch's films very much, indeed; I like his expressionist thing, very cult film.

AP: It is indeed. How many people have actually played the part here on stage in America?

DB: On Broadway, I think I'm third. In the rest of the country, they've had tours out everywhere, so I think altogether there must have been 10 of them up and down the country.

AP: Who was the instigator of you taking the part?

DB: As far as who took responsibility for putting me in? [*Laughs*] Jack Hofsiss, the director.

AP: How did it come about?

DB: I'd seen the play in New York at the tail end of last year. I thought it was a very good at the time. I came back to record the *Scary Monsters* album, and Hofsiss came to see me there and asked me if I'd be interested in taking over the role, as [Philip] Anglim was

ANDY PEEBLES, BBC RADIO, 1980

leaving. I said, 'Yeah, I'd love to do that.' I'd never done anything like that before. I'd certainly like that ... the challenge of it.

AP: A challenge indeed. A very demanding part. I was interested at the beginning of your performance where you stood on stage with the nappy on, if we can call it that; it seems to have been called that by most people in the press.

DB: Well, let's call it a loincloth, then.

AP: Loincloth, then.

DB: Let's not do as others do.

AP: [*Laughs*] Let's call it the loincloth, then. There's a sequence where [Dr] Treves is giving a narration and you suddenly go into that stance, which made me feel terribly sympathetic because that must have been dreadfully painful and probably still is.

DB: [*Laughs*] I suppose I ought to say that I do lots of exercises and stuff, but I don't. It came very naturally to me. I presume it's something to do with the mime training that I had earlier, it sort of worked on a physical level. But I've not had any trouble with my back or anything really. My hands got very stiff, actually.

AP: I was going to say, I was watching the veins stand out during the performance.

DB: Yeah, I've had trouble with that.

AP: It looked like intense pain. So, you are going to do this for how long?

DB: I shall stop on January 4th. I think if I continue doing it after that, it would seem a bit like factory work. I really just wanted to see what it was like doing a play anywhere, whether it be Broadway or wherever. There's nothing else on Broadway I would do, because there are a lot of techie musicals and whatever that I don't think I'd be very happy about doing. But this started off in Denver and Chicago for me, so we didn't know if it was going to get to New York. But it was the idea of doing a straight play which had the greater appeal.

AP: What sort of reaction did you get from the actors? I mean, inevitably, I suppose there must be one or two cynics around …

DB: No, they were great. Everybody. Every one of them.

AP: Did you fear that you would encourage, dare I say, the wrong sort of audience? That the Bowie music fans might come along literally just to see it as a performance and say, 'Well to hell with the play, but here's David and that's what matters to us'?

DB: Up until the first night, yes. That was the biggest worry … Not about what kind of audience, but what their reaction would be. But I think that's the fault of ours for not giving them enough credit, that they are responsible. There's that stupid word. They were interested in the play, they were concentrated, they really worked on understanding what the play was all about. And I think they enjoyed it, the majority of them enjoyed it.

AP: Well, I was sat next to a lady who originally came from England and planned her entire holiday around coming here to see you do the play. So that's a bit of an accolade. What about Britain, because the feeling and the feedback I've got from people I've talked to before we came, is that a lot of people will be sad that it looks as though you will never do it in Britain?

DB: Unfortunately, the rights are with another producer and director in England. It started in England, Philip [Anglim] first saw it himself at the Hampstead Theatre years ago when it was first put on with David Schofield, I think it was, in the Merrick role. And it's been on since at the National [Theatre] with Schofield, but it's been directed in a very different manner. I would have loved to have done it in England, but there's no way because there are no rights available to do it in England.

AP: How much research did you do? I heard a story somewhere that you'd actually been along to a London hospital and taken a personal look at the life of John Merrick.

DB: Yeah, that's the first thing … the whole thing happened so fast when they finally decided to take me as Merrick. I'd forgotten about the whole thing after Hofsiss had seen me. But I got a call within two weeks of having to go over and start rehearsals, so I couldn't do very much. So, I went to the London Hospital, and went to the museum there, and found the plaster casts of the bits of Merrick's body that were interesting to the medical profession, and the little church that he'd made, and his cap and his cloak. Nothing much you can get from that, just the general atmosphere that you get to feel something from it. I don't know what exactly.

AP: Do you know now what you feel or do you feel different things on different nights?

DB: Yeah, I find I take a lot of my day on stage with me, depending on what my day's been like. If I try and fight the day, I don't think I'm as credible as when I try and incorporate my daily feelings into the role.

AP: I was watching you doing the sequences sat in the bath, and you were still going through mime actions and picking up the sponge and what have you. I wonder what was going through your mind? Was it the same thing every night, whether you are so deeply involved in the part that it is the same thing, or whether you have different thoughts and views?

DB: I don't wonder much. I seem to keep some idea of a stranger being put into a new environment, and I keep on conjuring up new environments and I try and imagine what it would have been like in different places. I change the stage every night in my mind about what's on stage, and I concentrate on things that aren't really there.

AP: How much involvement did you have in the staging? Were you allowed to be …

DB: In my own characterisation, more and more I've been allowed to do it exactly the way I want to do it. Again, a precedent was set and so well defined by Anglim's original characterisation, or I guess I should say Schofield's original characterisation which became Anglim's, which is something that's so easily recognisable now, and the photos define the part as well fairly concretely … It's hard to fight the fact that it was his right arm that was longer, and the hips were at a particular angle, so the stance is very much an ongoing thing, it's gone through all the characters. But the voice I've changed considerably, I've made it much more of a London voice because I don't have actor's technique to talk in that sort of non-accent manner, so I just bring him back to a very London-type person.

AP: That's a cue for me to ask you, is London still very important to you?

DB: It has been because of Merrick, I think.

AP: Really? It's re-enhanced your interest in …

DB: I don't know about interest. It's not a city that I think I could live in – I still like to go back, but then again, I don't think there is a city I would be prepared to live in. Not sure if I'm anymore a city person.

AP: Do you have an interest deep in your mind in freakish phenomena and strange people, because if we go back in your career …

DB: I don't think it's that deep. [*Both laugh*] It's quite on the surface, really. Yeah, I am certainly intrigued by people who have either put themselves on the line or are on the line, unwittingly or unconsciously, or arrived at that situation. But that's a leftover from being a painter. I always painted people and things that were a little corrupted around the edges somehow.

AP: Did that ever worry you? What were your early influences – did you feel you had any?

DB: Not really. I never thought I wanted to do pictures or songs about people who were regular guys or regular people. It never appealed to me. There are enough writers and painters who do that kind of stuff anyway.

AP. Did you see Major Tom as being as a regular person in the very early days?

DB: I saw him as a person who thought he was a very regular person, but put in a situation that he couldn't handle, that would reduce him to something quite extraordinary where he has no intention of going back to the Earth. That was implicit in the song originally. I read the song that it was his intention not to come back, that it wasn't anything to do with Ground Control or failure on the part of the spaceship.

AP: Is it a song you're still very proud of?

DB: 'Proud' is not really … I don't know about 'proud'. I think it still means a lot to me. I think Major Tom does. [*Adopts an American accent as he pours a glass of water*] We'll just take a little break here.

AP: Did you see that as being one of the high points of your career? When one looks at it in terms of radio terminology, it's inevitably a piece of music that's going to be played an awful lot, and still is.

DB: Only that it was the first time that I'd been able to create a character that was very credible. I think for any writer, that's a high point. He preceded all the others, and I think one has a special place for him. I do, yes.

AP: And indeed, Major Tom has come back more recently, hasn't he, with …

DB: … 'Ashes to Ashes'.

AP: … a big success for you in Great Britain, which I hope will please you, still.

DB: Um … yeah. [*Laughs*]

AP: The British market, that is. I'm interested to talk to David Bowie in New York. We are here for a few days, but you're here on a regular basis now.

DB: What, in New York? Oh no, I'm not.

AP: Well, in America and doing a lot of travelling, but you're not in Britain as much as you were. Do you see the British market as being terribly important to you?

DB: Firstly, America isn't a place I come to very often. I'm not that fond of this place, either. [*Laughs*]

AP: Oh really? Aren't you fond of anywhere, Bowie? [*Laughs*]

DB: Well, it's okay. They know that as well. They have to live here! I don't mind working here again, it's a great stimuli as a place to work.

But as a living place, I don't know. I'm not at all sure about habitat, never have been.

AP: Naturally nomadic …

DB: Um. But England … what did you ask me about England? [*Laughs*] I can't remember.

AP: How important … was the English market to you now, the fact you had a Number 1 single …

DB: Oh, markets. Oh, God. I think I gave up the idea of markets way back when the whole process of business and selling records for records' sake and … when it became a question of what kind of content do you give an album so it gets higher sales? When that sort of great puzzle came up, I thought, 'Well, that's defeating the whole point of why I'm writing.' It just doesn't make any sense. And I wasn't enjoying … That was round about *Aladdin Sane* period, just before The Spiders's break-up. And that was one of the few albums where I put content in to try and accumulate record sales, which was a gross mistake all the way round. It's just something I didn't want to do. And I've found out since, of course. Then I got quite into the idea of, 'Well, they just have to take me for what I am' sort of thing, and I stuck with that.

AP: … succeed artistically …

DB: Oh, it's smashing that *Scary Monsters* has done so well. I'm really pleased. But it wouldn't have amazed me if it hadn't done … or sold like my albums usually do sell these days. [*Laughs*]

AP: [*Voiceover*] The incredibly honest David Bowie. You are turned to Radio 1 on a Monday evening. It's Andy Peebles this side of the microphone being straightened out and battered verbally by the man who I spoke to back in New York back in December of last year. We move now to the *Scary Monsters* album. Drug abuse is something which has riddled the rock business, and society in general, for a great number of years now, and I wondered whether that had some connection with a song called 'Ashes to Ashes'.

DB: I would never have wanted to be and tried not to be a banner-waver for any particular, quote, 'cause'. But I have seen an alarming amount of abuse, especially with heroin and the disastrous effects it has on people. So, when I was thinking of how I was going to place Major Tom in this. Hence, 10 years later on, what would be the complete disillusion with the great dream that was being propounded when they shot him into space 10 years ago and had such wonderful ideas. This great technology was capable of putting him up there. When he did get up there, he wasn't quite sure why he'd been put there, and we left him there. But now we come to him 10 years later, and we find that the whole thing has soured because there was no reason for putting him up there. It was an ego, a technological ego, which got him up there for no specific reason, and just added more disaster because it was a potpourri of technical ideas. So, the most disastrous thing I could think of is that he finds solace only in some kind of heroin-type drug … actually being that the cosmic space itself is feeding him with an addiction, and he wants now to return to the womb from which he came. It's also a nursery rhyme. It's very much a 1980s nursery rhyme. I think 1980s nursery rhymes will have a lot to do with the 1880s, 1890s nursery rhymes, which were all rather horrid, and had little boys with their ears being cut off and stuff like that. Well, I think, [*Laughs*] we're getting round to that again. I think the idea of the *Sesame Street*, nicer nursery rhyme is possibly outdated, unfortunately. Let's hope I'm wrong. I expect I am.

ASHES TO ASHES

AP: What about the diversification of interests? Have you found that easier to control? The fact that you're involved in a stage production here, and yet you still have the inevitable pressure of keeping up the output of music. How have you managed to mix the two, or indeed have you, at all?

DB: I think so, in terms of I don't have managers and stuff. I got rid of all that as well. I just have a couple of people who work with me, and it's much more on a real basis. I don't feel like an organisation or anything right now. Some of my contemporaries have got into that position and I think it's an unhappy one to be in. I'm not saying things are perfect, but it feels a lot more real. Yeah, I mean, there's not that much happening that I can't really look after. The play's in the evening, and I do my writing in the day. I can paint when I come home from the theatre, so it's all fairly logical.

AP: [*Voiceover*] All fairly logical to the mind of David Bowie, but to us lesser mortals, I would envisage a great strain. Let's move back now to the album *Scary Monsters*. And I asked David about a track which includes some excellent guitar work from the one-time leader of King Crimson, Bob Fripp. A song called 'Up the Hill Backwards'.

DB: That's a very odd piece of music because … what happens by the end of it, is that it actually makes some kind of commitment. But on first hearing, it sounds as though it's a very shrugged, almost cynical 'there's nothing we can do about it' kind of attitude, which is thrown at a very MOR-voiced [middle-of-the-road] track. So, it really sounds like the epitome of indifference. But, in fact, I've blocked it from beginning to end with the extraordinary, high-energy Fripp, quasi-Bo Diddley thing that happens in the beginning and the end, which bookended and gave it another kind of switch. It has far more power than it would at first seem, as a commitment. In fact, it has a very strong commitment, but it's disguised in indifference. These are all very personal readings of what I wrote. It's completely just my own very subjective point of view about them, and I'm more aware than most, I think, that a piece of music, once it's left the writer, really the knowledge of that piece of music ends there and it becomes public property and is interpreted, and correctly interpreted, by anybody who wishes to hear it. It's like a painting doesn't exist if it's locked up in a room. If it's not seen, is it a painting? Does it exist?

UP THE HILL BACKWARDS

AP: Can I talk to you about your method of songwriting? Because I've read that the Burroughs technique has been something which you've used a lot. We've been here over the weekend, we talked to John Lennon last night …

DB: Ah, lovely.

AP: … and John was chatting about working with you doing 'Fame', and I think you did 'Across the Universe', didn't you?

DB: Yeah, that's right.

AP: … and he played a bit of guitar on that.

DB: Yeah.

AP: And he said to me that he was fascinated by your technique of writing, and perhaps wished that he'd been able to do that as well.

DB: Really? It's not my … in fact, it's not really … Burroughs has got all claim to it and deserves it, but it was, I think, probably instigated by Lewis Carroll. He used to do cut-ups. I found that out fairly recently.

AP: Can you explain to us what a cut-up is? People might be interested to …

DB: Yeah. If you take some subject matter … [*Laughs*] … take a cup of subject matter…

AP: He's going to do this now!

DB: No, I can't. [*Laughs*]

AP: And come up with a new song!

DB: And you are talking about … what are we talking about? I've got to think of a situation. You're thinking, oh, let's go back to the Wall. The Wall keeps cropping up. So, you got the Berlin Wall and you've got different episodes happening outside of it. You're getting somebody trying to jump over the Wall. Then you write paragraphs. Well, this is what I do, anyway. This is only one example. I'd write a paragraph from the jumper's point of view. I'd write a paragraph from an observer's point of view on this side of the Wall and then an observer's point of view on that side of the Wall, so you've got three different points of view. And then I cut them up and I reshuffle them and I pull them out in three- or four-word phrases and put the parts together. And then from that, I can either take exactly what is laid out and utilise that as a new theme … you get some quite original little things coming out of it … a fourth point of view, in fact, that one hadn't thought about before … or, I can take it exactly as it reads, or I will then re-sort it out. There are no rules, there are no ground rules. I mean there is no, 'This is what it is, you are not allowed to deviate from that.' There's no rule system in it. It's a tool of writing; a way of writing to promote a new perspective on something that might have got stodgy. I don't use it all the time these days. I used to use it far more.

AP: Are you a quick songwriter when you want to be?

DB: Yeah, very fast. Yeah. I usually complete a song in about, I don't know … 20 minutes when I get going, but I might take two or three days building up different ideas and approaches to it. But the preface to it takes a lot longer than the actual writing.

AP: Do you often go back deep into your songwriting history to pick up on things again? Because one sometimes meets …

DB: Maybe that is so, but it's not a conscious thing. If one has a particular kind of perspective toward what you are trying to do, it's going to show through all the time, it's going to establish a style. I suppose if there's anything inherent in what I do, a style does come through, even though I seem to superficially change such a lot. There's definitely some tenuous link that goes through all the work that I do that can be identified as being me or what I've been doing.

AP: If we go back to the days of, back to Ziggy Stardust, I was very much wanting to ask you about 'Fashion' because we almost, well, we did work together in 1972 when you were on tour in Manchester. It's where I first met you …

DB: Yeah.

AP: … in the days when you had a very definite image. And the youth of Great Britain, certainly, seemed to think that the best thing to do was to rush off to the hairdresser and immediately look as near to David Bowie as they possibly could. What sort of feeling did that give you? Was it, when you sat and thought about it privately, a power thing?

DB: Initially, it was very morale boosting, [*Laughs*] let's put it that way. I think after a short while, though, it became quite … quite scary to live with that sort 'little mes', especially when it got so close to home, and it became something that was real in as much as there were a lot of people who found out where I lived and looked like me and came, in those days ... [*Inaudible*] ... and that was sort of scary because it seemed to intrude. And I thought, 'Well, I've created the damn thing, that's what you can expect is going to happen.' [*Laughs*]

AP: As you sit in front of me now, you appear very much to have shaken off the image ...

DB: I should hope so. [*Laughs*]

AP: I read in the press you'd said that in New York you could walk down the street and not be harassed, and people would say, 'David, how are you?' and you would say, 'Fine.'

DB: Yeah.

AP: That's something that obviously appeals to you.

DB: Oh, yeah, yeah. I mean, this is the perfect city for that. And Berlin is like that as well. Berlin even better in a way, because nobody will actually talk to you, either. [*Laughs*] Not only do they not recognise you!

AP: You were talking about people sitting in the garden a moment ago. Dare I bring the subject up – if we look at your career chronologically, the only odd thing that happened was the reissue of 'The Laughing Gnome', which is what made me think of gardens.

DB: Yeah. [*Laughs*]

AP: It's just gone through my mind. Was that difficult to cope with? Because I remember being as guilty as the next man about playing it on the radio.

DB: Oh no, not at all. [*Laughs*]

AP: The only thing that seemed to go out of sequence. Were you pleased about that? I mean, those were the days when people used to say, 'David Bowie sounds like Anthony Newley.'

DB: Oh, I did. I sounded strongly like … I thought he was a great role model. I was most impressed with him because he was the first one that didn't sing in an American accent. I thought that was very sensible. After [*The Strange World of*] *Gurney Slade*, um, I think that was the thing that registered most with me – Gurney Slade. There was something so delightful about that whole situation, invoking the things in his own imagination and putting them into a real form. I like that kind of manifestation.

THE LAUGHING GNOME

AP: We talked about John Lennon a few moments ago and your involvement with *Fame*. I think you describe that as being utter and complete plastic R'n'B.

DB: That album.

AP: Yes, that album. Was that a kick against what was going on basically in America at the time, when everything was high hat and four to the bar and very much disco?

DB: Oh, I don't think it was done in a spirit of anger. I thoroughly enjoyed the album. I liked the album a lot. I still do. I think it's a very good album. But it was plastic soul. It was something that I was reading from the clubs I was going to. And there was this new kind of R'n'B, it wasn't like the R'n'B I was weaned on as a teenager, it was …

AP: … dreadfully manufactured.

DB: It was manufactured, but I didn't dislike it. I didn't dislike it at all. It sounded right for the particular year that it was being done in, and it completely took hold of me and I wanted to produce stuff like that.

AP: Do you spend a lot of time listening to radio in New York? Because I've been here for …

DB: Not now. I think the radio is dreadful over here.

AP: Now, that's definitely what I think. It's very soft, isn't it?

DB: Ghastly.

AP: There doesn't seem to be much guts to it at all.

DB: There was one station called WPIX, but they crushed that one as well and put it back into Top 40 format. There are so little listenable areas for new music over here, it's disastrous. It's extraordinary. There are so many good bands over here starting work and trying to do the clubs, and coming from these suburbs of New York and whatever, and there's absolutely nowhere they can get any exposure on the radio. This lands lives by radio …

AP: Yes, it does indeed.

DB: So, if you can't get a hold in there as a creative artist, you've got no chance except to keep on playing the small clubs and hoping you build up a following big enough to carry you to a bigger audience, if you want or need a bigger audience. I don't know about that anymore, either.

AP: [*Voiceover*] David Bowie in conversation with me back on Sunday December 7, 1980. Ironically, and tragically, with mention of John Lennon the day before John Lennon was so brutally shot. We move back now to the album *Scary Monsters* – it's David's current album – and the hit single 'Fashion'. What were David's views on that song?

DB: When I first started going to discos in New York in the early seventies, there was a very high-powered enthusiasm and it had a natural course about it, which seems now to have been replaced by an insidious, grim determination to be fashionable, as though it's actually a vocation. There's some kind of strange aura about it, and I just wanted to capture that feeling in the song 'Fashion'.

FASHION

AP: Of the people who have come out of the New Wave scene in Britain, do you have any favourites?

DB: Yeah. Wire I like very much indeed. And I really used to like, well I still do like, Joy Division very much. Those two are, I think, my favourite British bands. Well, British-Irish. [*Laughs*]

AP: British-Irish, exactly. David, where do you go from here, because, as I said earlier on, there's a great diversification, you're doing all sorts of things. And I read with horror somewhere – this is only my opinion – that you felt video would be a great market for bringing you to your fans without perhaps the necessity of being on stage all the time.

DB: Oh, I don't think I quite put it like that.

AP: Is that a misquote?

DB: It's a misquote. It's a misquote. I know the content and let's change that around.

AP: Yes, please do.

DB: I don't fancy touring much, to be frank with you.

AP: You're bored with it?

DB: Bored? It's just facing up to the reality that it's such a demoralising and vegetating situation to have to spend so much time running for aeroplanes; and you can waste three months, and life is not that long, you know. And three months every year or so is a big portion of it, just to repeat the same show every night. And after the first couple of weeks, unless you're a positive philistine, there's no way that you can still enjoy doing the same show after two weeks on the road. So, I would rather smash it out for two weeks of really, really good shows, but centralise them in major cities and video out into in-circuit clubs at a lower door-admission price, so you get the same amount of people who are able to see the shows at a far cheaper rate. And I would be expending the total amount of energy that I could with enthusiasm just in a short period. It makes a lot more sense to me.

AP: It makes sense, but do you think your public would accept it?

DB: Oh, Christ, I don't care! I mean I just don't want to tour. I don't see why I should tour, because it's not giving anybody anything more from me, because if I can't do it with enthusiasm, it's going to show. And there's no way you can manufacture enthusiasm – well, there are ways, but I don't intend to go and do that situation.

AP: [*Voiceover*] I shall be interested to see what David Bowie eventually decides to do. I think it'd be a dreadful shame if we start missing him on stage. He's such a marvellous live performer. Back to the album *Scary Monsters*, and I asked David what was in his mind when he wrote a song called 'Teenage Wildlife'.

DB: I definitely set out to write an archetype. I've always been impressed with that kind of song. I've, from time to time, attempted to write those kind of songs. I think this is one of the more successful. I've tried to approach a young mind that is not forearmed to the hypocrisies that he will encounter and the stubbornness to change that people have, and to accept change and flow with it rather than become reactionary and fight against it, which produces the terrible conflicts that we find around us. It's also a warning for the young man not to develop his arrogance too quickly, because that's self-defeating as well, as we all find out as we get older. [*Laughs*] Nobody has ever asked for any advice; they always tell me what to do. [*Laughs*] And I, of course, always disagree with them because I'm as stubborn as they are.

TEENAGE WILDLIFE

AP: [*Voiceover*] If you've been listening intently to this programme, you'll have heard a very interesting view from David earlier as to the fact that once an artist has created a song, it then becomes public property. And I wondered what you made of a song on the album *Scary Monsters*, called 'Screams Like a Baby'. Well, here's David's view of that composition.

DB: I don't believe in this high-tech society at all. I don't believe it does exist. I think that's a great myth. I think the idea of high-tech songs, high-tech music, computer button, whatever, it's not like that. It's on a very emotional, people level, flesh and blood. One foresees it becoming even more terrifyingly real, anti-tech. The old symbolic street-fighting thing probably will not be as symbolic as it was, but will become reality; one can foresee it in the dreadful eighties. I lapse into this future nostalgia thing often. [*Laughs*] The evidence is by looking at any album I've made. That particular piece of music does reflect that. It's writing, taking a past look at, something that hasn't actually happened yet.

SCREAMS LIKE A BABY

AP: So having done *The Elephant Man* in New York, what do you see yourself doing stage-wise in the future? Is there anything in the pipeline?

DB: Probably, as I say, coming back to Europe at some point to do the minimal tour situation I would do. Maybe one south of England thing and one north of England thing. And do that from country to country over a two-week period, and do the same thing in America, as a commitment that I would still perform but only under my own regulations about how I'm going to perform in a restricted kind of area.

AP: It's good to come to New York and meet yourself looking happy [*DB laughs*] and pleased with life. And I think that's the situation?

DB: I think so, yeah. I'm a bit harassed because the play thing is hard daily. I find it hard to kick the part daily, and it's very intense doing the eight [shows] a week. It's not the physical thing, either, it's the emotional chronology of what happens to him during the course of the play. It sticks with you during the day, as though you're covered in apple sauce or something, and you've washed it off, but it's still sticky.

AP: You do think that when you've finished it, you will go and see the film and see John Hurt's performance?

DB: I shall go on holiday. [*Laughs*] Then I'll go and see the film. The last thing I want to do when I've finished this is go and look at a film of *The Elephant Man*. [*Laughs*]

AP: I think you'll enjoy it.

DB: I will, I know I will.

AP: David, thanks very much indeed for talking to us.

DB: That's my pleasure.

KID JENSEN, BBC RADIO

INTERVIEWER: KID JENSEN

While Bowie was looking to make hits and make money, he was also making movies. This period may be remembered as his *Let's Dance* years, but it's also the time when he appeared in *Merry Christmas, Mr. Lawrence* and *The Hunger*.

Bowie would go on to choose some real clangers, among them *The Linguini Incident, Yellowbeard, Absolute Beginners, Into the Night* and *Labyrinth*, although some have fared better over time and indeed gained something of a cult audience. But *The Hunger* is a good film, while *Merry Christmas, Mr. Lawrence* is a great film, in which Bowie plays a saintly British prisoner of war in a Japanese camp. He would later call it his 'most credible performance'. Despite that, and excluding *Labyrinth*, he would never take a leading role in a film again.

One reason was that he found all the hanging around on movie sets too boring. That was why he especially loved Nagisa Ōshima, the director of *Merry Christmas, Mr. Lawrence*. 'I've spent more time making movies sitting on my arse,' he said. 'Ōshima cancelled that out for me. Two takes and it was done.'[13]

Bowie always took mental notes on set with a view to directing his own movie. But, for whatever reason, it never came to pass – perhaps the only goal Bowie set himself which he never realised.

KID JENSEN: Last Monday, David Bowie invited me to his London hotel so that I'd be able to record a chat with him for this programme. It was my fifth recorded piece with him in 12 years. And I was really flattered at this meeting because it was, apart from his press conference on March 17, the only radio interview he'd wanted to do for quite a long time. Well, I met him on his own in his elegantly appointed suite, and he was looking very bronzed, very healthy and wearing a casual suit with an open-necked khaki shirt. What follows, after his current single, 'Let's Dance', is our recorded conversation.

LET'S DANCE

KJ: You are looking so fit, so tanned. What have you been doing to look so well?

DAVID BOWIE: I just got back from Australia. I was doing the promo videos for some of the tracks for the new album out there, and that was something like 116 degrees heat in the bush. But then I seem to have spent the last six months in hot climes. I was in Rarotonga before that on the Ōshima movie, so I've been back and forth from there, so I've inevitably got tanned.

KJ: I was going to ask you about the video. Presumably, 'Let's Dance', then, that single, was done in Australia too?

DB: Yes, that's right.

KJ: Who are those people?

DB: I wanted to work with aborigines but not in a clichéd context. I didn't want them to be dressed up in war paint or tribal gear, and that's something they're terribly against at the moment as well. So, I wanted to find a couple of just really pleasant-looking, young, modern people who happened to be aborigines, and I found these two in Sydney. One of them goes to a dance school and the other one is a boyfriend or something, named Terry and Jolene. And I just thought they're such natural stars, they're wonderful kids, they've never acted before in their lives. And they're just perfect for this thing that I wanted to do.

KJ: Right. Now, you're back in Britain. Do you come back often as a private person at all?

DB: No, well, I've been back quite a few times, yeah, privately. But only for a couple of days or a weekend or something.

KJ: Is that ever difficult for you to come back privately, though? Because there are always photographers at airports, waiting …

DB: Oh no, no, no, no. I have absolutely no problem coming in and out. I've been through London many times without people knowing. I mean it's very easy to avoid all that. I guess it's how much you want your photograph taken. [*Laughs*]

KJ: Do you still think of Britain as home, then?

DB: Er, no, I don't. No, I guess I've become far more international in terms of living. I feel quite at home in just about anywhere now, on a temporary basis.

KJ: Where do you spend most of your time?

DB: What is most of one's time? Over the last year I've been in London, New York, South Pacific, Australia, Africa and occasionally Switzerland. That's been *this* year. And this coming year, for the next six months, it'll be just about every city in the world.

KJ: So, it's not important to you to have a root or a home base?

DB: I don't feel, no … I'm not really a roots person in terms of home.

KJ: It's interesting to find someone as successful as you obviously are in your chosen fields, plural, to be as busy as you are. What keeps you going? Because you've had success, haven't you …

DB: Yes.

KJ: … and all that that means, but yet you want to keep working. That's a fairly gruelling schedule doing all this touring.

DB: Yes, it is. The reason I want to tour is that I've not toured for five or six years, and it really is exciting now again. It got to a point where I couldn't get very excited about doing the hundredth gig on a 200-city tour. I mean, it was just one tour after another. The excitement went for me, and it's taken all this time to get to a point where I really want to tour again.

KJ: In the mid-seventies you began experimenting, and recording too, disco, soul music, and now you've embraced this music again with Chic's Nile Rodgers, on the evidence of the single, anyway.

DB: Yes.

KJ: What has been the inspiration behind your current direction?

DB: When I went to Rarotonga to do the Ōshima movie, I wanted to pull out some cassettes and tapes to take with me for something to listen to. I found that my natural inclination was to choose mainly rhythm and blues from the fifties and sixties. I wanted to find stuff that I could play over and over again because in the South Pacific, it can get very boring.

KJ: That's a real *Desert Island Discs* situation.

DB: It really is, yeah. I was doing my *Desert Island Discs* in a way, and I found it was interesting to see what, in fact, I did choose. Everything from James Brown to Alan Freed Rock 'N' Roll Orchestra, Elmore James, Alma King. I surprised myself. I eventually got there. There was just about nothing representing the last 15, 20 years.

KJ: Amazing.

DB: And then I asked myself, 'Why have I chosen this music? What is it about this that makes me play it over and over again?' The fact was that it had such a human, emotional quality to it, without pinpointing a tight situation. It's a very non-uptight music. And it comes from a sense of pleasure and happiness. There's an enthusiasm and an optimism on those recordings.

KJ: Maybe we could take a break now and just hear a track that you would have taken to your desert island. Of all the things you remembered, is there something going in your head now like …

DB: Oh, Christ …

KJ: You mentioned some great names like Elmore James there.

DB: Yeah, okay. Alright, then. Try and find this one! [*Both laugh*] Bobby Gregg and his band playing 'The Jam'.

THE JAM (Bobby Gregg)

KJ: That was Bobby Gregg and his band and 'The Jam' that David Bowie took down to the South Pacific where he was working on a film a few months ago; because you were doing R'n'B yourself, weren't you, in the 1960s?

DB: Yeah. I desperately wanted to be a rhythm and blues saxophonist. I mean, that was my big thing. I wanted to be part of an equivalent of the Little Richard band, that was my ideal thing to do when I was about … actually, that was earlier. When I was about 13 or 14, that's what I wanted to do, so I played tenor with a few bands around town in those days. I got into one band, I think it was … now which band would it have been? God, I think it was a different band every week, or it was the same band and we changed the name a lot, [*Both laugh*] I can't remember. It all blurs. But I found out that I wanted to start writing my own material for that band, and the sax started taking second place to singing and writing songs.

KJ: Back in 1982 and now '83, working with Nile Rodgers, how did the two of you meet up? Did you know each other from before?

DB: We first met in a club in New York. No, I'd never met Nile before. I'd always thought his work was really good. It was just a wonderful bass and rhythm sound, and his guitar playing is also excellent. And we met in a club in New York and inevitably started talking about our own reference point. We wanted to find a common area, as one does with a new person, sort of find out what you like. And we both started talking about rhythm and blues stuff, and we both knew all exactly the same discs and records and bands. And when I had to consider who I wanted to work with on the new album, I thought, 'Well, let's give Nile a try, see if he'd be at all interested in working with me,' because of my own rediscovery of rhythm and blues stuff.

KJ: And he would have been aware, of course, of what you were doing in the mid-seventies as well.

DB: Yeah, very much so. So it was a good combination.

KJ: He knew the heart would have been there. A question I know the press would have asked you a million times, but I haven't heard the answer myself, is after so many successful years and records with RCA, you've changed. You're now with EMI America. Why the change?

DB: By the end of my contract with RCA, there was no love lost between us. I think the belief had gone in each other. I didn't believe in RCA, and they certainly had fallen out with me around the time of *Low*. There was no real interest in *Low* and many of the albums from there on. We just went through the movements of being artist and record company. I was really quite glad when I was able to terminate that particular contract.

KJ: I find that unbelievable because any record company, any other record company, would have been glad to take you on because you're the sort of artist who keeps lots of lesser-known artists afloat.

DB: I think familiarity had bred contempt. We were quite happy to take a short space from each other … a long space from each other. [*Both laugh*]

KJ: How do you react, then, to the numerous Decca and the RCA reissues that have cropped up in the last couple of years in the absence of new material from you, these sort of releases that in fact chart in the UK?

DB: I think they're horrendous. These compilations sound like they were done in about half an hour of a board meeting. The packaging is generally atrocious, and I find it most offensive.

KJ: What about the *Rarities* album, the Italian compilation, that came out? That as well?

DB: I'm not quite sure what the point of it is, except to maybe pick up a few extra bucks or something. If they'd wanted a compilation, they should have come to me and asked me to put something together for them, and I would have given them something very interesting, but of course they don't ask me these things, they just put them out. And I dare say they will continue to put out compilations of albums which I have absolutely no understanding of or control over.

KJ: Do you have a record yourself of all the things you've ever recorded? Do you have a collection of all your work?

DB: No, I'm not a very good back fan. I get a lot of stuff. My audience are really good like that. They send into the New York office an awful lot of stuff that they think I might not have heard, so I've heard and know about just about every bootleg that's been done. I've even had studio tracks from the early days that I didn't know existed come through to me, a very early version of, what was it, 'I'm Waiting for the Man', which I did in somewhere like … it was about 1970, a 1970s version of that, which floored me. I can't remember doing it to this day and it's definitely me. It's quite definitely me.

KJ: What about other memorabilia or paraphernalia, like a Stylophone, for example, that you used in 'Space Oddity'? [*DB laughs*] Anything like that?

DB: I probably have that. Things I've got … I've got, I think, every item of clothing I've ever worn. I always keep that stuff. Stuff like that I'm very reluctant to throw away. I've got all the very early Kansai [Yamamoto] costumes, all the early stuff from the Rainbow, and the stuff that was specially made and all the Dada-looking things. I've got all that.

ZIGGY STARDUST

KJ: What about the Ziggy Stardust period. That seems to be musically, for a lot of people today who always quote you, as being a prime influence. Does that seem – the Ziggy Stardust fellow himself – is he a long time ago in a far-off place or is he still fairly fresh to you?

DB: I find it very refreshing to look at. It was an extraordinary phenomenon in rock at that time. I can't really relate to the kind of enthusiasm I must have had for him at the time. I'm very much divorced from that situation. It is hard to connect with that, but that's been with purpose. I've really cut myself off purposefully from that situation, because for so many years it hindered my own physical and emotional state, and it was such a hard thing to try and live his life. [*Laughs*] It was not pleasant. So I really closed the door on him.

KJ: Now, as I said, people constantly quote you as being a major influence on their own music, notably Gary Numan, Japan, Human League. Do you see your own influence when you hear these records by these other people, particularly coming out of Great Britain?

DB: Oh, of course I do. But it certainly doesn't stop me from liking some of these bands. I really encouraged people to try and listen to or accept Human League, for a start. I was great fans of theirs from the moment they came out. I thought they had some very interesting things to say. Yes, [*Laughs*] I do see those influences.

KJ: Do you ever play any of the modern … are you aware, do you keep up to date with what's happening in this country?

DB: No, I get a lot of those things very second-hand.

KJ: What about the Bauhaus record? In a session for us, they did one of your songs, they did 'Ziggy Stardust', that later became a single. Have you heard that?

DB: Yes, I got that a couple of weeks ago. No, I'm not a great follower of modern music. I never was … my influences.

I purposefully have never listened to the music of the moment when I've been writing or working, because I wanted my stuff to come from a direction that wasn't involved with whatever was going on at the time. Or if I did listen to modern music, it was usually something right off the wall or something that nobody was listening to. And it would be ethnic music or even modern classical music. I guess when there was a proliferation of punk and New Wave music, I was listening mainly to Philip Glass and Steve Reich at the time, which was a lot calmer, more transcendental kind of music format. So, I try and run against the grain to keep my own writing sounding fresh and feeling fresh.

KJ: How about the Bauhaus single … what was your reaction to that? Did you enjoy what they had done?

DB: [*Laughs*] It was a shock to hear Ziggy Stardust being revived by anybody other than myself, I must admit that. I don't think it was that successful. I'm not quite sure why they did a cover version, but then again, I'm hardly one to talk, as my cover versions are usually quite dreadful. I can only think of a few that I quite like.

KJ: Name one, then we can play it. [*Both laugh*]

DB: 'Can't Explain' from the *Pin-Ups* album, I like.

CAN'T EXPLAIN (The Who)

KJ: I remember meeting you in France when you were recording that album.

DB: Yes, that's right, sure.

KJ: You've recorded with other people over the years, notably Bing Crosby and Queen and John Lennon. Is there anybody that you

can think of that you'd really like to do a duet with that you haven't
worked with?

DB: Absolutely no one. There never was in the first place. These
things just seem to come about. I've never really wanted to record
with other people. These things just sort of happened. I can't
think of anybody off-hand. I would … yes! It would be a lot of fun
with absolutely no purpose, but a lot of fun to make a record with
Kraftwerk. That would be fun.

KJ: Last year, our listeners would have seen you in a BBC television
production of Bertolt Brecht's *Baal*. What was it about this play that
attracted you to it?

DB: I think the role was much stronger in the reading than it was
in the actual presentation. Although, looking back on it, and having
seen it since its broadcast, I think it's a very strong piece of television
but not very accessible. It's not an accessible format to shoot that
long range. I mean his cameras, Alan's [Alan Clarke] cameras, were
almost in the next studio. Talk about long shots. And it was very hard
to see the action because the characters were so diminutive on the
screen. But the role itself I found an interesting role to get into;
I mean he was such a gregarious, loud person and such an emotional
cripple. When I look at roles, they either have to have an emotional
or physical limp. [*Laughs*] They're the kind of roles that interest me.

KJ: Presumably, you are turning down scripts all the time, ever since
you did the first movie and when you appeared on stage with *The
Elephant Man*, you must be inundated with scripts all the time. I was
going to ask you what you are looking for in a script.

DB: Up until *The Elephant Man*, it was the same role I was turning
down time after time. [*Laughs*] It's usually a green Martian who plays

rock'n'roll music, but *The Elephant Man* changed that. Now, it's a green Martian who limps. [*Both laugh*] The roles have been getting more interesting over the last few years, culminating with the Ōshima role of [Jack] Celliers in *Merry Christmas, Mr. Lawrence*, which to date has been the most fulfilling thing I've done.

KJ: And when will we see that?

DB: I think it goes to the Cannes Film Festival in May, and then probably opens up in London after that. I'm very excited about that one.

KJ: Is there any music at all in it?

DB: The music's from [Ryuichi] Sakamoto from Yellow Magic Orchestra, and it has a sort of Javanese feel because the thing is set in Java in a Japanese prisoner-of-war camp.

KJ: Now, working obviously on stage like *The Elephant Man* is a bit more like being on stage making music, as opposed to being on location doing a film. Do you know any stage fear at all? Because I saw you on television in America when you were doing *The Elephant Man* and I thought, this is really brave, and you carried it off with the same kind of conviction you would carry off performing music, perhaps.

DB: The first night of *The Elephant Man* was probably the most frightening stage thing ever.

KJ: Well, it is the most demanding role I have ever seen anyone take on, certainly.

DB: I was terrified before going on stage with that thing.

KJ: I think listeners will know that you played *The Elephant Man* without any kind of make-up. You were yourself on stage, you threw yourself into this character, and it was easy to forget that you were watching David Bowie – and I thought that that was a success.

DB: Yeah, the disorders were intimated rather than seen, yeah. I think that is the thing with John Merrick, the character, that the deformities were so awful that it would be hard to see past those deformities and see the real person. If that was what you were faced with on stage, you'd be continually looking at the make-up job and seeing the actor trying to come out of it – a problem, I presume, that John Hurt had to contend with when he did the film version. On stage, I think, it helped not to have the make-up. It didn't hinder it at all.

KJ: What about the other movie you've done – because you mentioned something you're pleased with, which is *Merry Christmas, Mr. Lawrence*, which we should be seeing in the springtime – what about *The Hunger*?

DB: *The Hunger*, again, was successful for me in the terms of the very thing I've just been saying. [*Laughs*] Oh, dear. It's a make-up job. [*Laughs*] I have to work through layers and layers of plastic, but I think the success of that is because he's an older man, about 300 years old, the make-up that Dick Smith did for that is so incredibly real that he made it work on muscle to muscle. If I move a muscle of my face it's reflected in the make-up itself and it's quite the most sensational make-up, it's fantastic.

KJ: You're playing an old, old man.

DB: Yeah. Well, he ages from his mid-thirties to 300 in about two and a half days, I think. [*Laughs*]

KJ: Why? Can you tell us?

DB: It's a little vampire experience, and his time clock goes wrong because he's not a real vampire, he was made into a vampire and, as we all know, real vampires can stay around forever, but the pretenders don't last above 300 years or something. It's a funny little piece.

KJ: And that is out this year?

DB: That comes out this year. I think that's quite soon, actually, about March or April release.

KJ: And Catherine Deneuve is in it?

DB: Catherine Deneuve is in it. And Susan Sarandon. Catherine is excellent, but Susan Sarandon, for me, is absolutely extraordinary. She's a great actress, fabulous actress.

KJ: And, again, I'll ask you if there's any of your music in the film?

DB: No, no, no. I've tried not to incorporate any of my music in any of the films where I'm supposed to be taking on the part of … a role. [*Laughs*]

KJ: Just to keep it totally divorced?

DB: Yeah.

KJ: I want to ask you about the new album, finally, now. Has this been a long time in the making? It certainly has been a while since we've had a new album out. Has it taken you long to record it?

DB: No, it was put together in three weeks because I had a very good idea of what I wanted to do, so it was a very simple operation to actually execute it in the studio. The arrangements were done before we went in.

KJ: Would you describe it as a dance album? The title track is certainly danceable. Is the album with a similar theme?

DB: I think you could dance to about everything on it, but really 'Let's Dance' is, by virtue of its title and the instrumental make-up, the only real dance track on it.

KJ: Is it all your own material as well?

DB: No, some of it is by others. I did a cover version of, well, half others, actually … a song that I did write with Iggy Pop called 'China Girl'. That's one of the tracks. One track that I didn't write is by, I think they're a London band, I might be wrong, called Metro.

KJ: They had a single out called 'Criminal World'.

DB: That's the song that I covered on the album. I always thought that was a wonderful song.

KJ: So did I. I remember that on Transatlantic Records. Really good. Wasn't that Peter Godwin, I think, who wrote the song?

DB: That's right.

KJ: Because I think he comes from Bury St Edmunds.

DB: Bury St Edmunds, is that right? [*Both laugh*] I thought it was London.

CRIMINAL WORLD

DB: I covered that one. Other than that … oh, 'Cat People', which I wrote with [Giorgio] Moroder. Yeah, the Metro thing is the only thing that I covered by somebody else.

DJ: Okay, and this album is coming out sometime mid-April?

DB: Yes.

DJ: Now, about the stage show, and this is what everybody can't wait to see, and it was sold out within hours of being announced in London and in Birmingham, and you've got some European dates as well … The Serious Moonlight Tour. Now the line in 'Let's Dance' – 'serious moonlight' – is it a whole concept, a moonlight or moonlit concept?

DB: Yeah, I wanted something which would give a general atmosphere to the tour. 'Serious moonlight', for me … it's the romanticism, it's the inherent quality of people being together, of a relationship between two people … I wanted to retain what I feel is the positive force on the new album, which is trying to see the world through the eyes of a couple. And I want to retain that kind of feeling for stage. It's on a more humanist level than anything I've done on stage before. It's not quite so icy.

KJ: That's what I remember best when you came with the *Station to Station* tour. And it was very icy. My palms were, in fact, sweating because the support was not an act as such but rather a film, *Un Chien Andalou*, and that was really unnerving …

DB: Yes, it was.

KJ: And I was thinking, 'God, what have we got in store here? What have I let myself in for here?'

DB: I was reflecting my own personality at the time, unfortunately. [*Both laugh*] Those days are long gone.

KJ: Are you going to be doing any old material on stage?

DB: I think I will probably be able to cameo just about every period that I've been involved in as a writer. I still find it very enjoyable to do a lot of the old material. I've changed the instrumentation on some of the pieces because they don't excite me as such anymore. So I've had to do something to make them exciting for me, otherwise I wouldn't be able to perform them with any real conviction, so I've made some allowances for that, but I've covered everything back to [*The*] *Man Who Sold the World*, I think.

KJ: Wow. Alright, well I'd like to thank you for your time here – and perhaps you might suggest a track … this is going to be difficult … but one of your older numbers that still gives you a kick on stage where you perhaps haven't had to change it that much.

DB: [*Pause*] Crickey. [*Both laugh loudly*] That's all I can say to that. Oooohhhh … I guess … yeah, I guess 'Rebel Rebel'.

KJ: Alright, we'll play out with that. And I look forward to seeing you in June in London.

DB: Okay. Thank you.

NEWSNIGHT, BBC TV

INTERVIEWER: ROBIN DENSELOW

Suntanned, sporting a coiffured, soul-boy haircut, writing with disco king Nile Rodgers, and singing hit after hit, all the while laughing. Of all the Bowie personas, this most commercial one remains one of his most unexpected. In hindsight, it's amusing to think that his most left-field turn took him to the middle of the road. Although, when talking about Bowie, 'commercial' comes with a hefty twist. 'Let's Dance' is dark disco, 'Modern Love' pits man against God, and 'China Girl' touches on heroin and imperialism via visions of swastikas. None of this was normal fare for any pop record, let alone tracks destined for the dance floor.

Bowie is caught here on the cusp of becoming the world's biggest pop rock star. He will subsequently spend the rest of the decade trying to escape the very thing he thought he wanted to achieve.

ROBIN DENSELOW: [*Introduction*] The new single, 'Let's Dance', shows Bowie changing again to New York Black funk-styles. It's his first release for EMI after 12 years with another record company, RCA, against whom Bowie now makes the remarkable accusation that they tried to dictate his style. EMI don't give lavish receptions like this very often. They won't say how much they paid for Bowie, but rumours range from £10 million to £17 million for a five-year contract.

DAVID BOWIE: Reportedly so, yes. I'm overwhelmed. [*Laughs*]

RD: Is that anywhere near accurate?

DB: Absolutely nowhere near accurate!

RD: Can you give us a more accurate figure?

DB: Of course not. [*Laughs*] The reason that we parted company, RCA and myself, were [sic] that we weren't really recognising each other's qualities to any endearing way. And I had such a general burst of enthusiasm from EMI that I couldn't resist.

RD: RCA really didn't like your last few albums, *Lodger* and things like that?

DB: No, they really didn't like those albums at all. In fact, one of the executives once suggested he get me another apartment in Philadelphia so I can go back to writing *Young Americans* and stuff, which is just not a very healthy atmosphere to write and record in.

RD: But yet, ironically, that's the sort of thing you've done with your first new record for EMI …

DB: Yes.

RD: … Not exactly *Young Americans*, a Philadelphia sound, but a Black New York style.

DB: Well, it's much better when nobody is actually telling me what to do. [*Laughs*]

RD: What about the new album? The single that's out already is very much more direct, much more rhythm and blues than the recent David Bowie output.

DB: Yeah, I got to a stage two years ago where I found that the experimenting that I was doing was eradicating a lot of the subject matter of my writing. But now I feel, for the next few years, I'll be concentrating on a lot more basic, earthier kind of material.

RD: More emotional songs?

DB: Yes, I think so – for me, anyway.

RD: Is that because of a change in your own outlook, own personality?

DB: Yeah, there's a gradual shift, I think, when you reach mid-thirties. I think there's a period when you have to decide not to try and grasp frantically for the feelings of desperation and anger that you have when you're in your mid-twenties. And, if you can relax into the idea that being mid-thirties is quite a nice place to be, with an amount of experience behind you, I think the perspective changes.

RD: How seriously do you take the business of writing pop songs?

DB: Very. I mean I always have. I still think it's one of the most direct, and can be one of the most important, of the art forms. Quite as important as … surely, I guess, it's replaced paintings in terms of defining one's society or culture. Quite definitely.

RD: In the past, your acting roles have very much been as an alien, an outsider in society. Are those the sort of roles you've particularly gone for?

DB: Yes, I always look for characters who have either an emotional or a physical limp … I don't really see my future in acting to a greater extent than my involvement now, so I really like to have characters that I can at least play around with.

RD: Do you see the acting as more important than music? How do you judge the two sides?

DB: They're both very different. Up until [Nagisa] Ōshima [the director of *Merry Christmas, Mr. Lawrence*] … I don't know, my experience my change from now on, but up until Ōshima, one is very much under the direction of somebody else's personality and vision, whereas with my own music, it's the reverse. So, I can't really equate them too much. But with Ōshima, I was given great freedom to interpret the role very much the way that I saw it.

RD: What about the future? Is it a question of picking and choosing different styles of music, different theatrical projects you want to go into?

DB: My immediate ambition is to direct something. For myself, I've had not a little experience with what is fast becoming the new school of film-making: learning. Learn as you earn, I guess. The promo film, the rock promo, puts its smack over in four minutes. But now I want to go into something a little more ambitious, maybe something around 30 minutes [*Laughs*]; 25 minutes would do.

RD: Is this a question of still wanting to prove something for yourself?

DB: One can't fight the urge to play around with film and video. It's a magic world when you can create that little world and portray its environment and the characters in it. It becomes obsessive.

LIVE AID, BBC TV

INTERVIEWER: PAUL GAMBACCHINI

Bowie had been one of the first names on Bob Geldof's list for what would later be termed 'the concert of the century'. Geldof's idea was to get the biggest star he could on board and, by doing so, convince everyone else to follow suit. Enter David Bowie.

Some days later, the Boomtown Rats singer called Bowie into the office of promoter Harvey Goldsmith to talk about the day itself.

'Everybody's doing three songs,' Geldof told him. 'But you're doing four.'

Geldof then asked Bowie if he wanted to stay to watch a short, unreleased film he had just been sent from a cameraman in Ethiopia called Brian Smith. Smith had been filming the drought and starvation for weeks for the Canadian broadcaster CBC, and had reams of leftover footage that was deemed to be too graphic for the public. Unwilling to consign the material to the editing floor, Smith spent his spare evenings in his hotel in Addis Ababa splicing it together, all the while listening to his favourite song, 'Drive' (aka 'Who's Gonna Drive You Home?') by The Cars. Only when he'd finished editing did Smith realise that he'd cut the piece to the song and that the two fitted perfectly.

'Seeing these images of people in this sump of human destitution, Bowie started crying,' recalled Geldof.

Bowie told Geldof he wanted to introduce the film on the day of the concert itself.

'You can't,' Geldof said. 'The BBC will never show it.'

Bowie repeated his request and said he would drop a song to make space.

'David, please,' Geldof replied. 'When you stop playing, people will go off for a cup of tea and it'll be hard to get them back, so you need to do those four songs.'

'I'm doing three songs and I'm introducing this or I'm not playing,' said Bowie.

'So, I didn't have an option,' recalled Geldof.

In fact, they both got their way. Bowie introduced the film and Geldof got him to sing four songs. His final number was 'Heroes'. Tens of thousands of hands went up in the air as hundreds of girls swayed on the shoulders of their boyfriends 'like flowers in the sun', recalled Geldof. Bowie then introduced the four-minute video.

'Suddenly, you see the flower of Britain start wilting in the sun at the misery of others,' recalled Geldof. 'The smiles fade. You can see the girls stricken as they try to slide off the shoulders of their boyfriends. People are just dumbstruck with the horror. And that's when the phone lines all over the world collapsed.'[14]

<After the performance, Paul Gambaccini spoke with Bowie for a short television interview.>

PAUL GAMBACCINI: David, you've been one of the most eloquent supporters of the Live Aid cause. Do you think this day has lived up to its potential?

DAVID BOWIE: I think it's surpassed it. The reception from the viewers throughout the world, the collaboration and cooperation between artists, managements, crews, the organisers … it's just absolutely superlative, it's been absolutely fantastic. I would love to see … it's probably not possible … but this kind of situation has to become an annual event, it really does. Ethiopia can only be helped to a certain extent in one year, but it has to be an ongoing situation, and I think a lot of us would pledge to do a show like this every year until starvation in many areas of the world, not just Ethiopia, was under some kind of control.

PG: Well, that's a good point, because so many people have said this can only happen once. You think this could happen again?

DB: Oh yes, I think so. I think everybody's had such a fantastic time. Certainly, I'd love to it again. I'd do it again next year like a shot.

PG: Rock music has had this potential for a long time. It hasn't seemed to be using it. Did it take Geldof or did it take the cause?

DB: I think rock music, the job it's done, is implant this kind of feeling within its audience for many years. So, when they're needed, they're there. You're not going to get that with many other kinds of media entertainment. Comedians don't have the same … you're not going to get them to turn up and dish their money out and send their money in. There's been a spawning ground for this kind of reception, this kind of activity for many years; I mean, it's so wonderful to see it actually get off the ground like this. A rock audience is a very healthy, thinking, sensitive audience.

PG: Do you think rock audiences and artists can shame governments and others to act?

DB: I damn well hope so. The inadequate action being taken by most governments in the world has been absolutely … and that, actually, applies to the actual government in Ethiopia. There's much talk of the government in Ethiopia preventing the stuff going out to the outlands because of political values. They want to keep a tight control over a certain area. Well, they've got to be shamed into actually distributing the food and increasing the worth of agricultural and farming education in those areas.

PG: You did something which was unique for this presentation, and that was, with Mick Jagger, you made a video which has not been seen and will not be seen. That's an example of another type of project which can be done. First of all, may I ask how you chose that song, and are there other things that people can do?

DB: We chose the song because I wouldn't do one of Mick's and Mick wouldn't do one of mine … no [*Smiles*] that's a joke. We chose the song because it's summer and for us the big summer song of all time was always 'Dancing in the Street'. And we thought, 'Well, that would be a gas, to do that one.' We didn't really think about doing it until we started reading all these reports and rumours that we were going to be doing a duet via the satellite. We knew beforehand that that was impossible, as there's a delay of half a second when you start trying to do that kind of thing. So we both came up with the idea of doing maybe a video that could be shown and, maybe, if it becomes a record after, we could donate the proceeds to Live Aid as well. So, it's a possibility.

PG: May we just remind viewers and listeners that though it is now late in the evening, the cause is still there, and the need is still there.

DB: It certainly is still there and [*Looks directly at the camera*] it doesn't matter if it's 25p, it doesn't matter if it's £1. Anything that you could manage is going to help keep somebody alive.

VIDEO JUKEBOX, BBC TV

INTERVIEWER: JOHN WALTERS

There's some debate about what was the first ever music video. One contender is 'The Little Lost Child', a series of photos about a poor girl's travails projected on to theatre screens while a live band played the eponymous song. Then there was a very short film made at the famous Thomas Edison Labs that showed two men waltzing as a violinist played. Edison Labs also happened to make the other contender, a longer piece called 'Annabelle Butterfly Dance', which featured the then-famous Annabelle Moore dancing in a flowing dress with small butterfly wings attached. What isn't in debate is when these music videos were made: 1894.

Of course, there were the Hollywood musicals and then, as early as the fifties, video jukeboxes were in existence in France, allowing bar-goers to pay a few centimes to not only hear but also watch artists like Serge Gainsbourg sing their songs. Come the sixties, Bob Dylan hurled his way through his lyrical cue cards with 'Subterranean Homesick Blues', The Beatles ambled around a field in a rather literal reading of 'Strawberry Fields Forever', and The Stones poked fun at their recent trial in 'We Love You'.

In other words, the music video has a surprisingly long history. But Bowie's role was significant in that he was one of the first to understand that this short film could be seen not as an afterthought to sell more records, but as a wholly separate art form.

'Bowie was the first to realise the video is a self-standing artwork,' says Glenn Adamson, former director of New York's Museum of Arts and Design.

Bowie's first effort in this area came in 1969, when he made a 28-minute-long promotional film featuring eight songs and a mime. Most were simply showing Bowie and his band, Feathers, singing and playing the songs, and were unusual but not ahead of their time. But one video was different.

Bowie had just written a song he knew was special, and he wanted to dramatise its odd narrative arc. 'Space Oddity' would feature Bowie as a silver-suited astronaut floating in space while a worried Ground Control technician tries to rein in his spaceman. The video ends on a happier note than the lyrics would otherwise suggest, with Bowie being pawed over by two women on his capsule bed. Some themes in rock'n'roll, it seems, remain eternal.

What's different here, argues Adamson, is that 'Bowie was the first to create an entirely fictional, narratively complex scenario, in which he was the star performer.'

This experimentation in video would continue throughout Bowie's life, all the way through to the end and the painfully prophetic 'Lazarus'. Here, John Walters takes time to go through some of Bowie's greatest video moments to highlight that Bowie wasn't just an artist of song and image, but an artist of film as well.

JOHN WALTERS: [*Introduction*] There were some artists for whom the video was not actually a new concept. David Bowie had been messing around with mime, dance and performance for years. He realised early on how important it was for an image to be recognised and imitated by admirers. In the early seventies, he bought primitive video equipment and made his own videos, while his stage act became more and more extreme. Bowie created the character of Ziggy Stardust, a war-paint and mime rock'n'roller, then, at the height of his success, he killed him off and moved on to different images, new experiments.

DAVID BOWIE: Sixteen. School leaving age. I went into an advertising agency, and I took night courses at art school. One thing that came out of the advertising thing, I think, was learning about storyboarding and putting your ideas on paper in chronological order. So, I was automatically, when I was designing shows, I was drawing the shows before I was putting the music together for them. And that really came out of advertising, I think. And that stayed with me. So, right from the beginning I was storyboarding videos.

SPACE ODDITY

DB: The first videos that I started doing properly were in collaboration with an English photographer called Mick Rock, who I found I had a lot of empathy with and ideas about what rock could be doing, what it could be saying. And our first thing that we did together was 'Jean Genie'. Looking back on that one, it looks sort of 'Beatle-y' now; it felt very new at the time. I think it was new in as much that nothing had been dressed like that for a few years. It was very Levi's and that kind of look. And we wanted to get a very graphic, white, almost *Vogue* look. Big faces, big bits of faces, eyes against stark white backdrops, things like that. And to throw in an environment, so we found a place, I think it was called the Mars Hotel in California somewhere – has to be in California somewhere – and we stuck the band in there.

JEAN GENIE

DB: Really, the sixties, when so much of the music was supposed to be pointedly instructive and informative, would overwhelm me and, through my theatricality of wanting to entertain, that sort of came in as well, and 'I'd better make this relevant to something'. And I think I've kind of been able to strip that off a bit now. So, I don't feel so much like some kind of information bureau with red hair. I think at the beginning I confused a lot of what I deemed art with what, in fact, was a very strong British vaudeville tradition. [*Laughs*] There's a lot of theatricality, which I probably put on a higher pillar than it deserved at the time. [*Laughs*] And there was a lot of music-hall qualities to a lot of things that I was doing. And now I'm less inclined to call what I do art – it's sort of populist entertainment.

BLUE JEAN

JW: When you are working with a director, do you find that a useful thing because you can trigger off ideas and you can take something?

DB: Yeah, very much so. With [David] Mamet, who is a great person for me to work with, he's incredibly generous in his allowing me to do what I want, especially at the beginning, when neither of us knew whether I could make videos or not.

JW: 'Ashes to Ashes', is that one?

DB: Yes, that's right. But I brought my drawings to him and I said, 'Look, I'd like to have a crack at this, can we try it my way? But there are things that I don't understand about video technique, would you help me out on special effects and things, and do you know how to turn the sky black?' [*Laughs*] This loud voice says, 'Yes!' So, we turned the sky black. But David has been excellent in those terms, technically. And he'll always continue an idea when I might wrap it up too quickly, he'll expand an idea that I might make too brief.

JW: What about wit, which there's a lot of, obviously?

DB: Yes, I think David and I are good for each other that way. We don't get too po-faced about it. Although 'Ashes' looks pretty po-faced. It was a riot making it … did turn out deadly serious, though.

ASHES TO ASHES

DB: One thing I've been sort of toying around with was the repellent and attractive qualities of the other side of the world, be it the Middle East or the Far East. How we are both drawn and repulsed by what happens, and who they are and why we even consider it 'us and them', but we're all one. That sort of basic idea came through firstly on 'Let's Dance', with the aborigines and the colonial English, and then in 'China Girl', and then finally in ['Loving the'] 'Alien'. It hadn't really occurred to me until that time that it was a subject that fascinated me a lot.

JW: In 'Let's Dance' … I like that mixture of the mundane, which is the early part of it, and then the red shoes. Where did they …?

DB: Well, they are two symbols, anyway — red shoes are for me, anyway. That's a found symbol, it's something that somebody else already created as a symbol and it seemed apropos for this particular video. One, they are the sinfulness of the capitalist society – a pair of luxury goods, red leather shoes. And also they are a sort of striving for success out of Black music – it was always, 'Put on your red shoes, baby.' Those two qualities I thought were right for what I needed as an object in that particular ... both the song and the video.

LET'S DANCE

JW: 'China Girl' was banned, of course. Did you think that was stupid or what?

DB: [*Looks up and lets out a breath*] I understand the concern. I do understand the concern. I feel very awkward about censorship, because I object very strongly to the chicks used in Page Three things. And I think it's because it's what they are surrounded by. It's easy enough to say, 'Well, somebody else can take their clothes off and that's called art, but because we appear in ...' That's one situation, where to be surrounded by so much death, hostility, violence ... to have that as the centre pearl for that kind of grotesque situation, I find very scary, especially coming back to this country, where it doesn't particularly happen like that on the continent much, although it is doing more, increasingly so. It's very startling to come back to it and see it, and it's very scary, I think. So, I don't know, you know, because we're just pumping it out on the ... and I don't need to use naked bodies in that particular context because, again, they are surrounded by other disorienting symbols which add up to some collective message which is not at all agreeable sometimes.

JW: And not perhaps what you intended anyway?

DB: Yeah ... I don't know, I find it an enormous dilemma, and I defy anybody to say that they don't find it a dilemma. I think it is a dilemma. If we knew how to deal with those particular situations, I think we'd know how to deal with a lot more situations.

CHINA GIRL

JW: The video you did with Jagger … when you were actually doing it, were you able to enjoy the song that much more as well than the actual performance? Was it different?

DB: Well, the difference … there was absolutely nothing premeditated about it.

> <*Bowie puts a cigarette in his mouth and a man comes to his side and strikes a match, which flares up. Bowie bursts out laughing and pretends to pull his eye out.*>

JW: Lies! [*DB laughs again*] You can't get away with saying that.

DB: [*Adopts a mock serious tone*] Absolutely nothing premeditated about it! [*Adopts a Cockney accent*] Worked in the rehearsal, John.

JW: And you did it very fast.

DB: Well, what we had intended doing … we were going to do a live satellite thing where Mick would sing in New York and I would sing in England. Then we found out that that half-second time delay thing really screwed it up. There was no way that we could technically overcome that so we could both sing together. There is no way around it. So, we decided to do a video together instead. We decided on the song that afternoon and we brought the band in. We started work at seven o'clock in the evening. We finished the record by 11:30 [pm], and we rushed down to the docks, and we started work in the docks at about quarter past 12, and we rolled through till 8 o'clock the next morning. So we did the record and the video within those few hours, which is a completely different way of working from the way I'm used to working. It was great. I know a lot of young bands work like that. [*Laughs*] Or say they work like that.

DANCING IN THE STREET

DB: I've heard it said so many times, 'Oh, when I hear that tune, I always think of the video.' But with me, I'm fortunate enough to be able to completely eradicate the video; if I like a particular piece of music, I can blank out the video that's associated with it quite successfully. But I think a lot of people have a lot of trouble with that, which is a shame because there was nothing more enjoyable in the seventies or the sixties or whatever than to be able to recreate different scenes in one's imagination for a piece of music.

JW: And keep them to yourself.

DB: And keep them to yourself. They become very private visions, and music was a lot more personal because of that, I think.

JW: What about the fact that these videos go into people's homes and you're there in people's homes. Does that demystify music and the characters who make music?

DB: You know, I don't know. I find it very hard to get inside the head of an 18-year-old these days. I don't know if it carries the same kind of mystic qualities that it used to for me. It does occasionally with me still. Yes, there are various pieces of music that I find quite transcendental. Not quite as raucous as it used to be, probably. I think Philip Glass has that same effect on me now that, say, Little Richard used to. But I needed that kind of loud, raucous thing when I was younger. Now, I'm looking for another kind of sensibility. I'm not quite so stricken with the idea of making a point. I don't think I'm quite as dogmatic anymore. I'm not quite sure that any point I have to make isn't being made quite as well by other people. And that maybe my most important point is that I can entertain very well, and I think I'm no longer finding it uncomfortable to reach that conclusion that I now find I'm very comfortable being an actor, an entertainer, without too much all-encompassing stuff to say.

NEWSNIGHT, BBC TV

INTERVIEWER: WESLEY KERR

One fairly reliable way to judge the quality of Bowie's musical output at any single point is to check out his haircut; here, his blow-dried mane makes him come across as a male Princess Diana.

The Glass Spider Tour has come in for a lot of flak over the years. Widely regarded at the time as cluttered and confusing, pretentious and over the top, it was always going to be hampered by the fact it was promoting one of his weakest albums, *Never Let Me Down*. Bowie would begin the show by descending from a 60-foot spider which stood atop the stage. When its bulbous body and vacuum-tube legs were lit up, it was some sight. The trouble was, much of the tour took place over summer, so the light show only became visible near the end.

On the other hand, the set and choreography had a seminal influence. 'It has become the blueprint for Madonna, Janet Jackson, Britney,' said U2's stage designer Willie Williams, who himself was inspired by the tour's towering centrepiece. 'There will be one set of costumes and a few songs, then there'll be a big scene change and the next thing. Bowie crossing rock'n'roll with Broadway was where it all began.'[15]

Even the way Bowie financed the costly operation, sponsored by Pepsi, would set the template for the future. Bowie certainly needed the financial help. The set was so large and complex that it took four days to assemble. That, in turn, meant he needed three separate sets to ensure he could meet the packed schedule.

Bowie would finish the tour exhausted. It's perhaps no surprise that his next incarnation would see him stripped of all frills and joined on stage by only a few mates.

DAVID BOWIE: It's the most physical tour that I've done ever, including the *Diamond Dogs* tour, the early seventies shows that I did. It's relentless. It never stops. I'm bruised as hell. I feel like a worn-out rag doll. But it's been just the most fulfilling tour I've ever done as well. I can't live without music, I mean I really can't. I love writing and recording music, and I really do enjoy performing. If I've cemented enough visual ideas with the music, that for me is really a fulfilling kind of performance. So, I couldn't live without those two things.

WESLEY KERR: You're well known for constant image changes.

DB: Yeah. [*Smiles*]

WK: Are they for you just a new suit of clothes or does it reflect inner turbulence?

DB: It certainly started off inner turbulence. It was for about four years there in the early seventies … an horrendous pit …

WK: What of drugs and …

DB: Yeah, a pretty stereotyped rock'n'roll lifestyle, which I was a right sucker for. But now, I think, hopefully, it's in the area of performance only. I hope I can work out my own psychological feelings and problems in the arena of music and performance, rather than drag my particular embitterments [sic] back into the streets and into real life.

WK: Which, then, after all these years, is the real David Bowie? Is it the lad from Brixton, the pop megastar – to coin a phrase – or …

DB: [*Rises from the couch*] I'll bring him on. [*Laughs*]

WK: … or is it the 40-year-old yuppie with a son at Gordonstoun?

DB: I think it's probably all of those … yuppie! Get out of here! [*Smiles*] I think it's probably a combination of everything I've ever done or ever been. It's an accumulation of all those things, you know. I don't know! I've not really fathomed out exactly … well, I'm now absolutely positive that I'm a songwriter and performer. That's one thing I do know about. But that's one of the few things that I actually do know about.

OUR TUNE, BBC RADIO

INTERVIEWER: SIMON BATES

On top of everything else, it turns out Bowie is a great dad. What would he say to his son, Simon Bates asks, if he failed his A levels?

'Never mind,' Bowie replies. 'Never mind.'

Bowie also turns out, surprisingly perhaps, to be a fan of Guns N' Roses, Kylie Minogue and his old Volvo.

Bates starts by asking Bowie about the time he said there were 15 great live acts capable of playing stadiums – who were they?

DAVID BOWIE: Oh, dear me. I can think of about five. [*Laughs*] I was being quite gregarious there.

SIMON BATES: Yes, you were!

DB: Fifteen great stadium acts?

SB: Not all 15, but five of them would be fascinating to hear.

DB: Stadiums?

SB: Yes.

DB: The Stones, without doubt, know what a stadium is all about. Springsteen, as a solo artist, is phenomenal in stadiums. I have a problem with the duration of his performance, which sometimes goes into a four-hour period and my attention span frankly isn't that long, but he certainly has a feel of being the self-imposed 'man of the people'. I mean he sets himself up in a way which is magic when it's put in front of 60,000 people. I've yet to see Prince in that kind of size, I don't know. One feels maybe that Prince would be, again, better in a more intimate surrounding. There's a delicacy with what he does which is kind of the antithesis of the very muscular performance you get from Springsteen. I anticipate that Guns N' Roses will be phenomenal in stadiums. They were unbelievable with The Stones. They got such bad press, but I thought they were wickedly brilliant, and they're a very dangerous band.

SB: Why do you say that?

DB: Some of their song references and all that. But there again, an artist isn't there to be morally right, politically right or spiritually right. If he does put himself up in that position, he's either aligning himself with a government party or he's paid to do that – he's an artist for the State or he's working for a dictator. I mean, we are up there to scream and shout about ourselves and at the world, and you make the best of it what you can, and they are certainly doing that, they are certainly doing that. They are young kids with very intrinsic LA street problems, and they capture … [*Laughs*] what a cliché … they do capture the pulse of their audience. They are their audience, there is no doubt about it. There is such a strong feeling of empathy between artist and audience with that band. They are the foremost street band in America in that way that, if you are 18, you tend to dress like that and you tend to feel like that, and they express it so well. And it makes them a fantastic stadium band. I think that's probably the answer – the stadium band, when it is an 'of the people' kind of artist, they tend to work the best.

> *<Bowie responds to rumours that he was supposed to appear alongside Kylie Minogue in the film* The Delinquents.>

DB: I think we can put that down to what is euphemistically termed 'a large artistic disagreement' with the producers in the way that it was going. The book that I had originally read and the film that I *hear* has been made … I have fortunately not seen it, so I cannot give you an opinion. [*Laughs*] I did see the rushes. [*Laughs*].

SB: Did you?

DB: That was the point that I pulled out, because they bore no relation to each other. The book that I'd read and the film that they were making had nothing to do with each other, and I just couldn't … I couldn't … I couldn't find any foundation for continuing working with them. They had their own way of wanting to do it, and it certainly wasn't mine.

SB: The book is a very charming, rather Edwardian, Australian book, that was required … [*Inaudible*]

DB: Interesting that you picked Edwardian. In fact, she [author Criena Rohan, real name Deidre Cash] came from a very strong line of socialist thinking. So, there was an effort to put her understanding of working-class Australian society in perspective through her eyes. And it was a committed effort and it was a wonderful little book, it really was a wonderful little book. And it should have been a little film. And it should have been an Australian film. There's no room in it for an American who says, 'I wanna get outta this country.' And you think, 'Oh, yes, please go away!'

SB: [*Laughs*] You have seen it?

DB: That was the rush that I saw, and it was that one line that just finished me off. And I will do something which is probably not popular, which is I will defend Kylie Minogue. When I was told that she was going to be cast as the female, I said, 'Oh, yes, she's a Chinese-Australian, obviously. It's completely the right kind of …' I was very cynical and then they showed me her test clip, and I thought, 'Do you know, if she gets the right leading man, she might actually carry this off.' And I feel very disappointed for her if, subsequently, it is a horror. Having spent a lot of time in Australia, I'm not so convinced she's just part of *Neighbours*, because over there she's fairly well known as an actress and she's done a lot of other work and we've seen a lot of her things in Australia from when she was like 10 years old. She's worked as an actress for a very long time, and she's more than competent, and she will survive it … she will survive it. I just feel sorry that it didn't go the way I would have loved to have seen it go for both her and the book. It was unfortunate.

SB: [*Voiceover*] Bowie's main hobby or obsession became fairly clear. And that is that he really is absolutely into travel in a big way. He owns an old Volvo which he's driven around Europe in. He actually has a yacht in the Caribbean. The yacht, I guess, must be a tax deal because he doesn't bother about it too much, but the Volvo he goes around everywhere in. Generally, he seems to be on the move always, leading a nomadic lifestyle. So, I asked him where this passion for travel came from.

DB: I think, like a lot of other kids, when I was quite young, people like Joseph Conrad really moved something within me that made me want to move. I mean the romance, the trepidations, the sense of adventure that was contained within that book [*Heart of Darkness*] and Rudyard Kipling; I have to admit, I know that's not quite the kind of name that one wants to throw around anymore – reactionary old fart – on the other hand, he wrote a good book and it inspired me. I've always wanted to travel. As a kid, Tibet was always somewhere I pictured as somewhere great to go.

SB: Have you been there?

DB: No, I still haven't been there. I got to know a lot of lamas. [*Both laugh*] When I had my three-minute flirtation with Buddhism, when I was an 18-year-old, I got to know one of the newly arrived lamas from the Potala called Chime [*Inaudible*] Rinpoche, who I believe is still here and does translations of the old Tibetan scrolls for the British Museum. I think he's their chief Tibetan translator there, and I do hear from him from time to time. I saw him about five years ago, that was the last time, I must admit. Running into him and finding this peculiar energy, which is a passive energy, the energy of the East, the energy of the Buddhist or the Hindu or the animist, I found it so entirely foreign to my code of conduct, my sensibility, that I really wanted to explore it. And particularly going to the East fascinated me from that point. I got to see some of it, fortunately – not enough as I'd like. I still haven't done China.

SB: You haven't done China yet?

DB: No, never been to China. Nearest I got was Hong Kong.

SB: What happens … when you're at home, do you get the feeling, 'Right, I must go book an airline ticket, go to the airport and go,' or do you get in the Volvo and travel off that way?

DB: Well, not to China. [*Both laugh*] But I have driven through all the great forests in Germany and down the Rhine and all that, through France and Italy in my own car, yeah. I drive considerable amounts.

SB: Do you stay in the two-up two-downs?

DB: I stay in *Gasthofs*, whatever's available. And when I'm in the East, I tend to stay very much away from the well-trod areas. I went to Bali just before Oz … well, actually, I went to Australia first on a trip before I started recording there with Tin Machine. I went there for a month with Melissa, my fiancé, and Coco and her boyfriend. And we went through the Kakadu National Park, and we explored the whole of the northeast and north of Australia. And we went up the Gold Coast, and that was just a fantastic insight into another kind of Australia – not like the bush.

SB: Do you take photographs?

DB: Yes, I took a lot. I do take a lot

SB: Do you take photographs of yourself?

DB: No, never.

SB: Smiling broadly at the camera … tourist …

DB: I'm not in one of them. No, I take real pictures. I just go for the shot. I want the volcano [*Laughs*] as it's bubbling over.

SB: It's geographical locations rather than churches or graveyards or …?

DB: I'm personally drawn to the romance or the history of the place and its culture, they are the first two things that inspire me. And inevitably, when I get there, it's the people themselves that become more important than either. When you start to meet the people [*Laughs*] … that's a lovely word.

SB: But aren't you [*Inaudible*] … immediately recognise you?

DB: Not in Indonesia. [*Laughs*] I don't have much of a problem in Java.

SB: But in Australia they recognise you?

DB: Oh yeah, in Australia. Well, that's another reason why one goes to north Bali and not south Bali, because south Bali has virtually been taken over by … it's sort of the Australians' Hawaii or Florida. I mean they just flock over there to Kuta Beach and Sanur. But once you get past the so-called art village of Ubud and start going further afield, it's pretty much, I would imagine, what it was like four or five hundred years ago.

SB: When you go to the national parks in Australia, does that make you more aware of green issues, are you concerned about green issues at all?

DB: Yes, I am – and, typically with me, I feel ambivalent about it, in as much talking about it worries me. How many times can you say a truth before it becomes dissipated? There's a point where you actually hear people say, [*Adopts a complaining tone*] 'Oh no, not again! We've heard enough about the bloody rainforest.' And that's the danger point, because then the issue just slips away. Ethiopia was so fashionable for that one year. It's as dire a problem as it ever has been once again this year, but it means naught, it's not alight, hardly gets a mention anymore. And that's the one thing that's so confounding about a truth.

SB: Maybe the cliché was in the question and not the answer. 'Environmental', again, is another word that's a turn-off word.

DB: But yes … he says, puffing another cigarette. It's something that now, because of others' efforts, not my own, and certainly in that particular area I'm a follower not a leader, but I have been made aware. And I was made more aware this time when I went to Indonesia; when I heard about the immense numbers of cutters that had been sent into Irian Jaya, and will probably hack that entire country down within a couple of years. And that's an enormous forest.

SB: Difficult question, but favourite country, and I don't mean favourite country to live, but if I gave you an air ticket now, where would you go?

DB: Currently this week, I think, either the east coast of Java or north Bali. The reason for that, as an artist, is that I probably produce my best work when I'm in a situation that I don't understand too well and an environment that I'm not altogether familiar with. I'm lousy when I'm in London or LA.

SB: Are you?

DB: Yeah.

SB: Why?

DB: The work becomes flaccid and it doesn't have anything and there's no substance to it. I try to write in Canada and, as much as I love Canada, it's very hard to get a vibe there of any consequence, unless you're forced to live there, I guess.

THIS IS NOT AMERICA

SB: [*Voiceover*] Let's talk about David Bowie's formative years, which is the sort of thing you see in *Q* magazine. About 20 years ago, there were lots of rumours flying around, I suppose fuelled by David himself, about whether or not he was sexually ambiguous. He often dressed as a lady, very often on stage, and there was an awful lot of doubt about just which way he was going. And I wondered when we were talking to David Bowie, if he was confident with being a bloke, really, these days. After all, there's an awful lot of hassle about sexuality in the 1990s, a troubled climate …

DB: Yeah, you know, I was a child of the sexual revolution. For me, I'm still very dubious about how a problem like AIDS possibly could be manoeuvred into such a way that it produces a new kind of reactionary mentality. It is indeed a terrifying and crippling disease, but we must also be careful that our concerns about that particular disease are, *at least*, altruistic.

SB: Are you talking about paranoia against gays?

DB: Yup. Also, ostracising certain elements of our society. I think it's a really strong possibility that that kind of situation could develop all over again.

SB: Ian Charleson [a Scottish actor] died recently, as you probably know …

DB: Yeah.

SB: … and he died of AIDS. And …

DB: Right now one of our great American artists, Keith Haring, is dying of AIDS and is contributing a lot of really good written work to that particular problem.

SB: But there was no public backlash here, nothing but sympathy for Ian Charleson and his family.

DB: Yes, as a personality. I think that when people are faceless, it's easy to hate them.

SB: [*Voiceover*] People often forget that David Bowie, the rock superstar, also has a teenage son and that teenage son is about to take his A levels. Taking your A levels is never any fun, and I asked David if he thought that Bowie Junior would pass those exams.

DB: I would hope so, I would hope so. He got a lot of O levels. [*Laughs*]

SB: If he doesn't get his A levels, what will Dad say?

DB: Never mind. [*Laughs*] Never mind. It's as simple as that. If I had anything important to stress to him, and I'm not so sure that I do, bar communication. As long as we communicate, I think that's the most essential factor. I'm not sure that whatever advice that I have to give is not tarred and stained by too many bruises from the past but maybe some of it is valid, some of it isn't. But I think one thing I would say to him, and I have told him, in fact, is that whatever decisions he makes now are not irrevocable. He does not have to wake up every day and think, 'What am I going to do for 40 years? Whatever decision I make now, that's it!' There's a lot of room for manoeuvring at this age, at 18 years old. It's a great age. And you should be freed of the feeling that you don't have to make those really important decisions now, because there's so much stress given to that. So many parents will say, [*Adopts an*

AUDITION REPORTS ON: DAVID BOWIE AND THE LOWER THIRD   (Tape 1 No.1)

RECORDED ON: TUESDAY, 2nd NOVEMBER, 1965 Producer in Charge: KEITH BATESON

HEARD BY TALENT SELECTION GROUP: TUESDAY, 16th NOVEMBER, 1965

ITEMS: "Out of Sight"; "Baby that's a Promise" (Orig); "Chim-Chim- Cheree".

INSTRUMENTATION: Lead vocalist/Leader: Davie Jones; Lead Guitar/V.B.: Dennis Taylor;
Bass Guitar/V.B: Graham Rivens; Drums: Phil Lancaster.

Quite a different sound. Especially in the Mary Poppins
number. Very helpful group although their drummer was late.
Useful and reasonably small.

YES

Routine beat group - strange choice of material. Amateur
sounding vocalist who sings wrong notes and out of tune.
Group has nothing to recommend it.

NO

Beat group trying for a more "family commercial" appeal. Not
bad, but lacks polish. I don't think the group will get
better with more rehearsal - what we heard will always be the
product. It's not outstanding in any way, but I have heard
worse groups broadcasting.

NO

A poor selection of material. Second number is very weird
and the treatment of Chim-Chim-Cheree kills the song
completely. Instead of being bright and gay the song becomes
a sad ballad - contrary to the lyric. The singer is a
cockney type but not outstanding enough. The group play
what they have to do with confidence but would like to hear
them put to a stronger test.

NO

An interesting group with an original style and off beat
choice of material. The lead singer could interpret a
beat number and a number like Chim-Chim-Cheree with
equal facility.

YES

An inoffensive pleasant nothing. I can't find fault with
them musically - but there is no entertainment in anything
they do. It'd just a group, and very ordinary too, backing
a singer devoid of personality.

NO

A very ordinary beat group. Instrumentally not bad but there
is a lack of dynamics, of drive and of personality. Singer
not particularly exciting. Routines dull.

NO

NO Confirmed by J.E. Grant 23.11.65

The notorious report by the BBC's 'Talent Selection Group' which came close to consigning
Bowie's musical career to the bin before it had even got started. A revisionist version of this
much-lampooned document might highlight the fact that several of the panel got straight to
the heart of what Bowie would eventually become: "weird", "contrary" and "off-beat".

Bowie's first appearance at the BBC was not as a singer but as a leader of a group of long-haired men fighting to end their 'persecution', featured on current affairs programme *Tonight* in 1964. The publicity ploy was a success and got him in front of the cameras.

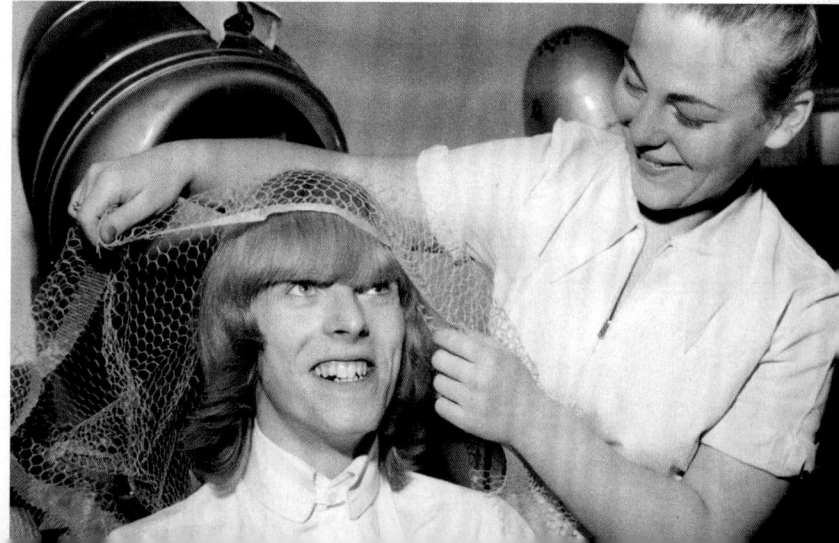

Above: Bowie outside the BBC on a cold March day in 1965 for the BBC Two pop programme, *Gadzooks! It's All Happening*. Bowie would perform 'I Pity the Fool' with his then-band, The Manish Boys.

Below: Bowie has a hairnet placed on his head by a hairdresser backstage at *Gadzooks!*, as part of publicity photos taken to create some 'controversy' around the band and their long hair. The group were apparently told they needed to cut their hair before the show and eventually reached a compromise which stated that their fee would go to charity if the show received any complaints (there were none).

Above, right: The *Cracked Actor* documentary captured Bowie as he toured America in 1974 at the height of his fame and drug addiction. Bowie looked glamorous and chiselled one minute, and then skeletal and anaemic the next. Director Alan Yentob said Bowie was fragile and exhausted but also prepared to open up and talk in a way he never had before. The documentary itself would spur a whole new style of arts films.

Left: The alien has landed. Bowie performs 'Starman' on *Top of the Pops* in 1972 – one of the most influential performances in music history.

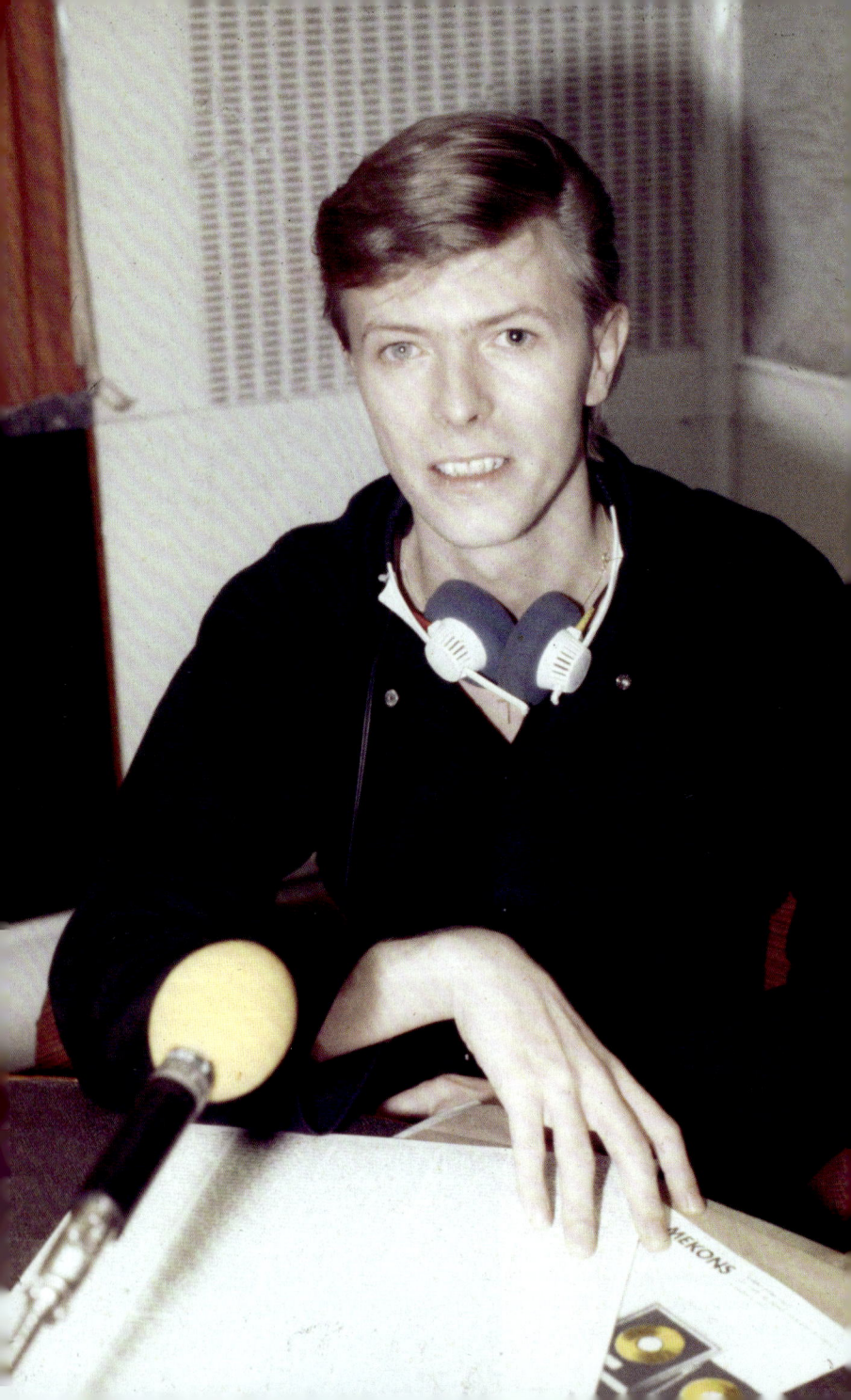

Left: Bowie was invited to guest DJ on BBC Radio One in March 1979. Among his choices were The Velvet Underground ('Sweet Jane'), Little Richard ('He's My Star'), John Lennon ('Remember'), T. Rex ('20th Century Boy'), The Doors ('Love Street') and Roxy Music ('2 H.B.' and 'For Your Pleasure'). Bowie showed his love of the 'new wave' with Talking Heads ('Warning Sign' and 'The Book I Read') and Blondie ('Rip Her to Shreds'), and if you look carefully you can see his copy of 'Where Were You?' by punk rock art collective The Mekons under his hand.

Suntanned and coiffured, Bowie is interviewed at Claridge's Hotel, London, for *Newsnight* in 1983. The mystery and distance that had made him so exceptional in the 1970s has been replaced for what would be his biggest-selling album, *Let's Dance*, and a string of chart toppers. "We're out of characters now, just into suits," he joked with journalists at the time.

Above: Bowie chats with Roger Taylor and Brian May of Queen at Live Aid in 1985. Princess Diana is in front, with Prince Charles in conversation with Bob Geldof to her left. *Below:* Bowie performed 'Heroes', 'Rebel Rebel', 'Modern Love' and 'TVC 15'.

When it came time for the grand finale with all the bands on stage together, Bowie bent down and charmingly asked Diana if she would like to join them. "I might be able to sing a bit of 'God Save the Queen' but that's as far as my vocals talents go," she politely quipped in reply.

accent] 'Yeah, you better shape up, boy. Shape up or ship out. Pull your socks up. Do this, do that.' I'm not a liberal father, but on the other hand I'm not an Edwardian or Victorian father – I don't know which was worse. [*Laughs*]

SB: Is that why you zigzag so much, from one thing to another?

DB: Oh, yes, yes, it's an adventurous way to live and it's not necessarily a good way for everybody. It's provided me with, ultimately, some of the best and worst moments of my life, but that's my choice. It's been wonderful to do, and no doubt I will continue zigzag for the rest of my life because I'm of that nature. I'm like that. I do that.

SB: Is there an artistic worst moment you can remember, a moment where you think, 'Oh my God!'

DB: Well, do you know I had to live with it … the re-release of *Laughing Gnome* almost crippled me. [*Laughs*]

SB: You might have to sing that on stage.

DB: Well, I did put the proposition forward. Well, I better get in first here. [*Laughs*]

SB: If they vote for it, will you sing it?

DB: I might use it as intro music. [*SB laughs*]

SB: [*Voiceover*] Let's talk about this business that Jonathan King was discussing in his column this morning. I wondered when I spoke to David why he decided not to perform any of his old material after this tour, why it was the end of the road for all the classic songs. I suppose also why he decided to embark upon the tour in the first place.

DB: It's a two-fold reason. One is the obvious one, that Ryko Discs and EMI have collaborated to put out between them all the old material that I had stockpiled over the last few years. When it came off RCA, I sort of sat on it, not knowing quite what to do with it, and I had approaches made to me by several big companies to put it out, but it was going to be packaged in such a way that I felt it wasn't the kind of quality that I wanted for my work. Having then seen the stuff that Reiko just did with Jimi Hendrix and Frank Zappa, I thought that I'd never seen archive stuff presented, cared for and digitally remastered like that before.
It was absolutely superb.

SB: Can you explain that, because a lot of people wouldn't know what you're talking about?

DB: Well, they transfer the tapes to digital process, which means you get pretty much the sound that was happening in the studio when you were actually recording them. And it's far superior to vinyl. And their research team is splendid. They, unfortunately, sometimes come up with tracks that you'd forgotten about [*Laughs*] and sometimes wished that they'd remained forgotten. But looking at them in a different light, some of them, it's quite fun to put obscure tracks on each of the new albums that are coming out. So, they wanted to do a compilation of all the best-known songs and stay away from hits, because I've actually not had that many. I've had two Number 1s, yes, in America, but things like 'Changes', which were never singles, are just as well known as, say, 'Jean Genie', or something like that. So, it was a combination of what you can call hits and favourite songs, and so they put an 18-track album together of that and they asked me if I'd be willing to support it. And I said yes, because I can think of a good use I can put this to. There has to be a point … rock'n'roll gets older, as myself and some of my peers have proven, we've got bounced into our forties now … that we can either follow the traditional way of working with our repertoire, which is like a Frank Sinatra or whatever, you go on forever singing your legacy of songs and all that, which is the way that it can go; or we can try to do the kinds of exciting and maybe risky things that we were known to do when we started working in music. So, I thought what I would do is do these songs for the very last time, purposefully painting myself into a corner and giving myself no option other than to develop more new material that makes *me* wildly excited to continue, if I'm going to continue, in music. As I don't want to be just taking those nostalgic walks through my career. This will be fun because I've never done it before. I've never done a show where I'm literally, in this particular instance, asking the audience to choose a song. And I will do exactly what it is that they want to come along and hear.

GOLDEN YEARS

SB: [*Voiceover*] We've been talking to David Bowie all this week as a result of an interview I did last Thursday week. We talked about the phone vote. You know the idea of the phone vote … basically what he's looking forward to is hearing from people who know his music and know him. He'd advertised the day that we did the interview that he'd advertised the phone number, so I asked him what the idea behind it was.

DB: I said, 'I think it would be great. I think I know what they want. I think I can guess about 10 or 12, but what do we do after that? There are some things that I'd like to do, like "Joe the Lion", that are totally obscure to most people and it's not really the kind of things that they'd want to pay to come and hear if this is their choice.' And they said, 'Well, the simplest way these days …' because the big thing in the States is the 900 [toll-free] line. And I said, 'Okay, if that's what you want to do, let's see if it'll work.' And the response has been, so far, dramatic.

SB: Have you any idea of what the most requested song might be in the back of your head?

DB: My presumption is that it would be 'Fame' or 'Let's Dance'.

SB: Not 'Heroes'?

DB: I don't know about Europe. Europe is a different kettle of *poisson*. I don't know.

SB: And you're going to give the money to charity.

DB: Yeah.

SB: Any idea which charity yet?

DB: Mine would be Save the Children fund, but I would like some of it split off to the Brixton community as well.

SB: [*Voiceover*] David still doesn't know whether or not it's going to be 'The Laughing Gnome' that gets requested as the most requested song to be sung on the tour by David around the world. [The *NME* launched a campaign to get voters to choose the song, and when it appeared that they were indeed about to win, Bowie scrapped the vote because it was being rigged. He later joked to *Melody Maker* that he had considered performing it in a Velvet Underground style.] He's been recording in Australia. We talked about *The Delinquents* incident a little earlier on, and he's been recording with Tin Machine. I wondered how that had been going.

DB: We did 25 songs in Sydney. My presumption is that 14 or so will go on an album, and I've left the rest of the guys … whilst I'm working, they'll be reworking some of the songs. We're taking a little more finesse over it than last time. The songs should be finished about mid-year completely, and mixed and all that. Then, hopefully, the album will come out in the latter part of this year and we'll be going out to support it.

SB: So this tour ends when?

DB: I believe, at the moment, it ends in August.

SB: Then you rehearse and do Tin Machine.

DB: It's snowballing a bit. My intention is then to go straight into rehearsals with Tin Machine for that late-year tour.

SB: Keep you slim, anyway.

DB: Oh, yeah.

MARK GOODIER, BBC RADIO

INTERVIEWER: MARK GOODIER

(BACKSTAGE AT MILTON KEYNES BOWL)

Bowie came in for some flak for 'Tonight'. He got even more flak for 'Never Let Me Down'. But the greatest amount of criticism he would ever receive was for Tin Machine.

Having lost interest in music and searching for something to rekindle the fire, he chose perhaps the most cliched of all avenues: a four-piece, guitar-based rock band. In love with the new sound coming out of America led by bands like The Pixies and Sonic Youth, he chose three friends in the hope that he could not only recreate that freshness and energy, but also lose himself in the anonymity of a group.

If Tin Machine wanted to recreate that Pixies sound, they never succeeded. But in hindsight, perhaps the sound was secondary. Bowie had killed off Ziggy, Aladdin Sane and the Thin White Duke. Now, he seemed intent on erasing himself. He dissolved into the soup of a grey band. Insisting they were a democracy, Bowie would only be interviewed with at least one other band member present.

It's tempting to see this as a form of therapy. After being revered as one of the most innovative artists of the twentieth century, he had suffered five or six years of fairly relentless criticism. He was no longer seen as cool or relevant. He had spent 25 years surviving on his own wits, with his head way above any parapet. Perhaps now he needed to share the burden and the criticism.

Tin Machine's LPs may not make the shortlist when it comes to Bowie's best albums, but it did allow him to put some space between himself and his eighties commercial period.

MARK GOODIER: It's a pleasure to welcome you to Milton Keynes …

DAVID BOWIE: Thank you, Mark. What a lovely place you've got here.

MG: Yes, it's absolutely marvellous, isn't it. Huge! It's almost like California or somewhere.

DB: I stepped off the plane today and I thought I was in Nairobi, it's unbelievably hot. What is it, 96 [Fahrenheit] or something this afternoon? Incredible, just amazing.

MG: Is this why you are here so early before the gig?

DB: I like to have a sunbathe… no, I like to just catch the bands. As they are working with me, it's disrespectful to not at least look at them. I liked the first band immediately, I thought they were great. Two Way Street. I thought they were really good.

MG: I don't know very many major acts who are headlining who bother to turn up. Does this mean you still buy records by new bands?

DB: It means that I get up at a reasonable hour. [*Laughs*] I do, yeah, I buy a lot of new records. I like music very much.

MG: What was the last record you bought?

DB: Well, the last one I bought was *Goo* by Sonic Youth about two weeks ago. It's only got three tracks on it that are worth a toss. I was disappointed because I like their stuff an awful lot, but now they seem to be backtracking on what they've already done. I think probably because it's the first major label they've been on, so I think they probably want to say, 'Well, if they missed it the first time around, we'll do it again.' But there are three good tracks on it and

I'm waiting for The Pixies', new album, which should come next week. Other than that, Dinosaur Jr. …

MG: Cocteau Twins?

DB: … Dinosaur Jr. have got a good album coming out. No, not Cocteau Twins, haven't got that.

MG: That's just about to come out. Okay, so, Sound+Vision … you look happy, you're smiling a lot. Are you enjoying it?

DB: Oh, ecstatic, Mark. [*Both laugh*] No, it's great, I'm having a ball. But I'm working with Adrian Belew, he's a very funny guy to work with. It's a very buoyant show. I mean the 'after-show life' … generally … you can't really say that about working on a tour, but this has been wonderful because both Adrian and I do get up, as I said earlier, at a reasonable hour, and we've been able to get out and about. Every city we've been to, we've gone out of our way to make each town worth going to. I know a lot more about Cleveland than I knew before. [*MG laughs*]

MG: The thing about this is that, regularly, tour travelling is not the kind of ideal travelling to see places.

DB: No, it isn't. I don't know what's made the difference. I guess because we are taking the bus such a lot and it feels a lot more sort of civilised. When you're just flying from gig to gig, you feel as though you possibly are in 'big business'. You can kid yourself that you're just on a holiday tour when you're in a bus, and it feels a lot more sort of real.

MG: This tour might also be …

DB: It's also a lot more dangerous, [*Laughs*] I think! I'm wondering if I shouldn't have gone by plane after all!

MG: You don't like flying, though.

DB: I loathe it, yeah.

MG: Well, I would imagine this tour would be good fun also because it's a greatest hits tour. I mean you billed it as the Bowie fans' choice.

DB: It is fun because of that, but it wouldn't be if I thought I had to go back out on the road at some point and do them again. Half the motivation for doing this is that I could do it with enthusiasm because I won't be doing these songs again. There are songs, frankly, that I really had a hard time getting it up for. It's difficult to sing 'Changes' and 'Rebel Rebel' and all those things and not think, 'Heavens, I've been doing these for 20 years.' But because it's the last time, I can really get excited about them.

MG: That's very good. Let me ask you about the phone line that you opened and people voted for their favourite Bowie song. Did they actually affect how you planned out your set?

DB: Eighty per cent of it. I thought I'd do 80 per cent of their choice and 20 per cent of mine, just because I can. I think the annoying thing was that it was fairly predictable, in a way, but I guess I asked for that. The songs that we were asked to do were pretty much what I guessed … I mean, I'd already put half of them in the programme. [*Laughs*] If I say, they'll probably ask me to do 'Space Oddity', then heh, sure enough, you know we got 'Space Oddity'! But that's fine, that's alright, because not everybody knows very many of my albums, that's okay.

MG: I think you're being rather modest.

DB: No, it's true. You'd be surprised.

MG: So, did you in any sense have to relearn some words for these old songs? I mean you haven't played all the old songs …

DB: [*Adopts an American old-timer's voice*] Every single one of 'em, Mark! Every single one of 'em. Yeah, things like 'Ziggy Stardust' I'd almost forgot. I purposefully almost tried to forget that because it was so representative for me of an era that has gone; it was so '72, '73. It was hard to, kind of … but, surprisingly, that has become one of my favourite songs to sing on this tour … out of character just as a straight song … it's really a nice song to sing.

MG: You seemed also, when I saw the Tin Machine tour, to be enjoying a very small audience tour. This is completely different. Will the Tin Machine project come together again?

DB: Oh, it's already … we've finished the next album. We did that in January this year, and it comes out end of this year, and then we go out on the road February next year.

MG: Are the Tin Machine albums quick albums, as opposed to David Bowie albums that sometimes take quite a long time?

DB: Yeah … I don't know, I don't know mine take that … I mean *Let's Dance* took me about three weeks. That's not really very long. I'm not known as being a guy who goes in for … because I get bored too quickly. If it's not sounding good in about three or four weeks, then I'd rather just stop doing it. But no, this last album with Tin Machine, it took about five weeks. That's because we wrote an awful lot of stuff, and we've knocked it down to 14 tracks, so we're very happy with that, and we're terribly excited about working next year, really excited. I can't wait. This is a helluva band, it really is.

MG: So, that's your excitement post all these greatest hits?

DB: Well, yeah. I mean, I like reading a lot as well. That keeps me excited. I've just been very disappointed, as the book that I went for today has been out of print for three years.

MG: For three years?

DB: Yeah, I had a copy of it and I lost it on tour, and I went back to Foyles and they said it's out of print. So, if anybody out there's got a copy of *The Renaissance Artist at Work* by Bruce Cole, please send me it.

MG: Send it to me and I'll pass it on.

DB: Yeah, do that.

MG: Part of this tour is playing in Eastern Europe, and dates which were added after the Wall came down. That must be quite exciting.

DB: Is it? I suppose so. I'm fed up with all that. I mean, I'm not really interested.

MG: Why did you add the dates, then?

DB: No, I mean I like going to the east, but all the Wall business, it's such a load of hyperbole about it. There's going to an awful lot of problems with that particular situation. Still, it'll be nice to see what's happening now. Won't be the Berlin I remember, though.

MG: Okay, two more questions. Films ... what's coming up?

DB: Got any? [*Laughs*]

MG: I haven't got any good scripts. Now you're asking, I'll work on one. Seriously, you're obviously offered so much stuff, there must be something you want to do.

DB: Daily! [*Laughs*] I can't open my doors anymore! I'm doing a comedy [*The Linguini Incident*], as it happens, just after the tour, a quickie, with Rosanna Arquette and Kelly Lynch, who was in *Drugstore Cowboy*, which I'm quietly, as all rock people are, terribly excited about, [*MG laughs*] because nobody ever offered me a comedy before because they always saw me as being very po-faced. But I met the director, and we had a couple of drinks together, and I got the part. [*Laughs*]

MG: I think he obviously had a sense for good business.

DB: No, no, no, no. Rock stars are traditionally dreadful box office.

MG: This may be a question you can't answer because the people I've asked it before have found it very difficult. But do you have a favourite of your own songs?

DB: Do you know, it's an awful … that's a dreadful … Well, at the moment, yeah. There's a song on the next Tin Machine album called 'Goodbye Mr Ed', which I'm particularly … there's an enigmatic answer. Yes, a song you've never heard before. [*Laughs*] A song that's not even out yet and won't be for six months. 'Goodbye Mr Ed', that's my favourite song.

MG: There's a hot tip from David Bowie! Thank you for your time.

DB: My pleasure.

NICKY HORNE, BBC RADIO

INTERVIEWER: NICKY HORNE

Tin Machine was to last four years. Here, the band is about to release its second album, which would be heavily criticised and prove to be the beginning of the end.

Despite the critical reaction to Tin Machine, the band's impact on Bowie was significant. He emerged from these chrysalis years as if reborn, making a series of distinctively different albums throughout the nineties. It was as if he had released himself from the weight of being David Bowie, paradoxically giving himself the space to go back to *being* David Bowie – someone who would experiment for a whole side or write a hit tune or do whatever the heck he wanted.

For most of the rest of his career, Bowie would defend Tin Machine's music. When he largely gave up trying to defend the bulk of the music, he still defended the time as allowing him to exorcise his past and recapture his fire.

NICKY HORNE: [*Voiceover*] David Bowie is currently in Los Angeles finishing a new Tin Machine album due for release in September. I spoke to him a few days ago via satellite. First, I asked him to look back on last year's greatest hits tour. Was he happy with the result?

DAVID BOWIE: For me, aesthetically, it was the best show that I ever did, without doubt. Looking back at it, it was pretty stunning in visual terms. I had one of the neatest, tightest and most enthusiastic bands that I've worked with in many years. That's the Adrian Belew band. Overall, I thought it was a really great way of bowing out from those songs.

NH: And what was it like for you, so many years on, going on stage and playing all those greatest hits?

DB: A song can only trigger memories; it doesn't become completely Pavlovian. The memories are triggered maybe during rehearsals … you get all kind of as weepy as I ever get, anyway, about songs. 'Ah! Do you remember this old chestnut?', you know, and sentiment overflows and we wipe our eyes and then we're fed up with the damn thing in about seven days with continually playing it. [*Laughs*] It tends to get like that on any tour for me. And with older songs, for me, it's really hard to sing them with any degree of enthusiasm or integrity after a bit because, frankly, it just becomes like a discipline, because you've got to do that song that night because it's expected of you. But when you've been doing it for eight months every single night – or, well, let's not cheat, say four times a week – it's really hard to conjure up its potential magic, and you just have to rely on the song itself to produce the magic that it had inherently in the beginning. But there again, having said all that, by the time you get round to the last five or six performances and you realise it's the last time you're ever going to sing them again, I think it's a real watershed of emotions, because you're putting away an awful lot of creative life there. It was a real tough decision to make. It's an easy cop-out at the end to say, 'Well, that might have been the last time.' But this was for real. I mean, that was it.

NH: But was there any point, David, during that tour, especially towards the end, where you knew this was going to be the last few performances of 'Suffragette City' or 'Changes' or any of those, where you thought, 'Hang on a minute, I'd actually like to keep singing these'? Was there ever a point where you thought you might change your mind?

DB: Frankly, in that way, maybe only a couple, and they come from the very late seventies period. Things like 'Ashes to Ashes' and, let's see … things like 'Sound and Vision', which were kind of new to me because I hadn't actually played 'Sound and Vision' on stage ever before. So, for that tour, it was still fresh for me, that song, in a way, as a performer, because I hadn't been doing it for 16, 20 years. So, it was kind of a shame that they had to go. But, [*Adopts a Yorkshire accent and laughs*] when you've got to go, you've got to go. And they had to go as well. [*Adopts a director's tone*] Follow all the other little songs through the door into time … and get covered in cobwebs.

NH: Why did you make that decision to just consign them to that little box and tie the string and put the sealing wax on?

DB: [*Laughs*] Because I'm that sort of little runt.

NH: No, you're not.

DB: I am. [*Still laughing*] I am, I tell you. I suppose it was some creative exercise for myself. I didn't want to find myself in that position of having to just continually be bringing them out. I didn't want a career that … well, firstly, the word 'career' has always scared the shit out of me, because it's not something I really ever wanted. I wanted to be a working, practising artist. Sorry, [*Adopts a mocking tone*] artiste. I didn't ever see the time when I'd be dragging out old songs to say, 'Do you remember this old one?' So, as I thought I never wanted to do that, maybe I should do something about it. So I did.

NH: Interesting response. There was some criticism that, at points, it became a little, how can I say it, mechanical to do all the oldies, just churn them out like a jukebox.

DB: Someone's always going to complain, aren't they?

NH. Okay, well, let's move on to Tin Machine. But first, can I ask you, David, because I haven't had the opportunity to ask you this before, what are you trying to achieve with Tin Machine?

DB: Well, what we have achieved is a really first-class stage band that we all feel we have a terrific collaborative effort within, and producing the kind of music that I think, frankly, we wanted to be involved in and wanted to be able to buy for ourselves if we were listening to music. That was basically the premise of the band, is 'What's the kind of music that we'd like to buy?' And that's what we set out to create and, indeed, is what I feel that we have achieved on both the first and second album.

NH: What makes it so important for you, David, to be part of a band rather than Bowie with a band?

DB: Because I haven't done it before.

NH: That's a good answer. I think many people admire the fact that you want to be part of a band.

DB: They should try being in one before … [*Laughs*]

NH: I mean people do admire you for trying to be part of a band, but I think there are other people who might say that it's a little naive for you, as David Bowie, just to be a singer in a rock'n'roll band.

DB: I know, but it's fun, isn't it? [*Laughs*] I don't know about all that. I just find it a lot of fun and hard work, and really, it's such an effort in being involved with three other people who have an opinion. It's good for me. [*Laughs*] It's really good for me. Not only have I picked three guys who have opinions, but they're all egoists, so [*Laughs*] it's doubly hard – who gets to wear the nice suit? 'No, David, you're not going to wear white, you'll wear black like all the rest of us.'

NH: Do they really tell you what to do? Come on.

DB: Yeah, absolutely. Absolutely. Well, it's not for me to say. You know something, I think all that stuff about David Bowie having a bunch of musicians with him – [*Adopts a gossipy tone*] 'And do you know something, he probably pays them salaries' – is something that's going to go with this band just for time. Already, I've had people coming up to me and saying, 'It's amazing you've actually done a second album.' The process is more important, and us working as a band, being a band, playing live as a band, making records – over time it just becomes a band. At the beginning, of course, I expected that. I'd be foolish not to expect that. You know something? That'll pass.

NH: You've always had an uncanny knack to shock your audience with your changes. And I think the first Tin Machine album certainly shocked a lot of your fans.

DB: It shocked me. It shocked me. It shocked me because I found there were so many raw nerves on it, in listening to it. There's a lot of … oh, a lot of anxieties beneath the surface of that, and I think all four of us felt that, partially because we knew we were going into a dangerous area, really, to explore this kind of venture. It was an odd thing to do, I think, that showed in its writing. I guess there's not quite so much angst … oh, God, I haven't used that word in years … on this second one.

NH: Tell me about that. Tell me how it's different from the first?

DB: I think putting ourselves into Sydney, Australia, had a real cohesive effect on all of us. Two of the guys hadn't really travelled that far before. They'd never been to Australia. Well, actually, I'm the only that had been to Australia. Finding ourselves out there in a completely unknown place – we didn't know anybody – brought us well into our own circle; and we relied and looked to each other an awful lot for support and encouragement to get through that six-, eight-week period that we were out there. I think that was the duration of it. Out of that came an awful lot of interior writing, so there's probably a little more inner writing on this album than there was on the last one. Although, for practical purposes, I suppose some people called it aggressive or abrasive or whatever, it still carries that air with it. It certainly has that kind of aggressive manner. Be interesting, actually, to see what people think of it, I suppose. I know we like it.

NH: I think, going back to the first album, I think it surprised a lot of people because it was so abrasive. And I take your point about wanting to sail in dangerous waters, but I think a lot of die-hard Bowie fans were really surprised by how abrasive and unapproachable the album was.

DB: Yeah, I expect they were.

NH: That's exactly what you wanted, though, wasn't it?

DB: It's not what we wanted so much, Nicky, it's the way that it turned out. We hadn't a clue how it was going to turn out. We just knew what we wanted to do for ourselves, and how it did turn out was an album that really … I mean, we were smacked in the face with it as much as our audience. I mean, it's not a pleasant album to listen to.

NH: Were you disappointed that it didn't do better in sales?

DB: Oh, God, I thought it did *phenomenally* well. I thought it might just do a few thousand. It was spectacular that it even approached a million worldwide. Frankly, it's only in the last few years that I've actually sold any albums at all. Everything I've sold since *Let's Dance* has sold umpteen bucketful millions more than anything I did in the seventies, the so-called 'important' albums. In those terms, it was all incredibly unbalanced. But this time, to have this particular album, which was almost precious to us in as much as we didn't know what we'd gotten ourselves into, and to see it do so incredibly well was really, really encouraging to us.

NH: It's fascinating that you should say that, that your albums, the *Let's Dance* album and the albums after that, sold bucketloads and yet the earlier albums didn't.

DB: I know. I think that's the way with a lot of artists, you know. Dylan has much the same thing. Everybody knows about him and everybody knows his songs, but at the time he didn't sell records. It was incredible, it was almost like the whole thing was word of mouth. Sometimes the artist becomes bigger than the work that they do, or something, it's a peculiar situation.

NH: And you think that happened to you?

DB: I'm not sure if that precise situation happened to me, but it's certainly logistically what happened to me; the more commercial stuff certainly did much, much better than the stuff that was less commercial. Going back to my own favourite period, which was the

Low–Heroes–Lodger – and I must include *Scary Monsters* of the early eighties – that stuff, all four of them put together, didn't achieve anything like the kind of album sales that, say, *Tonight* or something like that made.

NH: So, what do you consider to be the yardstick of success as far as you, David Bowie, are concerned?

DB: Whether I'm being truthful to myself as an artist, if you want to talk in artistic terms, but that can spill over into all areas of your life.

NH: Can you extrapolate on that?

DB: No. [*Laughs*] But I certainly repeat the maxim that, to me, it's terribly important that I can live with what I'm doing as an artist comfortably and, in some cases, happily. Not necessarily comfortably – no, that's not true. Sometimes I have to live with something uncomfortably, but at least I know it's come from some kind of root of honesty.

NH: So, Tin Machine was an uncomfortable process …

DB: Yeah.

NH: … that in the end made you happy. Is that what you're saying?

DB: Yes, that's right. That's well put. Well put, Nicky! [*Laughs*]

NH: Thank you, David. [*Laughs*] Would you like to interview me now?

DB: That's my pleasure, Nicky!

NH: Tell me, finally, as we wrap up the thing about Tin Machine. The new album … when can we expect that?

DB: It comes out on September the first, and we're going to be touring on … I can't give the exact date, but it'll be around October when we start a mini-worldy kind of thing. Once again, we're keeping the audiences way, way down.

NH: What kind of venues will you be playing?

DB: I think we'll probably be somewhere between one and three thousand, something like that.

NH: So, when will you be coming here to Great Britain?

DB: Those dates haven't actually been set at the moment.

NH: And what's the album called?

DB: *Tin Machine.* [*Laughs*]

NH: That's … original.

DB: Yeah. And it doesn't even have a 'two' after it.

NH: Well, David, we look forward very much to the new album, and, in fact, I look forward very much to hearing it and talking to you at length about it, track by track.

DB: Smashing. I really look forward to that.

NH: Thanks once again, David.

DB: Thanks a lot, Nicky. That was really good. Bye-bye.

WOGAN, BBC TV

INTERVIEWER: TERRY WOGAN

Terry Wogan was once asked who his most difficult interviewee was in 50 years of broadcasting. 'David Bowie,' he replied. In fact, Wogan found his guest so evasive that the exasperated Irishman said, 'I thought a solid slap would have helped the situation.'

In truth, Bowie simply appears to be trying to pretend that he is just another guy in the band, Tin Machine. It's an impossible situation for any interviewer, let alone the audience, to accept.

'I didn't hit him, of course,' Wogan added. 'But it came close.'[16]

TERRY WOGAN: Good to see you. Thank you for joining us.

DAVID BOWIE: [*To the audience*] Good evening, Ron. Evening, Ron.

TW: [*To the audience*] Evening, Ron. [*Whispers to Tony Sales*] This guy who is fronting … is he okay?

DB: [*Makes an overt move to look at the time on his watch*]

TONY SALES: Yes, he is. You mean this man here? [*Points to Reeves Gabrels*]

HUNT SALES: Reeves, Reeves Gabrels.

TW: Yes. Hi, Reeves. Good to see you. Because the guitar he was playing … it didn't look like a real guitar he was playing. I suppose that's not a real guitar he had.

TS: Well … Yes, that was a real guitar.

DB: No, it's my lunch, Terry.

TW: It's your lunch, is it? [*Laughs*] Look, how are you all getting on? Is it all working out alright, Tin Machine?

DB: We have colour problems. [*Audience laughs; DB is wearing a lime green suit and TS is wearing a bright red jacket*]

TW: I thought it was just me.

HS: [*Points to his sunglasses*] I'm going to have to keep these on.

TW: It's new – new for us, anyway – to see you part of a band rather than just fronting a big spectacular.

DB: Yeah, yeah.

TW: Why did you decide to do it?

DB: It gives me a new insight into washing habits. [*Audience laughs*]

TW: You all share the same shower, do you?

DB: No. [*DB laughs*]

TS: [*Inaudible*] Same laundromat.

TW: So, who brought you together? Who is the moving force in you coming together? [*DB points to TS*]

TS: Well, David and Hunt and myself have known each other for close to 17 years, and then David got acquainted with Reeves, and we ran into each other, and he told me about Reeves and maybe we should all just get together and have a play. And we did, and the next day we thought, 'Well, let's keep playing.'

TW: Was it a deliberate attempt for you to go into another direction?

DB: Hello, Ron! [*DB shouts out into the audience again*] He's just a mate of ours from Dublin.

TW: Yes, I've got a few mates in Dublin as well. [*Audience and DB laugh*] Left a long time ago. Was it, from your point of view … you wanted to go in another musical direction. What happened?

DB: We just got around to jamming, really. It just felt like a good thing to do, so we're just doing it to death.

TW: Yeah. What are you trying to do? [*DB laughs loudly*] Because I'm one of the older guys. What kind of stuff are trying to do here? Are you trying to go back to the roots of rock'n'roll, or are you trying to create a *new* sound or what?

HS: We're going back to having fun. That's a movement. Getting back to having fun.

TW: But it's going to involve a lot of stuff on the road? A lot of touring?

DB: A lot of movements on the road.

TW: Well, you won't get far on the road if you don't make any movements. [*Audience laughs*] You'll get knocked down, for a start. [*More audience laughter*]

DB: That's right, Terry.

TW: Are you going to do albums or personal appearances or what?

TS: Yes, we're going to do some personal appearances very shortly.

HS: We're doing a TV show right now. [*Audience laughs*]

TS: We started now! [*More laughter*]

DB: We're doing a tour in November; we're coming to England to tour.

TW: Excellent. Well, we're glad to see you. Thank you for joining us.

TIN MACHINE: Thank you.

TW: And I hope it's a great success. Tin Machine.

OUR TUNE, BBC RADIO

INTERVIEWER: SIMON BATES

Bowie was not one for looking back, but, at this time, he finally reunited with his greatest musical partner of them all, Mick Ronson. The two had performed together on stage at the Freddie Mercury Tribute Concert the year before, and now Ronson joined Bowie on his latest album, *Black Tie White Noise*, for a song they used to perform more than 20 years previously, Cream's 'I Feel Free'.

Ronson knew he was dying; he had stopped treatment. A few days after this interview, at the age of 46, he would be dead of the same disease, liver cancer, that would eventually kill Bowie.

Three days after Ronson's death, Bowie was due to appear on a US chat show. He asked the host, Arsenio Hall, if he could say a few words after his friend. After praising his musicianship and influence, Bowie became clearly emotional and simply said, 'I miss him.'

'They planned to do all sorts of things together,' said film-maker and friend Jon Brewer. 'They just ran out of time.'[17]

SIMON BATES: [*Voiceover*] After a long and controversial involvement with the experimental group Tin Machine, David Bowie has now resumed the solo career he abandoned after the release of *Never Let Me Down* in 1987. The new album, as adventurous and eclectic as anything he's done in his 30 years as a professional musician, was started at the beginning of last year when his forthcoming marriage to the Somalian model, Iman, inspired him to write some spiritual music for their wedding service.

DAVID BOWIE: I guess that was the real plunge that caused this to be a solo album. Because of Iman's parents being Muslim, and her whole family is Muslim, and my family is Church of England, Protestant, whatever, however lapsed, and we were marrying in a church in Italy, it was important for me to find something that also had no representation of institutionalised and organised religion, of which I'm not a believer – I must make that clear. And so, I started writing music for the service that, again, tried to reflect and incorporate the feeling that I felt that we had as a relationship and what our relationship meant to us. It was strictly instrumental, just to try and find those passions and those spiritual feelings that we had with each other. Doing that opened this virtual floodgate of other emotions and things that I wanted to say and delve a bit deeper into the last two or three years of my life. By virtue of that, it became an album of writings, and even incorporating other people's songs to reflect the ways I felt about things. I mean, 'Nite Flights' by Scott Engel [aka Scott Walker] for me, was an absolute summary in a way of what our relationship was; it was something neither of us had really expected, and probably didn't want, but had happened at our age, Iman at 37 and me at 46. Probably the last thing that both of us thought would ever happen to us. And it's a hell of an exploration and a kind of adventure, and you don't know where it's going to take you. And that song really felt like it, this kind of dangerous territory

that we were embarking on. 'Oh, crikey, what have we done now?'
[*Laughs*]

NITE FLIGHTS

SB: [*Voiceover*] David Bowie's version of 'Nite Flights', first recorded
by the Walker Brothers in 1978. Bowie was moved to write the title
track, 'Black Tie White Noise' during the riots provoked by the
Rodney King verdict. He couldn't have picked a more dramatic
moment to arrive in Los Angeles.

DB: I got in with Iman the day the riots started, and was here during
the duration of them; and the feeling of both the inevitability of the
riots because of the decision and the numbing quality of it all was
quite … I think it really illustrated that so many people in America
feel that they are unfairly imprisoned within the lower rungs of
society, and it's a prison from which they see no real escape. It really
felt, because of that, like a prison riot more than anything else, or
the beginnings of a revolution. My understanding of what's been
happening in America, Blacks are now worse off than they were
even five, six years ago. One obviously pins a lot of hope on the new
administration to not burst that bubble of enthusiasm that swept
them into power.

BLACK TIE WHITE NOISE

SB: [*Voiceover*] 'Black Tie White Noise', a duet with Al B. Sure!
As well as responding to the LA riots in the song, Bowie also
acknowledges the enduring power of Marvin Gaye's classic state-of-
the-nation album *What's Going On*.

DB: Yeah, it's a straight out-and-out homage to him, because I think
of all Black music, I guess, that album by Gaye was really a milestone

in the Black voice being heard in the musical arena. It was such a stunningly committed album, and because of the nature of the subject matter of that particular track, I wanted to pay some kind of due back to him.

SB: [*Voiceover*] Bowie's co-producer on *Black Tie White Noise* is Nile Rodgers. Their last collaboration was in 1983 on the most commercially successful album of Bowie's career, *Let's Dance*.

> <*The interview then includes an interview with Nile Rodgers, who says the big difference to the two albums was that now Bowie, who was paying for the album out of his own pocket, didn't care about the cost. 'Let me know when it gets to somewhere around three million bucks,' he told Rodgers.*>

YOU'VE BEEN AROUND

SB: [*Voiceover*] On David Bowie's new album was 'Jump They Say', a song that was partly inspired by his stepbrother, Terry [Burns], who was to take his life after a long history of mental illness. And that's where we pick up our conversation with David Bowie in this series of three exclusive previews.

DB: I've attempted to at least get near the situation of his suicide, which, for me, was absolutely incomprehensible, and probably something I refused to accept for quite some time because I hadn't made any contact with him, and I felt probably very guilty that I hadn't made any physical contact. I've lost that guilt now because I don't really believe that anything would have prevented this suicide. I'm not naive [enough] to believe that one man can really save somebody who is in such a state of absolute depression … that it can really be done. Everybody does have, in the end, control over their own lives, and over their own destinies. But it has bothered me an awful lot. The song is not biographical by any stretch of the imagination. It's my impressions of what I believe I felt about Terry, and in conjunction of how I felt about myself metaphysically jumping into things. So it was really a combination of both of us. There is a philosopher, whose name I wish I could remember, who said that one creates the doppelgänger so that you can inflict one's own fears and guilts and passions and the darker sides of one's personality on to that doppelgänger and then you kill him, and hope, by doing that, you no longer retain those weakness and faults yourself. I feel that's probably played not a small part in my life: the idea of the doppelgänger as being somebody that I can inflict my own fears and paranoias on. Artists are really messed up, you know. [*Laughs*]

JUMP THEY SAY

DB: Over the years, it seems I've mythologised my stepbrother far more actively than he actually took part in my life. I know that, one, he did guide me to towards reading a lot more than I read, and steered me to areas that I wouldn't probably have found on my own, things like Jack Kerouac and Beat authors. And I know he had an interest in jazz, but I've subsequently read that I've said that he took me to jazz clubs, which is not entirely true. I would have loved him to have taken me to jazz clubs, but I just used to take myself to jazz clubs. I did in fact take *him* to a Cream concert at Bromel Court [Bromel Club, in the Bromley Court Hotel], which would have been, I guess, 1967, something like that. I was very disturbed because the music was affecting him adversely, because his particular illness was somewhere between schizophrenia and manic depressiveness; and I know that he was getting to a pretty tranced-out state watching Cream because I don't think he'd ever been to anything as loud as that in his life. I remember having to take him home because it was really affecting him.

SB: [*Voiceover*] It's a mark of Bowie's lasting affection for Cream that he's chosen to revive one of their earliest tracks on the new album. 'I Feel Free' was a song he used to play during his Ziggy Stardust days, making it a perfect choice for a jubilant reunion with his old mate from The Spiders from Mars, Mick Ronson.

DB: I thought, 'Well, if Mick and I are going to work together, let's try and make it mean something, at least for us, give it some depth.' I just picked on that one because that was an encore number that we used to do. The approach was dictated by the musicians I was working with; I mean, there was no way it was going to be a copy of the Cream version. The guys infected it with such life that it was just a joy, because I was a little cautious about approaching that song because it's such a classic to Cream fans. But I really like the version we did. I think it's whole new reading of it, and I think it's very successful.

I FEEL FREE

SB: [*Voiceover*] David Bowie's version of 'I Feel Free' featuring Mick Ronson on guitar. Most of the other musicians on the album were working with Bowie for the first time.

DB: Barry Campbell, the bass player, is totally new. He's a guy that Nile wanted to work with for a few months. He'd found him working in a club in New York as a bass player, and I don't think Barry had done any studio work before, so he was a first-time-out, young guy. Great! Wonderful bass player. Drummer – who coincidentally is also called Campbell, Sterling – Sterling I'd known for a long time actually because he was the drummer for Duran Duran at one time, when Duran were touring with me back in … was that the '83 tour? I think so. I think Duran did a stretch with us up in Canada on tour and he was their drummer at that period, so I knew Sterling. And then Philippe Saisse is a French man who's been ensconced in New York for about eight years. I guess he's the only session man that we used in as much as the others are kind of working musicians outside of the studio, and he's a wonderful talent; he's been on more albums than one can think of. And the other guys: I guess Lester Bowie somewhat falls in the category of a Miles Davis type – he's an older guy, he's eccentric and plays much in the same style as Davis.

LOOKING FOR LESTER

DB: Lester is incredible – he's quite experienced. We only brought him in because it was such a jive thing to do, like, 'The Bowies together, at last.' Then, he was such fun that we let him on 50 per cent of the album by the end of it. We'd only written him in for one song, just to kind of get him to guest on it. But he was great, really great. He was also uncontrollable. I mean, he wouldn't listen to any of the tracks. We'd say we want you to do this track and he'd say, 'Don't play me no track. I'm going out there, just pump it through the speakers.' And he would just play immediately [once] it started. He wouldn't know what key it's in, nothing. And he'd just play and that was it. And you'd have to grab what … and when you finished the take, he'd say, 'That's it.' 'How about another take, Lester?' 'Oh, alright, but just start it from the middle. Don't tell me where you're going to start it from.' Anything to put him off his guard. He would make the situation so he was just jumping in at the deep end all the time. He was an extraordinary man to work with. A man had to follow him around because he wouldn't listen through headphones, he'd have it playing through the loudspeakers, and so you had all this dreadful leakage coming through his microphone, when you could get him on the mic, so you had to … there was one take where we had one guy following him around with a boom because he was wandering all over the studio. [*Laughs*] I mean, he is something else.

<The interview then includes more conversation with Nile Rodgers.>

SB: [*Voiceover*] In an album chock-full of surprises, perhaps the most unexpected track is Bowie's version of the recent Morrissey song, 'I Know It's Gonna Happen [Someday]'. So, why on Earth did he pick that one?

DB: Well, he nicked one of my songs, so I nicked it back again. [*Laughs*] It's a fair cop. He did a lovely parody of 'Rock 'n' Roll Suicide'. He uses the same chord sequence at the end of this particular song on his last album, *Your Arsenal*. Coupled with the fact that Mick Ronson produced it – I could see what was going on there. I thought, 'Well, okay.' And the sentiment of that song is not dissimilar to the sentiment of 'Rock 'n' Roll Suicide', which is just have some kind of faith and things will work out. So, I kind of knew where it was all coming from, and I thought, 'Well, okay, if I were to do that song, I would do it like I would have done it in 1973, '74'; so I've done a kind of a [*Inaudible*] derision. But he did say, 'It's very grand!', [*Laughs*] which I would agree with him. It is very grand!

I KNOW IT'S GONNA HAPPEN

MIRACLE GOODNIGHT

DB: That's just a relationship song, there's nothing very deep. I think the nicest thing about it is the riff, it just doesn't stop. It's one of those things that really grabs you and there's no point going to anything else because the riff is strong enough to carry the whole piece, which indeed it does, [*Laughs*] to the point of repetition. A very simple song.

> <*The interview then includes more of the conversation with Nile Rodgers.*>

SB: [*Voiceover*] David is feeling very happy about his music, and that happiness has been intensified by a spiritual rejuvenation.

PALLAS ATHENA

DB: Maybe something that's been reverberating within me for some time, and maybe something that I'm acknowledging – not only, in a way, publicly, but also to myself. But when one does turn oneself over to God in terms of that one doesn't have control over life or the circumstances or relationships or anything to the degree that one wishes one could exert, I think it's inevitable that you eventually get to the realisation that there is not necessarily something that we can conceive of as a plan, but that there is an order in that which we perceive of as chaos, and that order comes from God. And I guess there are some voices given to that on this album, maybe not in such a pontificating manner. I'd hate to think that I was a deliverer of polemic. I'm really not like that. I work on intuition and impression. Impressions more than anything. I think my writing has a lot to do with my impression of life rather than an accurate, clarified view of it. I'm not a Dylan. I'm not somebody who can sit down and stoically write a clear picture of what is happening. But I can leave a very strong impression of how I feel about things … too strong, sometimes. [*Laughs*] But this one I really feel is a fairly accurate reflection of my state of mind. It doesn't have the same pain as some of the other albums. There's almost a joy in there, which is nice to see peeking through at long last.

SB: [*Voiceover*] The diversity of this album couldn't be more apparent than when you contrast 'Pallas Athena', Bowie's affirmation of his faith in God, with 'Don't Let Me Down & Down', his soulful interpretation of a Moroccan love song he recently discovered.

DB: It was an Arabic album that was lying around the house when Iman and I first met, and it was one of the songs that we were playing all the time. I adored it. I thought it was so quirky and sweet. They did it in 3/4 with, I don't know, bazooka and gong, or something. It was a really strange little song. [*Laughs*] I put it into 4/4 and made it an R'n'B ballad, and it kind of worked. When I took it into the studio and played it to Nile, [*Laughs*] he couldn't believe that we could make a song out of it that would be recognisable, but I saw this germ of beauty in it and I think it's a very sweet song.

DON'T LET ME DOWN & DOWN

<The interview includes more of the conversation with Nile Rodgers.>

SB: [*Voiceover*] Well, Bowie might adore that song, but he does have mixed feelings about what he calls the bonus track on the album, 'Lucy Can't Dance'.

DB: [*Laughs*] That's my least favourite track on the album. I can't help but tell the truth about that one. I didn't want to put it on the album, you see, but my record company really liked it a lot and, as we're new to each other, I didn't want us to fall out quite as soon as … well, no, my track record's not bad. But I do tend to inevitably fall out with the record companies I'm with, and I didn't want it to start this early. So I said as long as it wasn't in the body of the album, but if I could put it on as a bonus track, I'd let them get away with it. I like the lyrics, don't get me wrong. The lyrics are good. I just find the tune so incredibly twee.

<The interview includes more of the conversation with Nile Rodgers.>

LUCY CAN'T DANCE

SB: [*Voiceover*] Opening the album as an instrumental, 'The Wedding Song' is reprised as the concluding track, this time with a Bowie vocal celebrating his marriage and his new-found contentment.

DB: I see this album as something that had to be written because of my initial wanting to write the church music. But it's not about the wedding – that was a starting point, but it's far wider, far more diverse than that, because it prompted me into writing a lot more about the subjects and about attitudes and emotions and whatever that had been going through me in the last two or three years. I found that it became a source of woodwind and keyboard instruments that dominated the album. I guess that would be a reaction to working with the highly aggressive guitar orientation of Tin Machine. I don't know whether it's polarised the situation, but I would imagine that I may vacillate backwards and forwards in the future between Tin Machine and maybe a wider berth to other avenues that have sort of been opened up to me in solo albums. And again, as always, which is always the most exciting thing, I haven't a clue what I'll be doing next.

MARK RADCLIFFE'S GRAVEYARD SHIFT, BBC RADIO

INTERVIEWER: MARK RADCLIFFE

Bowie had just finished touring his *Outside* album with Nine Inch Nails (NIN). The American industrial grunge band were the bigger pull in America at that time, but singer Trent Reznor couldn't bear to be the headline act over his hero. The novel solution was that Bowie's band would gradually come on near the end of NIN's set and the two bands would slowly merge. Reznor said that looking over to see Bowie sing his song 'Hurt' was one of the greatest moments of his life. The two ended up working together, and produced one of Bowie's best songs of the nineties, 'I'm Afraid of Americans'.

Reznor had been at the height of his drug addiction at the time of the tour, so when he bumped into Bowie some years later, the first thing he tried to do was apologise for his behaviour. He didn't even get to finish his sentence. Bowie gave him a big hug and told him, 'I knew you'd come out of that.' 'I get goosebumps right now just thinking about it,' Reznor said.[18]

Bowie tried the same approach of merging bands with Morrissey on the next tour. It didn't work. Morrissey took off in high dudgeon one night, without any explanation, apparently annoyed that this approach deprived him of saying goodbye to his audience. In public, Bowie was diplomatic at being left in the lurch with no support band, but behind the scenes he was said to be seething. When Tony Visconti and Morrissey later suggested to Bowie a duet on 'You've Lost that Lovin' Feelin'', they never heard back.

MARK RADCLIFFE: Right, we're in New York with David Bowie. We'll have the current single from the album, then we'll get rid of the boy, Lard, and have some proper questions.

THE HEARTS FILTHY LESSON

MR: 'The Hearts Filthy Lesson', which is the current single from David Bowie's new *Outside* album. And just looking at the sleeve to that, which we'll be coming to, do you remember *George and Mildred* David? Do you remember that?

DAVID BOWIE: It doesn't look a bit like Mildred.

MR: No, but there's a George element there.

DB: It's the mac.

MR: Tell us about the Diary of Nathan Adler, art detective. [The album *Outside* was subtitled *The Nathan Adler Diaries: A Hyper-cycle*] So, no holds barred, it's a concept album?

DB: Absolutely. Brian had thought that concepts albums [*Laughs*] – concepts albums! – there have not been many around recently, and there's probably some very good reasons for that.

MR: Brian being Brian Eno?

DB: Oh, is that what his last name is? [*Laughter*] Little fella, bald head, very intelligent. We just thought we would do something that really is sort of out of use at the moment. The idea of doing a concept thing, we thought, would be an interesting way to get involved back in music again.

MR: Well, you've never shied away from concepts in the past, have you?

DB: No.

MR: People shy away a bit because they think they're going to get accused of being pretentious, but you once said you wanted to start a school of pretension anyway.

DB: I think I did! [*Laughs*] Very successfully. You know the thing with concept … every album is a concept album. It's very rare that a band or an artist will put together just a bunch of diverse songs. There's usually a thread running through an album, except you're not supposed to use the word 'concept', you know. But we thought we'd bring it back.

MR: And it's not linked by lots of dialogue with you putting on different voices?

DB: Absolutely … different hats!

MR: So, for the uninitiated – which is everybody at the moment, because the album's not out – what's the concept?

DB: I think what we were trying to do in musical text and words was just to do a summary of what it feels like to be around in 1995. And to kind of get you through it, the narrative and the characters were really a thread. You don't really need to take any notice at all of the narrative and characters. You can treat all the songs autonomously, as just separate pieces. It's really about the audience having their own interpretation, which I'm very much in favour of. Really, I sort of feel that my intent is not really that important.

MR: I mean, there is a basic story behind it, isn't there?

DB: As loosely knit as possible, because I don't really want to tie the ends up – just like life, keep it untidy – because I don't know where it's going to go on the next album, because we're going to keep this series of albums going through to 2000.

MR: So it's a 'to be continued', then?

DB: But it might not even have narrative on the next section. We might just break away from the form of it completely. It's very much going to be dictated by what the year feels like. That was the year that was, with a back beat.

MR: It's all very oblique, the content, but there are some murders that go on. It does take place in a town that is nearby.

DB: Yeah, we took the idea of ritual art, which is so prominent, especially the last 10 years in the visual arts, and just extrapolated on that and thought, 'Well, how far out could it go?' You get to the point maybe where murder itself was considered a fine art.

MR: Right, well, it's got pretty close.

DB: Yeah, there have been some extraordinary stories subsequent to our putting the album together, in fact. There was a Dutch artist called Rob Schulz, who got his legs blown off by, apocryphally, a fellow artist just a few months ago in Holland.

MR: Was this the bloke who then got put in a bag and thrown on the …

DB: No, that was … [*Laughs*]

MR: Who was that, because he got shot and got thrown on the autobahn or something?

DB: [*Laughs*] But that was just hype. No, no, it was art, you're right. [*Both laugh*] His name is Chris Burden and he came out of

San Francisco and he did that in 1975. And, in fact, became the subject of a song I wrote called 'Joe the Lion'.

MR: Oh, I always thought that was about your son.

DB: No, no, no.

MR: But the concept is loosely set not far from here, fictitiously …
Oxford Town[ship].

DB: Yeah, New Oxford Town, which doesn't exist, in New
Jersey, which does exist. We just felt we needed a landscape for
the whole thing. The whole thing was written in the studio in an
improvisational way. You kind of just develop … as I was improv-ing
over the music, I was just working all these ideas that I had in my
head and it just became a landscape with characters.

MR: People are already drawing parallels with *Diamond Dogs* …

DB: Yeah! There's an [*Inaudible*] of that in it.

MR: … a nightmare vision of not the future now, but the present.

DB: Yeah, I think when you are as old and sage and wise as I am,
that you look back … I've done so many albums now that I can kind
of draw from my own albums now, that I very rarely go outside of
my own work in a way, and I'm able to use a lot of the ideas from
the past and recontextualise them like now, and they kind of say
something different.

MR: When you go for a big project like this and you get all these
high-flying ideas and get carried away with it, is there anybody close
enough to you to say, 'Hang on, Dave, we've gone right over the edge
this time – you can't do that'?

DB: No, thank God. [*Both laugh*]

MR: It's entirely up to you.

• • •

MR: David, Menswear [a band] mean anything to you, Menswear?

DB: Yeah, ah, yeah.

MR: Right. [*Laughs*] What do you do … do you get records sent over because you do keep up with stuff, don't you?

DB: No, I know a record shop. [*Laughs*]

MR: Oh right, so you do …

DB: No, I buy a lot. I generally listen to everything, all the time. I like keeping up with what's going down. Not much of it … you know, you only end up with a couple of things at the end of a year that actually stay with you. I'll tell what I love this year, what I've got to admit, is one that never saw the light of day, Scott Walker's *Tilt*. I thought that was absolutely extraordinary.

MR: Now, I'm a Scott Walker fan and I couldn't get on with that at all.

DB: Really? There's a couple of skippers there, there's two or three tracks that I would go past, but I thought some of the writing was absolutely brilliant.

MR: I found it a bit scary, that, but perhaps that's not a bad thing.

DB: Oh, it's wonderful.

MR: Anyway, we were talking about sandwiches before there. Somebody has delivered you … it's like enormous … a skyscraper of a sandwich.

• • •

MR: What about you, Lard? Have you had any sandwiches recently?

RILEY: No, just beer, basically. A bit of wine.

MR: They do a good beer sandwich place just down the road.

RILEY: Fabulous beer sandwich. That's what it's known for, isn't it, New York.

DB: Actually, because it's America, it's beer and sprouts. [*Laughter*]

MR: Essential. Right, we'll have the title track from David's new album, then we'll send Lard out for beer and sprouts sandwiches.

OUTSIDE

MR: As we've already mentioned, you've been working with Brian Eno again. People have kind of gotten dewy-eyed and nostalgic for your old Eno collaborations, pleased to see you back with him again.

DB: Yeah, Brian and his wife came to my wedding in '92 and inevitably, we started talking about what we're doing in music. Once again, our ideas about what we needed to do and what we enjoyed doing were exactly the same. It was just like having a weekend off, those 12 years or so we weren't working together. As soon as we got back in the studio, it was as easy as falling off some logs.

MR: What does he give you that other people don't give you?

DB: I think it's because he's inventive conceptually. He makes it more of some kind of game format in the studio. The first that we did, he brought over some material from London, some high-coloured material, and we redecorated for the first day.

MR: So, were you a haberdasher in a past life?

DB: Sort of. Well, we've even done that. That's how we got round to me doing wallpaper really, was Brian and I for some benefit thing, for War Child, that Brian was organising. We decided we'd do a bathroom interior decoration stall at the end of the gallery. We didn't have time to do it, but we were going to have wallpapers and tilings and stuff that we'd designed as an installation.

MR: [*Laughs*] It just seems an unlikely thing that you'd want to do – redecorate the bathroom. Did you try it at home, put it up to the wife and say, 'What do you think of this?'

DB: Several times a month, yeah.

MR: [*Laughs*] Just seems odd. Anyway, going back to the studio, this was in Montreux, yeah?

DB: Yeah, we also did an awful lot of work in New York as well, backwards and forwards. So, we got the band in to help redecorate. We thought we'd better do some music as well. But we started as a series of Brian throwing out different ideas for characters for us all.

MR: Yeah, you finished up being a town crier?

DB: A 'griot', I think was the word, which is an African storyteller to tell stories.

MR: Oh right, so everybody in the band gets a different part to play, do they?

DB: Yeah, what happens is that they forget the parts as soon as they start playing, but for those first 15 seconds when they start playing they come in in character, so the music doesn't become just a regular jazzy or bluesy, you know, one of those awful jams where it's inevitably a 12-bar blues. So, they come in from spacey places.

MR: What were some of the other parts – like milkman, painter and decorator?

DB: Almost, yeah. One guy was a disgruntled ex-member of Clash, that was his part. So he was supposed to play all the notes he wasn't allowed to play when he was with them, for instance.

MR: [*Laughs*] So, how does that work? That affects the way they play?

DB: It definitely does, yeah. And also it takes their inhibitions away. You know, at a party, for instance, you've got these really quiet, rather sour in-laws and you say, 'Well, let's have a game of charades.' Then you give them something they know and they suddenly become different people, and it's almost the same kind of thing. You give them something to break down their inhibitions and they do things that maybe they wouldn't have done. It's a nice way of working.

MR: Obviously, in the past, people are familiar with the big concerts when you'd play characters – Ziggy and Aladdin Sane, the Thin White Duke, and all that. Do you feel more comfortable yourself performing at one remove with a character in between you?

DB: Actually, funnily enough, no. As you saw from the show the other night, we're doing the stuff from *Outside* just as songs. I'm very happy just … I really have fun with the music now. My whole attitude about going on stage is, if I'm not having fun, I'd rather not be doing it. So, I go out very carefree. Really, I have no expectations from audiences. If they are, as they were last night, really listening then great – really, a fabulous audience – that makes it even better, it makes it really good.

MR: One of the things people also know about you is that you used to write lyrics by cutting them up and pasting them together. And you said you still had a bit of cut-and-paste sessions in that, do you do a lot of it on your Apple Mac now?

DB: Yeah, yes. It was an American writer, William Burroughs, who really initiated that style of writing – cutting up phrases and retrieving that strange information that maybe the subconscious knows about, all that Freudian stuff. I've used the same method since the early seventies, but now I've got a program for the computer that does it for me, and much faster. So, I'm swinging along into that now.

MR: Right, and you put this band together for this album. One of the names I was really interested to see was Mike Garson, pianist extraordinaire. Never a man to play two notes where he can get a couple of thousand in.

DB: He's the only guy that I would trust with the same space that a lead guitarist would normally take. He plays so eccentrically, and really knows no bounds, that if he does play a solo, it's going to keep the attention as much as any guitar player.

MR: We're going to play another track from it, 'We Prick You', which is one you've chosen. Is there anything you want to tell us before we play it, or shall we just play it?

DB: It's just dotty. [*Laughter*]

WE PRICK YOU

MR: Blur, do they mean anything to you?

BOWIE AT THE BBC

DB: Yeah, I like them a lot. I like their [*Adopts director Damien Hirst's accent*] new video ['Country House'] by Damien Hirst, the well-known sheep herder.

MR: I haven't seen that. I've been told it's very Benny Hill.

DB: It's very colourful. It's very British. I'm not sure how it'll play in America, but … it's just so bright and daft. I like it a lot.

MR: Yeah, because Americans might (not) go for it. Because we were talking about, like Portishead, who just won the Mercury Music Prize, who have been getting some bad reviews for their live gigs in the States …

DB: Yes, I think it's tough over here for British bands. They [Americans] hold a lot of store by touring in the States and about working the stage and all that, and I think they kind of expect you to deliver … I don't know. I think it's difficult for some of the newer British bands if maybe they haven't had that much performance experience behind them.

MR: Like Portishead, I read some reviews of Oasis from the States, and the thing they couldn't get their head round, the American audience, was that they stood still.

DB: Yeah.

MR: Is that a problem, do you think?

DB: Well, [*Laughs*] yeah, I guess it is, isn't it?

MR: That's why Alvin Stardust never cracked it. [*Laughter*] We were talking about Suede, of course, you're well familiar with them.

DB: I don't know. Did they come over here, Suede?

MR: They came over with The Cranberries, didn't they?

DB: Yeah, yeah. Oh yeah, Cranberries did quite well.

MR: Cranberries did quite well, and Suede, who were supposed to be headlining, didn't do quite as well. We were saying that maybe the Americans have never quite gone for that androgynous thing, really.

DB: No, I don't think so. Well, except, there again, with the newer bands probably, people like Trent Reznor, for instance, or Billy [Corgan] out of Smashing Pumpkins, there's a move toward that particular persona, I think.

MR: We were talking about the kind of records that form the basis of your understanding of American music – what would they be?

DB: The first three that really mattered to me of white artists were the Village Fugs [later known as the Fugs], Frank Zappa and the Mothers with *Freak Out!* and The Velvet [Underground] album. Those three really became the nucleus of my listening in the sixties.

MR: And it's really sad that Sterling Morrison [guitarist with The Velvet Underground] has died.

DB: Yes, that was very sad.

MR: Did you see The Velvet Underground when they got back together again and did that tour?

DB: I tell you, I saw, even funnier than that, when I very first came over to the States in about 1970, one of the things that happened … I heard that The Underground were playing in New York. This was a magic event for me and I was all on my own, it was my first trip over here. So, I went to see their gig [*Laughs*] and during the break I got to speak to Lou, and I was, 'Ah, great,' and I was going on and on about his writing and he was nodding, 'Yeah, yeah,' and then halfway through he said, 'Look, Lou's actually left the band, I'm

Doug Yule.' [*Both laugh*] And he looked identical to Lou, the guy was the spitting image. It was such a comedown because I was thinking, yeah, he's as good as I thought he was on stage.

BRIAN ENO TRACK FROM 1973

MR: I was talking to David Bowie while that was on and we were both wishing that Brian Eno would do a bit more songs, would do a bit more singing.

DB: I think he's got a great voice. It sounds slightly insane, his voice. He does very good pop songs.

MR: Yeah, I love it when he does that. I love the other stuff as well, I'm not knocking that. I wish he'd do a couple more songs. Also, I never realised this, you've got northern roots.

DB: Yeah, I've got this really annoying habit that if I'm with somebody from the north country, I start lapsing back into that way of talking, because my father was from Yorkshire and my mother was from Lancashire, so if nobody from the north is around, I'm [*Adopts a strong London accent*] back in London again, you know, and I'm down there. But as soon as, like with Damien Hirst, for instance, he's from the north country and he said, [*Adopts a Leeds accent*] 'I didn't know you came from the north country?' I said, 'What do you mean?' He said, 'Well, you're talking with a Yorkshire accent.' I said, 'I'm sorry, it's like sitting in a room with my dad listening to you talk and I just lapse back into it.' It's really hard.

MR: Now, this tour that you're doing. After we finish this show tonight, you're on the bus to Toronto. Now, I'm quite surprised. Why do you want to go on a coach?

DB: Because it's got no wings. [*Laughs*]

MR: You've still got a terrible fear of flying?

DB: I don't like it at all. I mean, I never got easy with it. I did stop for about six years, I never flew anywhere. I had to go everywhere by liner – well, not on the ground, but when we hit a sea. [*Laughter*] Sometimes I didn't know the difference. But now I've gotten back into flying, but I don't like it. I do it as little as possible.

MR: Right. This tour, you hooked up with Nine Inch Nails. How did all that come about? Are you a fan of theirs? Are they a fan of yours?

DB: Yeah, I think they're terrific, especially the second album, *Downward Spiral*, I think that's great. Over the last few years, it's been quite noticeable in this country, America, that a lot of the new bands are quite influenced by a lot of the British acts from the early seventies – T. Rex, myself and Roxy [Music] for instance. And Trent, particularly, was talking a lot about the work that I did and the work that I did with Brian. So, on spec, when Virgin, the record company, asked me if I would support the album with a tour, I said, 'I'd love to, but I'd like to take someone out with me.' And I gave Trent a phone. He'd just finished something like a 12-month tour, but said if he only had to do it for six weeks, he'd love to do it. So, he's on with me and we're working together on stage as well.

MR: It's quite an interesting thing, because they do a set and then there's a transition, isn't there?

DB: Yeah, it works so well for both of us because the audiences are so entirely different from each other. His is very industrial-oriented, mosh-pit kind of audience, and so we've got about a 30-minute spot where we both work together and kind of introduce the audiences to both our ideas that kind of touch where we have a point of common ground.

MR: It is quite interesting to see you sometimes doing Jacques Brel torch songs in front of this mosh pit of industrial goths.

DB: It's fantastic. They body surf to Jacques Brel, [*Laughter*] which is very late twentieth century, wouldn't you say? [*Laughs*]

MR: Very deconstructed. Post-post-modernist. Post-post-ironic.

DB: Yeah, post-post-ironic, yeah.

MR: We'll talk more about the show in a moment. We're going to play 'Hallo Spaceboy'. This is the one where there's three drummers, [*Laughter*] two of theirs and one of yours.

DB: Yes, we were standing around for a few more, [*Laughter*] but we only came up with three drummers.

MR: You want to get the lads club, the local pipe and drum band, you'd have 14 drummers.

HALLO SPACEBOY

MR: 'Hallo Spaceboy' from the album *Outside*.

DB: [*Adopts a funny accent*] Hello, Mark.

MR: One of your character voices, we haven't got all the effects to do that.

DB: That wasn't me, actually, that was the other Mark.

MR: Right. Oh, was it? Obviously, on this tour you played most of this new album, a lot of unfamiliar stuff.

DB: Everything. Everything. I mean I think only maybe people who know my material really well would even recognise a lot of the old ones, because they're the more obscure tracks that I've never done live, the majority of them, like 'Joe the Lion' and 'Teenage Wildlife' and those sorts of things. So, in a way, I guess it's really tough on the audience, and I'm just really appreciative of the way that everybody is listening over here, it's great.

MR: In a way, you sort of burnt your bridges because you did the Sound+Vision – the greatest hits – Tour. You said, 'Right. That's it out of the way, I'm not going to play these again.' So, you had to move on from there really, didn't you?

DB: Absolutely. That is the reason I did it, because I didn't want to settle into having to do those because they were expected just to keep working as an artist. You want to set yourself new parameters, and for me it was really important to keep pushing where I could go musically.

MR: You looked back over some of the albums in the eighties and said, 'Actually, I must hold my hands up now and say actually some of them really weren't that good.'

DB: There's two there that I've always been disappointed with, and it's partly because of my indifference towards making them. I wasn't friendly with music anymore after *Let's Dance*. I didn't like that period. That whole period for me was really a depressing period artistically. So, I had big problems with *Tonight* and *Never Let Me Down*. But of the 25 or so albums I have made, those are the only two that I'm not too keen on.

MR: Did you ever feel like the knack of writing songs had deserted you?

DB: No, it's just lack of wanting to bother.

MR: Why was that, then?

DB: Because I felt like I was in the mainstream, [*Laughs*] and I felt, I'm going to be locked in here, I'm going to have to please people, and all that. I fell foul of that, but when I then decided just to please myself again, everything started going okay again.

MR: Did you ever come close to jacking it in totally?

DB: Not really. I don't think I'd ever do that, but I did do a lot more visual arts instead. I painted and sculpted a lot during the eighties as opposed to doing music.

MR: So, what did you do to get back into … In a way, you become very vulnerable because instead of trusting your instincts, you start to look for a direction and, okay, you may latch on to some industrial thing, you could hear Bavarian oompah one day and think, 'Ah, I'll do that!'

DB: I think so. I think that is a danger, but fortunately I got friendly with a guy called Reeves Gabrels, who is now my guitar player almost on a permanent basis, in the mid- to late eighties – about '87, '88 we kind of hitched up. And, at that point, he was a godsend, really, because Reeves said, 'What you're really best at, and what everybody enjoys about what you do, is when you get experimental and just follow your own nose about what you should be doing.' And he got me into that frame of mind again, I guess. Plus, my own dissatisfaction with what I was doing. That's when we formed Tin Machine, precisely to do that – to break down all idea of what it was that I was. Everything I've done from that point, with Tin Machine included, is work that I really stand by and work that I really adore.

MR: Were you disappointed when people … because Tin Machine got a right slagging, didn't they?

DB: Yeah, but you know something, those albums sound really great. They sound really great. I'm really proud of a lot of that work. No, I like everything I've done since around '88, '89.

MR: So, you enjoying being back on stage? You look like you were enjoying the other night …

DB: I'm having a ball.

MR: … doing your puppet dance.

DB: Well, yes, that's a new step, you know. It's very good. It took me hours to work that out.

MR: Well, he's been doing that for years but by accident, the boy Lard. [*Laughter*] What's your pre-gig ritual? Does it take you ages to get ready? No people smoking in the same room? Choose your own clothes? Do you do your own hair? What do you do?

DB: I turn up. I'm only wearing a tank top, [*Laughter*] so it's not exactly a 10-hour procedure.

MR: So, you don't go through any elaborate thing like that?

DB: Shopping, generally. [*Laughs*]

MR: Do you?

DB: Yeah, depending on the city, I go and have a walk about.

MR: You don't have a team of acolytes and stylists around you, who sit there with you …?

DB: I've been looking for some acolytes.

RILEY: I'm not bad with a bit of hair gel. If you're struggling on the tour, I can tease it up nicely. It's not a problem. Can you let me go?

MR: With the greatest of ease, the boy Lard. With the greatest of ease.

WHERE THE WILD ROSES GROW (Kylie Minogue and Nick Cave)

DB: That's really good, that.

MR: You like that?

DB: Yeah, I like that a lot.

MR: We've been talking about Tindersticks and Lee Hazlewood and people like that. You're saying that Julian Schnabel …

DB: Yeah, Julian Schnabel, the painter, I did a film with him recently on Jean-Michel Basquiat, a young Black painter that committed suicide in the eighties. I played Andy Warhol. But Julian just before that had done an album himself. He did it with … who was it now … ah, Bill Laswell. Bill Laswell was the band.

MR: Great bass player.

DB: Yeah, fantastic band, and it kind of has the same quality. It's like that [Leonard] Cohen–Lou Reed feeling. I'm not bad, actually.

MR: Are we going to see that film in England?

DB: Yeah, New Year it comes out.

MR: Is it true you played the part in that film with the original Warhol wig? You went and got his gear?

DB: Yeah, we got all his stuff from the museum set up in Pittsburgh. They lent us everything. It was really kind of spooky because nothing had been cleaned, and his clothes still had the … aftershave smell, and …

MR: Oh, thank God for that.

DB: Everything. Yeah, it was really odd.

MR: And what about the wig? Was that authentic?

DB: [*Laughs*] That was a genuine wig. And it was made by somebody like JoJo Wig Creations on Broadway. [*Laughs*] He obviously got really junkie wigs.

MR: And you found his make-up kit that he used to patch up his face with when he was out and about?

DB: Yeah, the kind of little bag he used to carry around. When he took it to the hospital with him for the last time, it had his notebook and addresses and old, torn up cheques [*Laughs*] and a little stick of pancake he obviously used when he went out shopping.

MR: What about the film, are you pleased with it? Have you seen it?

DB: I've not seen it, nothing, no, because as soon as I finished working, I went straight off to rehearse for the tour.

MR: So, we see the film in the New Year. You're on tour. The important news for listeners is that you are going to play in England.

DB: Yeah, yeah, yeah, and it's going to be real soon as well. Hopefully, it's going to be November. But we'll have an official announcement, hopefully, Thursday this week.

MR: That's going to be with Nine Inch Nails as well?

DB: No, as I say, Trent would only do the first six weeks, so we're working through some other ideas for England and Europe.

MR: So, you're looking for another band to do the same thing with?

DB: Yes.

MR: Any ideas?

DB: Yeah, lots.

MR: Okay. We're going to play … what about Tricky?

DB: I love Tricky. I think they're great.

MR: And you wrote that thing in _Q_.*

DB: Yeah. [_Laughs_]

MR: So, you're going to turn into a rock journalist? You're going to add that to your …

DB: Only if I can do it my own way. _Q_ magazine are really cool, though; they just let me ramble on.

A FOO FIGHTERS SONG plays

MR: Dave Grohl. That's his new band. And they did that cover version of 'The Man Who Sold the World'.

DB: Yeah, it was incredible to hear that.

MR: Did that bring a new audience to you for this tour?

DB: I don't know. The only two things that they recognise are 'Andy Warhol', which was covered by Stone Temple Pilots, and this one that Kurt [Cobain] did. Yeah, so I guess they are partly … very much responsible for bringing people to this stuff.

MR: [_To Riley_] I'm sorry you're having to sit here. You're sat there looking gormless, aren't you?

* References an interview with Tricky in _Q_ magazine – although the article is so surreal, involving cut-up language and dream sequences where the two musicians appear to scale the wall of a sky-scraper, that 'interview' is probably not the right word to describe it.

RILEY: Well, that's my job.

MR: You've obviously got your eye on David's half-finished sandwich.

RILEY: That's nice. Looks like a nice sandwich.

MR: Why can you not do anything useful, seeing as you've come all this way?

RILEY: Well, what I was thinking of doing was going out on the streets and talking to people.

MR: It's looking good, yeah. I'm liking it so far.

RILEY: All these New Yorkers, because we're in New York, aren't we?

MR: Brilliant.

RILEY: What I'm going to do is go out with a microphone. I'm going to talk to them, you see. I'm just going to stop and talk to the local colour.

MR: Yes.

RILEY: I'm going to do that after the next tune, I think.

MR: Okay. Fantastic. Vox pops with the boy Lard on the streets of New York. In the meantime, the Pixies and 'Debaser' from the *Doolittle* album. And you used to play this?

DB: Oh, yeah, yeah.

MR: With Tin Machine?

DB: It was a wonderful band, The Pixies. Reeves Gabrels's old buddies.

DEBASER (The Pixies)

<Marc Riley New York vox pop follows.>

MR: We're going to have another track from *Outside*, this is 'A Small Plot of Land'. Is this about your dad's allotment in Tadcaster?

DB: It is, yeah. Flat cap and a garden shed.

A SMALL PLOT OF LAND (an avant-garde jazz song reminiscent of the sound Bowie would later use on Blackstar*)*

MR: It's alright to fade it there, is it?

DB: Well, there's another 17 minutes, Mark, [*Laughter*] but you got the gist.

MR: There's going to be heavy rotation on that. [*Laughter*]

DB: Well, it's the next single. [*Laughter*]

MR: A wise choice, there. 'A Small Plot of Land' on *Outside* by David Bowie. We're with David Bowie in New York for about another 11 minutes, after which it'll be Wendy Lloyd. So, where do you live then? You don't live in New York. You're homesick for England occasionally. Where's home?

DB: Well, I come back and see my friends frequently throughout the year, and on tour you never really know where you are. I'm just here all the time now. During the course of the year, Iman and I like to spend our time all over Europe and all over America.

MR: Where's your main house, is it in Switzerland?

DB: Yeah.

MR: And what about your son, Joe [now known as Duncan Jones], because he's at college in the States?

DB: That's right. He's just started his doctorate in philosophy so he's going to … I don't know [*Laughs*] … what do you do when you've got philosophy? I suppose you write a lot.

MR: Whose idea was it to change his name from Zowie back to …

DB: Well, actually it was circumstances. At the time, I found it a lot easier to attract his attention in a crowd by calling him Joey as opposed to Zowie, and people wouldn't … because they know Zowie, especially in England, immediately. If I used 'Joey', it didn't attract attention to him, so it's kind of stuck.

MR: Right. And you spent quite a lot of time as a single parent because you did bring him up, didn't you?

DB: Yeah, yeah.

MR: Was that difficult? Because you had a lot of famous battles against drugs and all kinds of things, so does that make it easier or more difficult?

DB: [*Laughs*] The thing is we never really had, I guess you call it, a celebrity-type life. Joe was never exposed to all that because I've actually lived quite quietly, believe it or not. So he hasn't had to go through that. Maybe some of the children of my contemporaries, or whatever, have had to go through different things. But it's been a pretty regular life here.

MR: And what do you do when you're not playing? You're obviously on tour at the moment. We know you paint and you write and all kinds of things. What do you do when you really want to … do you ever get a takeaway curry, take your shoes off, put them on the coffee table and watch the darts championships on the telly?

DB: No, I've built a radio station at home and I broadcast to the living room.

MR: [*Laughs*] Just sit there playing all your favourite records?

DB: Yeah.

MR: That's pretty much what I do.

DB: Yeah, it's like this, all these tape machines.

MR: Do you have a boy, Lard? Have you got a feckless lump of lard you can wheel in from the suburbs of Gstaad?

DB: I've got a shop mannequin, then I throw my voice … stereo mics.

MR: Now, that is a smart move, because I could have just put him in a flight case …

RILEY: Don't give him any ideas, David, please.

DB: You told me you did keep him in a flight case.

MR: It has been known. This is a crass question, but of all your albums, apart from the most recent one …

DB: [*Spells it out*] C R A S S. Yeah, okay, got it.

MR: … apart from the most recent one, because that's always the one you're most interested in, have you got one that you look on more fondly than all the others? Or do you want a bit of time to think about it? Shall I play a record and you think about it?

DB: Yeah.

MR: Alright. We'll have some New York Dolls. And you had some wild times with the Dolls in your time, didn't you?

DB: Yeah, they introduced me to New York [*Laughs*] in only the way that they could.

MR: Some of the few people who outdressed you at the time.

DB: And outskated me. The first band I saw in roller skates.

MYSTERY GIRL (New York Dolls)

DB: Songs for falling down to.

MR: Absolutely. So, you had some wild times in New York with them, did you?

DB: Yes. [*Laughs*] Yes, I fell down a lot.

MR: Your favourite album out of all yours. Can you answer my crass question?

DB: Yes, somewhere between *Diamond Dogs* and *Lodger*.

MR: Right, those two. So, you're off to Toronto. How long does that take on the bus?

DB: Three and a half decades. [*Laughter*]

MR: Do you get your own fancy bus with a four-poster bed, or do you travel with the boys?

DB: Yes, we've got a bus where we all have … it's a democracy … four-poster beds. All on the same bus, just piled high. It's a very tall bus. [*Laughter*]

MR: And we can look forward to seeing you in the UK, probably as early as November.

DB: Yeah, really looking forward to that.

MR: If you can find a new band.

DB: Thanks a lot, you guys.

MR: No, thanks very much. And David Bowie's new album *Outside* is out on the twenty-sixth. We'll finish tonight – we've been debating about this – and we decided to finish with the Sex Pistols from *Never Mind the Bollocks*, '77, and this is 'New York'.

LATER ... WITH JOOLS HOLLAND, BBC TV

INTERVIEWER: JOOLS HOLLAND

One night in 1995, Britain's biggest band of the decade found themselves up against one of its greatest Rock Gods in the gladiatorial
confines of *Later...* The decision to choose who would start and end
the show fell to Mark Cooper, the show's co-creator and producer.
Cooper chose Oasis for both. It's a decision he now regrets. Here's
how he recalls that evening.

"We have Oasis, who are the biggest thing in the world, they're
in their pomp, and they rule Britain. Then, we have Bowie, who is
kind of on the skids. He is canonised now – deservedly so – but at
this point he's coming off two Tin Machine albums and there's a
sense of him trying to find himself again. *Outside*, the album he came
on to promote, is very much a brave album. Its primary influence
was perhaps Trent Reznor of Nine Inch Nails – there was a trip-hop
influence, there was a noise influence, too. It was an arty record and,
arguably, a difficult record in many ways. But Bowie had never been
on the show before and it was a huge coup. The show was always
about balancing the sense of past and present and we were spoilt for
riches. So, there they were, facing each other across the room, in a
gladiatorial set-up in true *Later...* style.

"I used to be obsessed by what songs the artists would perform.
I was happy with what Bowie was going to do but Oasis' choices were

bewildering. They were going to perform Slade's 'Cum On Feel the Noize', 'Wonderwall', and 'Round Are Way', which was disappointing.

"On any other week, the main focus would have been welcoming Bowie onto the show for the first time, but I decided to start and end with Oasis. If I had my time again, I probably wouldn't do it that way."

The main problem was Liam Gallagher, Cooper remembers:

"Liam turned up late and apparently he was off his tree. The band said that he'd been on a bender for three days. They hadn't seen him for all that time. So, when we came to the rehearsals, Liam just about staggered through, his voice palpably going, looking like he'd just climbed out of a haystack. He went up to the canteen for some chips and a BBC coffee in a paper cup looking pretty hangdog and he wasn't really talking to the others. Noel was certainly pissed off with him.

"I was going back and forth as to who would start the show. You had David Bowie, a true British great, and Oasis who, in my view, were performing the wrong songs. Obviously, with Liam singing 'Cum On Feel the Noize' – he has a voice like an oxy acetylene torch, it's one of the great driving voices of British rock'n'roll – it's a different proposition. Oasis went for the take and Liam struggled, in my view rather poignantly; his voice came and went, and it was kind of a unique version. When they finished, I was called down from the gallery. The band's management, their plugger and Noel Gallagher were adamant it wasn't good enough. Liam skulked off and left the building to recover somewhere – and they went again. This was really galling because to me, because *Noel* singing 'Cum On Feel the Noize' was not the same thing.

"And then David came up with 'Hallo Spaceboy'. The sound was so dense, so punchy and loud, and you were instantly reminded that here was one of the great front men. He looked glorious. He was pushing 50, but he looked amazing in a white shirt, very slender, very handsome, hair quipped up. The drummer was just pounding the drums the whole way through. It was an enormous sound on overload, and Bowie was at his operatic best.

"One of the odd things about the night was that Oasis were so wrapped in their pomp that they didn't notice Bowie. Noel didn't speak to Bowie all night and that was unusual, almost like they were wary of each other. If I were Oasis, I'd have been thinking, 'God, we are performing at 75% against a titan.' Bowie was just so good. In performance, you were reminded of what a titan he was. His performance of 'Strangers When We Meet' was one of his best performances on *Later*... When he finished, there was a wonderful, exhausted-but-triumphal sigh from him, a kind of 'Phew!', because it's a big vocal and an epic song, one of his great ballads of loss and regret. He was fantastic. Oasis, in comparison, weren't able to deliver who they were at that point in time."

JOOLS HOLLAND: And now I'm coming over this way because we are now going to chat with one of the greatest artists of English popular music. Ladies and gentlemen, David Bowie. [*Applause. Jools Holland and David Bowie sit down at the piano.*]

JH: A funny old thing, a piano.

DAVID BOWIE: Who's driving?

JH: Well, it's a left-hand drive, this one.

DB: Okay.

JH: We're very excited by your new record, which you're playing songs from, *Outside*.

DB: Thank you, Jools.

JH: And you're back, reunited with Brian Eno for the first time since *Heroes* and *Low*.

DB: 1979 was the last time … yeah '79 was the last time we worked together.

JH: Sixteen years?

DB: Sixteen years.

JH: Why back together with him?

DB: I ran into him at my wedding. [*Laughs*] We got really quite excited about what we both wanted to do in music, and it took us only two years to get it together to actually come to the studio. '94 we did that.

JH: Did you go back to Berlin to do it?

DB: No, mainly New York and some work in Switzerland, but the majority of it in New York.

JH: I believe you put lots of words into a computer and scrambled them. Is that right?

DB: Yes.

JH: tell us, how does that work?

DB: I use bits of poems and pieces, articles out of magazines and newspapers. I retype them out and put them into the computer. It's got a randomiser programme in there. It spews it all back out again, and I make of it what I can, what I will.

JH: Well, that brings us to a little bit of archive footage of yourself.

DB: Good.

MOONAGE DAYDREAM

DB: As you can see, on that particular sequence I'd just undergone a thing with a weight-gain product.

JH: [*Missing the joke*] Where did you gain any weight? I didn't see …

DB: That was the bigger me … [*Laughs*] Hah, bigamy! That's how these new songs get written.

[*Inaudible chat*]

JH: That was 'Moonage Daydream' from *Cracked Actor*. On the *Outside* record there's a lot of characters on the record and quite a distinct narrative on the story.

DB: Yeah, you can take that as you want. It's not necessary to follow the narrative. I sort of left that way behind. Because we are doing songs in a straightforward stage show, I'm taking them on autonomously as separate pieces, just as songs. But if you want, you can try and pull the narrative out of the bits that are there.

JH: A lot of people like this new record very much.

DB: Thank you.

JH: A lot of people are coming to the tour. But some people are moaning minnies and are saying, 'Why isn't he doing old songs, the old songs that we know and love?'

DB: Well, if they didn't know that I wasn't going to be, they must have been living under a rock.

JH: That's your answer?

DB: Yes.

JH: Well, that's good enough for me.

[*Laughter and applause*]

JH: Good enough for all of us. David Bowie, ladies and gentlemen. Thank you very much.

DB: Thank you, Jools.

THIS IS YOUR LIFE (JOHN PEEL), BBC TV

John Peel arguably saved Bowie's career not once, not twice, but three times. The first occasion was when Bowie was rejected by a BBC audition panel at the very outset of his career. Such decisions were to kill many a fledgling career, since the BBC monopolised the airwaves. But, in Bowie's case, Peel stepped into the rescue to pull some strings and ensure the 18-year-old was given a rare second chance. Bowie recalled the moment when he appeared by video to honour Peel on the popular light entertainment show *This is Your Life*.

DAVID BOWIE: Hi, John! [*Peel smiles*] I remember around 1965, I did an audition for the BBC and I failed, and the report said, [*DB adopts a classic BBC accent*] 'This vocalist is devoid of personality and sings all the wrong notes.' [*Audience laughs*] So, in your inimitable manner and with tremendous enthusiasm, you got me back on for another audition, which I passed the second time around, which gave me freewheeling access to a lifetime of singing all the wrong notes. And I guess there's a lot of us out here who would like to thank you, John, for having faith in us and what we've been trying to do. So, from all of us, thank you very much.

Peel was clearly delighted to see Bowie, especially since the last time he had tried to have a word with 'my mate David', he'd been told to fuck off.

Many years before, Peel had gone backstage to chat to his old pal. But this was in the years following the assassination of John Lennon and a more anxious Bowie had since hired a former Navy Seal-turned-karate-expert to be his bodyguard.

As Peel edged towards the dressing room, he found his path blocked by a muscular and menacing figure.

'Where the fuck you think you're going?' the martial arts expert asked.

'Just to have a word with my mate, David,' squeaked Peel.

'Like fuck ya going to have a word with him,' came the response.

'Since then,' wrote Peel in his memoirs, 'and surely well beyond the New York karate expert's intention, I've not had a single word with David.'

The second time Peel saved Bowie's career was in the late sixties, when no one was playing, let alone buying, Bowie's records. 'We kept Bowie alive for a couple of years,' said Peel. 'He went through a bad patch of not getting very much work and people not paying a great deal of attention to him. He did a lot of sessions during that time.' Despite giving him air play, Peel was surprisingly not a great fan during this period. It was only when 'The Man Who Sold the World' and then *Hunky Dory* came out that the DJ became a convert. 'I just liked the idea that he was always a step or two ahead of the game,' Peel said.[19]

The third and final time Peel affected Bowie's career came one night after a concert. At this point, Bowie was vacillating between being a rock singer and a mime artist. Peel was upset to see his friend at the foot of a bill or, as he would memorably recall, 'below that lowliest of God's creatures, an Australian sitar player'. Peel decided his friend should be spared any more humiliation and told him to stop his act because nobody liked mime. 'You were right,' Bowie said later, 'no one in the world likes mime.'

HAPPY BIRTHDAY DAVID BOWIE, BBC RADIO

INTERVIEWER: MARY ANNE HOBBS

It was the most emotionally raw moment of David Bowie ever caught on tape. A deep intake of breath, a loud exhalation, silence, yet more silence and then tears. 'You really got me there,' Bowie said. Those 30 seconds were so long that the BBC later had to edit it down to prevent the emergency dead-air tapes from kicking in.

The cause of such a heartfelt reaction was a crackly message from across the Atlantic by a 54-year-old singer from Ohio. Scott Walker had a supremely odd career, perhaps only rivalled by Bowie himself. Once part of the Walker Brothers, songs like 'The Sun Ain't Gonna Shine Anymore' and 'Make It Easy on Yourself' made them mid-sixties rivals to The Beatles in terms of the sheer numbers in their fan club. But Walker rejected the fame to go his own, unique way. 'Imagine Andy Williams reinventing himself as Stockhausen,' the *Guardian* once wrote. It was the sort of career trajectory that Bowie adored.

'The one [message] that really killed me was Scott Walker,' said Bowie afterwards. 'That really got me. The man has got such great integrity and doesn't deviate from his particular vision. He's someone as selfish as I am in that he pays no attention to the audience and just does what he wants to do. He's someone I've looked at when I think what should I be doing.'

MARY ANNE HOBBS: David Bowie, it's lovely to see you.

DAVID BOWIE: It's lovely to be seen. [*Laughs*]

MAH: Personally speaking, I was in a blind panic about my age when I was on the cusp of 20, but 50 … how does that feel?

DB: Ironically, I don't think I'd have thought about it unless so many people brought it to my attention. [*Laughs*] I feel awkward about it. It's one of these things I've never done before, so it's like putting on a new suit in a way and getting used to it and easing into the idea of it. I feel good enough to say that I wished I'd been 50 years ago. [*Both laugh*] It seems daft, but here in Neasden, I mean in New York, there's not really a big age thing. It's probably more an English thing than an American thing in a way.

MAH: In your rehearsals for Madison Square Gardens, you recorded some exclusive tracks for us, which we're delighted to have. We're going to begin with 'The Man Who Sold the World'. What still turns you on about that song?

DB: I guess I wrote it because there was a part of myself that I was looking for. Maybe now that I feel more comfortable with the way that I live my life and my mental [*Laughs*] state and my spiritual state and whatever, maybe I feel there's some kind of unity now. But that song for me exemplified how you feel when you're young; you know there's a piece of yourself you haven't really put together yet, and you have this great searching, this great need to find out who you really are.

THE MAN WHO SOLD THE WORLD

SUPERMEN

DB: Wow. That was very strange to do after all these years. I really haven't done that for so long. Interestingly enough, the riff that I use on that [*Hums the tune*] I actually revived on the new album, *Earthling*. I used it on one of the songs on that. You've got to spot it! When I was a baby, I did a rock session with one of the millions of bands I had in the sixties – it was The Manish Boys, that's what it was – and the session player doing the guitar solo was this young kiddie who'd just come out of art school and was already a top session man, Jimmy Page. He'd just got a fuzz box and he used that for the solo, he was wildly excited about it. He was quite generous that day and he said, 'Look, I've got this riff but I'm not using it for anything so why don't you learn it and see if you can do anything with it; so I had his riff and I've used it ever since. [*Laughs*] It's never let me down.

MAH: So, David, scores of top international celebrities were clamouring to wish you a happy birthday

DB: Including Fred Nietzsche. [*Laughs*] Oh, I'm dreading this!

MAH: We also asked them for a question. Robert Smith, I think, starts at ground zero.

ROBERT SMITH: Hello, David, this is Robert Smith from The Cure. Why did you choose the name Bowie when you changed your name? [*Sings 'Happy Birthday' at high speed*]

DB: You let me off very lightly, Robert – I'll give you a big kiss tomorrow night. There was a band in the mid-sixties achieving worldwide television fame called The Monkees, and there was an English guy in them called Davy Jones, and I was just David Jones at the time. And I just liked the idea that, one, it was a Scottish name, and the other, that it had images of the Bowie knife and that the Bowie knife was sharpened on both sides so it cuts both ways, so I thought there was something terribly ambiguous about the name. So I opted for that.

MAH: Many of your celebrity fans bottled out of asking what they really wanted to ask, like a really tough question. Brett from Suede got kind of halfway there and backed down a bit.

DB: Well, he's tall enough for the job.

BRETT ANDERSON: Hello, David, this is Brett Anderson from Suede. There's lots of things you could ask, isn't there, like Tin Machine and that, but I just wanted to know about one really brilliant song that I've always really loved, which is a very early song of yours and it's always been one of my favourite songs, called 'Let Me Sleep Beside You'. I want to know what you think of it and why you don't play it? Have a happy birthday. See you.

DB: How did you know about that song? I guess it must have been released on something. [*Hums the tune*] Good riff! Thank you for reminding me about that, Brett. [*Laughs*] I might use that riff. I'm the ultimate recycler. It sounds like it might have been influenced by Simon & Garfunkel, but gone a little heavier. I still thought I might have a chance at being a romantic songwriter, which never actually proved to be my forte. Do you really like that song? You are a funny bloke, Brett! You really are.

MAH: [*Laughs*] Here's a man who once said that Ziggy Stardust changed his life. I think you would call him very reverent indeed.

IAN MCCULLOCH: Hello, David. This is Ian McCulloch. Tell me this. Between the Ziggy Stardust and Thin White Duke years, how decadent did decadence get? Which song other than your own do you wish you'd have written? Have a great birthday. Love on you!

Above: Bowie with Jools Holland in 1995. In this first appearance on *Later... with Jools Holland*, Bowie performed 'Hallo Spaceboy' from his *Outside* album, an alternative version of 'The Man Who Sold the World', and 'Strangers When We Meet' (from *The Buddha of Suburbia*). In total, he would appear on the show three times.

Right: On *Later... with Jools Holland* in 1999, Bowie performed 'Ashes to Ashes', 'Something in the Air' and 'Survive', both from *Hours*, and 'Cracked Actor', complete with cigarette in hand. *Hours* would be the first album to be released by a major artist as an internet download.

Right: Two days after his headline set at Glastonbury, Bowie returned to the BBC before a largely invited audience of a few hundred people at the BBC Radio Theatre in Broadcasting House. The intimate surroundings, his never-better voice, and a range of songs from the greats to some surprises, made this one of his greatest live performances to be caught on record.

Bowie is interviewed by Jeremy Paxman for *Newsnight* in 1999. The interview subsequently became famous as the one in which Bowie chastises Paxman for not fully grasping the oncoming influence of the internet.

Headlining Glastonbury on Sunday 25 June 2000 – the night that Britain remembered just how fortunate they were to have David Bowie. At the end, Bowie told the audience, "We made it. What a wonderful evening. Please be safe. We really love you a lot." Bowie had contracted laryngitis a few days before and wasn't even sure his voice would last. As it was, he played 17 songs and a four-song encore.

Above: Bowie is interviewed by John Wilson for *Front Row* in New York in 2002 to coincide with the release of his album *Heathen*.

Below: Sitting at the piano with Holland as the monitor shows footage of Ziggy Stardust, during his third and final appearance on *Later... with Jools Holland* in 2002.

Above: Appearing on *Parkinson* in 2002, alongside Tom Hanks. Bowie performed 'The Loneliest Guy' from his *Reality* LP and 'Ziggy Stardust'.

Below, overleaf: Bowie would return to Parkinson in 2003. Ahead of the recorded interview, the studio audience were treated to a rare delight in rehearsals when Bowie sat down at the piano and, unaccompanied, sang 'Life On Mars?' Even the production team were left stunned. "It's those genuine musical moments that make it all worthwhile," said the show's producer, Danny Dignan.

DB: Thank you very much for the question, Ian. How decadent was it? Well, I tell you, some days I wore green *and* red. It got that bad. What was the second question?

MAH: Which song do you wish you'd written?

DB: Oh, Lord. It's governed by the moment. The one that comes straight to mind immediately is 'Shipbuilding'. I think it's one of the most beautiful songs written. A stunning piece of work. Makes me cry just the opening bars. Specifically, the Robert Wyatt version. I just think it's the most tragically beautiful song.

MAH: I suppose you've had a pretty reckless existence. Did you ever think that you'd make it to 50 and still be a sane man?

DB: I didn't want to make it to 50. It seemed so unglamorous. Who'd want to be 50? There's a certain point when you're young, if you're nuts enough, you go into auto-destruct. You half want the whole thing to end because it's better to go out at 30, in sort of a ball of fire or smoke. But once I saw that I couldn't do that, that I'd survived it all, then it became unusual because I'd never thought about it. I really felt kind of redundant until I was about 43, 44, then I started to feel there might be some point in getting old.

MAH: So how long does it take you to get over a serious night on the booze now, David?

DB: About 24 hours. [*Laughs*] But I actually don't drink anymore, I'm afraid to say. I'm aware I'm talking to an English public here, but I'm afraid it happens no more. [*Laughs*] No, I stopped drinking many, many years ago – and everything else, as it happens.

MAH At which point did you decide, this is it, the booze has got to go?

DB: I think just waking up day after day realising that I hated my life. You get to a point where you think, 'Well, I can't put up with this anymore,' and I just did something about it.

MAH: I guess middle age carries a terrible stigma …

DB: I'm over middle age. [*Laughs*] I'm long past that!

MAH: But you know, it's like The Sex Pistols got leathered for reforming at age 40.

DB: Quite right.

MAH: Is there anything that you wouldn't actually now dare to do at age 50?

DB: Yeah, quite a lot, but I'm not telling you. [*Laughs*] I don't know. That's a really good question. No, I think I'm daft enough to have a go at anything, really.

ANDY WARHOL

MAH: 'Andy Warhol' … it's a role you've already played once in your life. You've also chosen to record an acoustic version of the track from *Hunky Dory* for us. Tell us a bit about Andy. What fascinated you about him?

DB: I think it's the same kind of thing that fascinated every art student back in the sixties – the fact that this guy was as well-known as the work that he did. In fact, probably more people knew the name and the look of Andy Warhol than what he actually did. When I first met him, I took him this song and I played it to him and he was gobsmacked, I think. He absolutely hated it. He was cringing with embarrassment. I think he thought I'd really put him down in the song, and it really wasn't meant to be that. I guess it was an ironic

homage to him. He took it very badly, but he liked my shoes.
I was wearing a pair of shoes that Marc Bolan had given me, brilliant canary yellow, semi-wedge heel, semi-point rounded toe. Seven and a half, they would have been. Anyway, he liked those because he used to design shoes when he was in advertising, so we had something to talk about.

MAH: Mick Jagger once said of you, 'You should never wear a pair of shoes in front of David Bowie.' I don't know what he was referring to.

DB: I know why he said that. [*Laughs*] He showed me an album cover that he was going to do, using an artist called Guy Peellaert, and I immediately rushed out and got Guy Peellaert to do my cover too. [*Laughs*] He never forgave me for that, because mine was *Diamond Dogs* and I can't remember what his was.

REPETITION

MAH: 'Repetition' from the album *Lodger*. David, that's an extraordinary version of it.

DB: I wanted to pick a couple of songs that really were probably the least well known of my songs. Particularly this song I wanted to try acoustically, because it was so much an electronic song on the album and I wanted to see what it was made of, just as a song, when it was really stripped down and just became an acoustic piece. And it's interesting to see how something that really is so minimal works quite well as a straightforward rendition … I know it's weird, but it's Reeves [Gabrels], what can you do with him?

MAH: What do you think the David Bowie of 25 would have made of the David Bowie of 50?

DB: I think I would have driven myself mad because I wasn't used to having happy people around. I think I would have wanted to put me in a box and nail me in because I think I would be too exuberant for the 25-year-old. I kept very much to myself at the time, and I spent much more time on my own than I would with other people; I read too much. I think it's the other way around now.

MAH: Do you have a favourite period where you look back over your career, I mean favourite hairdo or a favourite make-up job, a favourite Lycra catsuit maybe?

DB: [*Laughs*] I was never actually a catsuit ... did I wear catsuits? I wore kitten suits, I think. I don't know. I always tie them to characters. I don't really think of them as outfits and stuff. For me, if I see an outfit from the past in some photograph, it reminds me of the entire character I was working with at the time. For me, an outfit is an entire life experience. [*Laughs*] It also is when you're younger, I think. An outfit is much more than just something to wear – it's about who you are; it's a badge, it becomes a symbol. A friend of mine, George, when we were real young, we used to buy our shoes at Denson's in Lewisham, just under the railway bridge ... it was [the shop] Denton's, but the shoes were Denson's high pointers, if I remember rightly. It was about '61 and we prided ourselves on being the first kids in the area to have Italian shoes, 'winkle-pickers' I think they were vulgarly known as, but they are actually called high pointers.

MAH: [*Laughs*] We've got a bit of a shoe fetish going on here, haven't we?

DB: Yeah, [*Laughs*] I'm big on shoes. And then we were pipped by a much smoother guy in the sixth form called Gavin. I mean, even the name, Gavin ... he was so cool. He went into advertising. He had

Chelsea boots. They were so kind of elegant because they weren't pointed and they had elastic sides. We were so crestfallen.

MAH: I guess you are responsible for the hairdressing disasters of tens of thousands of teenagers …

DB: Disasters?!

MAH: … who decided to experiment with henna for the first time to get the Ziggy Stardust look.

DB: Well, more fool them. They should have used … now what did I use? Schwarzkopf, was it?

MAH: So, we're back to some top international celebrity questions. Here's the boss from U2.

BONO: [*Adopts a south London accent*] 'ello, Spaceboy! Major Bono 'ere. Can you hear me? Can you hear me?

DB: Yes, me dear.

BONO: Is something going wrong? Something going wrong, alright, you're 50 and you look 15. Is there a picture of you somewhere that tells the real story, your Dorian Gray? And if there is, who would you have paint it? Happy birthday, David. You're a prince of a man. The world should kiss your arse.

DB: Thank you, young B. You can be first in line. [*Laughs*] He's a lovely little bugger. He's a very generous guy. He sent me, just before Christmas … it wasn't a Christmas present, he just thought I'd be interested … he sent me two wonderful bios on Samuel Beckett. On one of them Beckett's got a hairstyle not dissimilar to the one that I'm sporting at the moment and on the inside he wrote, 'This man's got your haircut, and I'm sure he's got a pair of stilettos somewhere.' [*Laughs*] He's a funny bloke. Funnily enough, I did a thing on the internet today, and I was going through photographs for it, and I found this photograph that was obviously taken very early in the morning after some gross party back in around 1973, '74; and there's me, David Johansen and Cyrinda Foxe lying on the floor fast asleep amidst all this unbelievable trash and rubble. We just look like three totally finished, homeless, out-of-it meth drinkers. It's the most unbelievable photograph.

MAH: [*Laughs*]

DB: It looks like three people who will never pick themselves up again.

MAH: Of course, not everyone wanted to ask you questions, David. Some just had a personal message they wanted to deliver by carrier pigeon.

DB: Oh no!

SCOTT WALKER: Hi, David. This is Scott Walker. I'm coming to you via a very crappy, old, handheld tape machine, so I hope it's alright. I'm going to be a devil today and not ask you any questions. I'm certain that, among the many messages, there'll be those about how you always embraced the new and how you freed so many artists, and this is, of course, true. Like everyone else, I'd like to thank you for all the years, and especially for your generosity of spirit when it comes to other artists. I've been the beneficiary on more than one occasion, let me tell you. So have a wonderful birthday and, by the way, mine's the day after yours, so I'll have a drink to you on the other side of midnight. How's that?

DB: [*Sucks in his breath then breathes out loudly. There's a long pause.*] Wow. [*Another long pause and the sound of him moving in his seat*] That's … that's amazing. Oh, I see God in the window. [*Laughs*]

MAH: [*Laughs*] He's the boss isn't he, Scott Walker? You've absolutely got to love him.

DB: That ... you really got to me there, I'm afraid. That's ... I think he's probably been my ... my idol since I was a kid. That's very moving. I want a copy of that!

MAH: You can have it. You can take it away.

DB: I'm absolutely ... that's ... that's really thrown me. That's ... thank you very much.

MAH: It's interesting to hear Scott talking about how you freed so many artists, and I think that's true. You were the first androgynous icon. These days people think nothing of blokes in frocks and full make-up. I mean everybody's done it, from Kurt Cobain to Eddie Izzard, but there were times when ...

DB: I don't think much of it, either. [*Laughs*] Sorry.

MAH: [*Laughs*] But times were very, very different when you were showing off your sexual ambiguity. I bet you couldn't stop off for a cup of tea anywhere north of Soho, could you, really, without being battered.

DB: Well, you could, but you took your life in your hands. [*Laughs*] Again, so much runs with wanting to be provocative, making a point of being confrontational, that you kind of did it more out of bravado as much as anything else. I mean, the two feelings that were running through me were, one, that I wanted to make people aware of me, and the second thing was that I refused that I would have to live any kind of life that was behind closed doors, and all that. Again, in reading, I've been fortunate enough to see how many people have been so screwed up because they had to live their real lives in a strange, dark, twilight kind of way. I just knew I was never going to do that, and I think, frankly, it was the right thing to do.

I would still say that that is one of the most important things to do with one's life.... that you can't hide who or what you are; and you'll enjoy yourself, in the long run, much better if you sort of come clean from the beginning.

MAH: Your influence has been incredibly broad. You feel it in dancing, the rock'n'roll arena, and even in fashion. You must have killed yourself a couple of years ago when all the supermodels were shaving their eyebrows off.

DB: Yeah, I tell you what, I'm much more of a fan of music – I'm the ultimate fan. I get so excited about a sound that strikes me, that really catches me and makes me dance inwardly. It's a life force for me. Music always has been, and I always will be this kind of 12-year-old kid. Fashion doesn't do that to me in the slightest. It's just stuff to put on. I see it much more as something with which I dress up the different characters that I still come up with. I've gone back to doing characters on *Outside*. I enjoy it, I really do enjoy it. Now, I feel a lot safer about it because I don't become them off stage. I do think fashion is funny, really, fashion. It's so nonsensical. We don't have to do it. It's one of those things like cuisine – we just have to eat, we don't have to put a little dress on it. [*Laughs*] Broccoli with a pair of stockings on. It's totally unnecessary, and that's what makes it amusing.

LADY STARDUST

DB: This, I think, is a really lovely song and it sounds good even today. I like this one; I think it's a good bit of songwriting. I think it was probably one of the first songs I wrote for Ziggy. I was trying to do this concoction based on an American guy called Vince Taylor who came over to Britain, who was totally out of his mind. He was a failed Elvis-type impersonator in America, but he went to France via England and made himself a kind of Elvis over in France, and then one night went out on stage dressed as Jesus and said that his music was over and that he was going to save the world. Vince is no longer with us, I'm afraid, but I hung out with him for a while over in London and he was quite out of his tree. I remember that, one day, he took me down Tottenham Court Road and he had a map of the world, and he laid it out on the pavement and showed me where all the Martians were going to land; and we were kneeling over this map in the middle of all of the rush-hour pedestrians, and I was thinking, 'What is this bloke at? He's out of his gourd!' And then I lost track of him. Somebody like that stays with you. He became sort of the role model for Ziggy – he was one of the many. And then I pieced together bits and pieces of other artists and they all became this rather grand, stylish lad, Ziggy.

WHITE LIGHT/WHITE HEAT

MAH: David Bowie with 'White Light' on Radio 1. A live favourite of yours. I think they're all flinging their pants down the front when you kick off with that one, aren't they?

DB: Well, I think it's a lot of older girls who are throwing my pants back at me that I'd left in their rooms many, many years ago. The Velvets [The Velvet Underground], along with Scott and a number of others, were really a very, very big influence on me musically. A funny story about The Velvets … I told Lou this for the first time in rehearsals the other day. He could not believe this. When I first came to America, very early seventies, a friend of mine said, 'Ah, The Velvets are working down at the Electric Circus.' So, I went down and had a look at them and they were wonderful; they did all my favourites, 'Heroin', you know, all the finger-clicking songs, 'White Light' and 'Waiting for the Man' and all those things, and it was so fantastic. After the show, I went backstage, Lou Reed came to the door and I started talking to him about all the music and how much of an influence they'd been on me, and I seemed to be the only bloke in Britain that had ever heard of them, and all that. And we chatted for about an hour, and he was wonderful, a really nice guy. A week later, when I met my American friend again, he said, 'What do you mean you talked with Lou Reed? He left the band years ago!' I said, 'But I sat down and talked with him.' He said, 'No. That's Doug Yule, the guy who took over.' And I said, 'God!' And when I told Lou the other day, he said, 'You know, I did a book signing the other week and I looked at the back of the crowd and I saw Doug Yule at the end of the line waving at me.' [*Laughs*] Now I think Doug Yule has become more mysterious than Lou Reed in a strange way – the enigmatic Doug Yule.

MAH: I suppose we couldn't do a show like this without including some token northerner, so here he is.

MICK HUCKNALL: Hello, David, you cockney git. This is Mancunian Mick Hucknall. Tell me this, how do you react to music journalists when they judge your career? It's great to see people celebrating your career this way. I want to wish you a happy birthday and much success, and I think you're wonderful.

DB: Well, I think you're wonderful too, Mick. Thank you very much. My immediate reaction to all that kind of thing is that I just look around at my life, my friends and family, and I feel good about that, then I really don't have much to say about any of the rest. I've really had such a wonderful life, all in all – incredible experiences. And I've got away with murder. [*Laughs*] I really don't have any right to be heavy on anybody who wants to judge my life, as long as they judge their own as well.

MAH: Who else but one of the Pet Shop Boys would have the brass neck to ask a question like this?

DB: [*Laughs*] I wonder which one?!

NEIL TENNANT: Hello, this is Neil Tennant. David, do you regret saying in the early seventies you were bisexual? And were you actually bisexual at the time?

DB: I wish I'd said, Neil, that I was tri-sexual, but I never did. It was a joke that came too late. [*Adopts tone of a curious reporter*] 'Tri-sexual … what does that mean, David?' It means I'll try anything. Alright, Neil?

MAH: [*Laughs*] That kind of leads us neatly on to the next set of questions, which, of course, are about sex because everybody wants to talk to you, David, about sex, I suppose. Who was really hitting on you in those days? Was it girls or boys?

DB: It was rather the other way around, if my memory serves … well, my memory has never really served me well, but if it serves me at all, I think I was hitting on everybody. [*Laughs*] I think it was that way round because I felt that I had a real sex problem … I couldn't get any! [*Laughs*]

MAH: I don't believe that for one minute.

DB: Er, no. And so you shouldn't. No, I had a wonderfully irresponsibly promiscuous time. It was just heaven. Actually, it's not bad now. [*Laughs*]

MAH: What about the worst sexually transmitted disease … do you remember what it was and who gave it to you?

DB: I never had one. [*Laughs*]

MAH: Really? [*Pause*] Let's hear some more music from the Tin Machine era; this is 'Shopping for Girls', obviously Brett Anderson was hedging his bets a little, he didn't want to upset you considering you're 50 and all but, you know, he wasn't too keen on Tin Machine. How do you remember Tin Machine yourself? You were really belligerent about it at the time, as I recall.

DB: I'm still incredibly belligerent about it. [*Laughs*] No, I'm not belligerent about it. I see it in a very different way from everybody else because I went through it, and I know how much I needed that experience. I'd just given up writing towards '87, '88. I was very indifferent to music. As I say, that was my real period of crisis. I feel that I just didn't know what I was supposed to be doing. I just made a major decision to plunge myself into something that was *the* most unexpected thing I could do, just to shake myself up – and it certainly did that. Publish and be damned.

SHOPPING FOR GIRLS

MAH: Right, time for some more top international celebrity questions. Damon was going to ask you a question about your embracing of commercialism in the eighties, but he bottled out.

DAMON ALBARN: Hello, this is Damon. Happy birthday, David. Hope you're enjoying your own *This is Your Life*. I've got lots of questions, but one I've always wanted to ask you is why you've never written a musical? You've always *almost* written musicals. Anyway, happy birthday.

DB: I have written a hundred musicals in my head, but the thing that always puts me off is actually going along and watching a musical.

They are always so bloody awful that I never actually finish one off. It always ends up on Broadway, and that's the most depressing thing [*Laughs*] about it all. I don't know. I had in my mind there must be some way of working a travelling musical, something that works in rock arenas. I guess that may be something that is maybe a last working ambition that I would like to accomplish without it slipping into that awful saccharine thing of Broadway.

MAH: Ian McCulloch asked you a little bit earlier about excess, but I think that's probably the subtext of Shaun Ryder's question too.

SHAUN RYDER: Hiya, David. It's Shaun from Black Grape. Are you still enjoying yourself, dude? Happy birthday, Dave. You're a cool dude, man, big time.

DB: Ah, that's very nice. Thank you very much. Love the band. I really do. They're a very exciting band, I think. Yeah, I do enjoy myself, and I enjoy myself probably within the realms of more moderate existence.

MAH: I have to say to you that one of my favourite documentary pieces that's ever been made about you is the *Cracked Actor* documentary, which I think is a magnificent piece of work. It did look like you'd swallowed a chemistry set … the scenes in the back of the car there. What sort of combination of drugs were you taking in those days? Did it look like one of Elvis's prescriptions?

DB: My drug intake was absolutely phenomenal. I was seriously addicted. *Cracked Actor* is extremely painful for me to watch because I know what my interior life was like, and I was unbelievably screwed up. I can't tell you how bad life was for me. I guess it's one of the ironies of having that kind of success, is that everything on a material level couldn't have been better. I mean, my music was going down well. I had a wonderful audience at that time throughout America. It was quite phenomenal. And everything else about my life, about me and about how I felt and how I thought about myself, was just awful. Absolutely the worst. It was just one of the worst periods of my life, the whole mid-seventies.

MAH: I tell you what, I bet you had one of the most exciting bathroom cabinets in the western hemisphere.

DB: So I've been told, yeah. My old mate, my old mucker, Eno, always said the thought process is the aeroplane that you can crash and actually walk away from it. I don't put myself on the edge physically anymore because [*Adopts an elderly tone*] I like this old frame of blood and guts, and I want it to remain around for just a little longer.

MAH: Perhaps long enough to see one of the young contenders of 1997 come into their own. I'm talking about Placebo, who you've championed for a long time, David, and I think we've got a word from them.

BRIAN MOLKO: Hi, David, this is Brian from Placebo. Now that we've done around 10 gigs and that we've opened for you several times, I would like to know when we're actually going to get a chance to collaborate on a recording, because that would make us very, very happy.

DB: Thanks, Brian. I think they're a wonderful band. What Brian doesn't know is that I'd love to produce Placebo. I don't know why, but there's a lot about Brian and the way he works and what he's doing and his single-mindedness that really reminds me of me at his age. I think he's an extremely talented writer. I think his potential hasn't been met yet. I guarantee that they're going to be a major band.

MAH: David, you were very famously and seriously ripped off by your management in your early days. You should be a phenomenally wealthy man, but I assume you're not. You probably don't have to worry about where the next bag of chips is coming from, but I doubt you own your own bijou cluster of islands in the Caribbean.

DB: I would say that I'm rich, not wealthy.

MAH: You are also the first artist to float yourself on the stock market.

DB: [*Laughs*] I feel like a hot air balloon.

MAH: What do investors get? Are they looking for some used underwear or are they going to get a slab of royalties?

DB: I quite seriously never talk about my financial business.

MAH: God, miserable git! [*Laughs*]

DB: It's a nice story to have out there, though.

MAH: So, let's end today, David, with a couple of tracks for the fans, 'Aladdin Sane' and 'Quicksand'. That's a double whammy if ever there was one.

DB: I'm so pleased that I thought about doing 'Quicksand'. It was somebody in the band that said I should do it. I'd forgotten all about it, and since I've done it for you guys, I've started using it in the set now, using it on stage, because I'd forgotten it. It's a really lovely song. I really like that one, and I'm really knocked out that [Robert] Smith is doing it with me. Smith and Jones together, at last!

THE LUNCHTIME SOCIAL, BBC RADIO

INTERVIEWER: JO WHILEY

Most Bowie fans think of *Never Let Me Down* as Bowie's worst album. It's pretty clear why. Bowie had lost his mojo because he'd lost his love of music, at least making music. What wasn't clear until this interview was that he'd fallen so far out of love with music, that he had considered quitting entirely. In fact, he had insisted to BBC's Mark Goodier just a few years after *Never Let Me Down* that he had never thought about quitting.

Here is Jo Whiley's memory of that day.

I remember being obviously quite daunted at the prospect of interviewing David Bowie. I was in the studio on my own, the producer had gone. I was just sitting there prepping for the interview, writing down notes, writing down questions, head down – door opened. I presumed it was my producer, and I suddenly hear this voice go, 'Er, is it alright if I smoke in here?' And I looked up and it was him, David Bowie. No one had brought him in. He'd just come in on his own, plonked himself down, sat there, and he did everything he could to make me feel completely relaxed. He was so friendly, he was just absolutely lovely. And the chat was great.[20]

JO WHILEY: It's Radio 1, the *Lunchtime Social*, and today I'm well chuffed to say my guest is David Bowie. Hi, and welcome along.

DAVID BOWIE: Hi, Jo.

JW: Hi. What is your history with this place? We are in a new building from where you might have been to Radio 1 than at any time in the past.

DB: Yes, this is the first venture. The coffee's even worse here than it was …

JW: Yes. [*Laughs*] It's diabolical!

DB: What's this? Is this squash?

JW: Yes, you have to drink orange or lemon squash when you come here. You don't touch the coffee at all!

DB: It's in the book.

JW: Were there John Peel sessions and …

DB: Yeah, I did a lot of that stuff in the old days. Funnily enough, the things that we did with John were mainly live performance things, and they were done in a theatre complex. They were a lot of fun. John was great about helping new acts, which of course we were in that time – about '68, something like that. I think we did some of our very first performances with John, before we were actually on the road.

JW: You seem a very contented kind of bloke these days. Like you're enjoying yourself.

DB: Yeah, isn't that disappointing? [*Laughs*] It's the bane of the writer, you know, because we are not supposed to be able to write when we are all happy and content. So, I'm thinking about getting back on drugs and things.

JW: If you could.

DB: Yeah, maybe just aspirin or something.

JW: [*Laughs*] I've got some Migraleve in my bag.

DB: Ibuprofen are really quite tasty. [*Both laugh*]

JW: Just the two at a time!

DB: Yeah! Two of the 400s.

JW: Does that not apply to you, then?

DB: What's that?

JW: Just the idea that you do produce better material when you're depressed or angst-ridden.

DB: Well, the most obvious example for me is that *Low* was really a completely drug-free album, and it was the immediate end of a spell when I was really trying to kick drugs, and I believe that *Low* is probably some of my best work, so I'm not really sure about that maxim. I think it has more to do with enthusiasm for what you're doing. If you have a genuine, real kind of motivation for making music then I don't think anything either helps or hinders, really.

JW: But how do you continue that motivation after a *few* years in the business, David?

DB: Nothing can help it but one's own natural enthusiasm. I don't think you can create a kind of a synthetic enthusiasm for music. I think you either love music, or you go off it a bit. [*Laughs*]

JW: Have you been off it at certain times in your career?

DB: Oh, yeah. It's probably more 'off me' than actually going 'off music', because even in the period that I believe I wrote practically nothing of any validity, which was, for me, the last part of the eighties, I hated being a writer in that period …

JW: So, what work are you talking about?

DB: None of it was produced, that's the thing. I made virtually nothing after … what was the album called … *Never Let Me Down*. And that I didn't like as an album. And I really didn't record anything during that period. I was still listening to music, but other people's music, very intensely, and kind of burying myself in stuff that I liked at the time, which at that period – Pixies and Sonic Youth and all that sort of middle-eighties music – that I thought was overwhelmingly fresh and lovely.

JW: So, that kind of kick-started you again?

DB: Yeah, it did really. The shows were massive, they were all stadium shows. It was, I suppose, a success in material terms. Well, yes, it was a real success in material terms. And the albums were selling far better than they should have done, but I just wasn't … I had a moment where I really just wanted to quit completely. But that's an actual process for any artist, the ups and downs of things.

JW: Well, you must go through it over and over again.

DB: Yeah, yeah.

JW: Do you not worry that your time will come and people will stop taking notice of the stuff that you're doing now, and it's like, 'Oh, maybe I should stop'?

DB: I think if we weren't selling albums and we weren't playing performances, I wonder if I would still bother to write. I often question myself about that: what are my real motives? I think every artist does. You always say that you're writing strictly for yourself, but I think it's probably a fallacy, if not a lie, to say, 'If nobody bought my records or came to our shows, I'd still write because I'm only doing it for me.' I'm not really sure about that. I've never known that, fortunately. [*Laughs*] Immodestly, he said. So I don't know. But we shall see.

<*Whiley asks Bowie where he gets the inspiration for writing.*>

DB: I think environment has a lot to do … with me as a writer.
I really soak up the places and the people and the events of wherever I happen to be, and I've got a natural curiosity about life. I tend to go out an awful lot. I see everything that's happening.

JW: You just don't like missing out, is that it?

DB: I just love it, you know. I'm not a recluse, I'm not that kind of person. I don't go and hide away somewhere. I'm always in some town, somewhere, seeing a bit of theatre or a band or a club or cinema or anything.

JW: And that is what inspires you?

DB: I guess just having some links with the society you're in.

JW: Don't you get hassled when you go out?

DB: No, never.

JW: Don't you?

DB: Never. I have a great time. But there again, I travel … I'm a quick, mobile, intelligent [*Laughs*] unit. I don't travel with a lot of people, either myself or my wife or maybe a couple of friends or whatever. But I don't go out as a crowd, so it's really easy for me to get around.

JW: Do you go out in disguise or anything?

DB: I don't have to, no. I don't bother with that.

JW: Don't you?

DB: No. No handkerchief on my nose.

JW: [*Laughs*] Have you met Michael Jackson?

DB: Yeah, I've met him two times. He's come to a couple of shows.

JW: What's he like?

DB: I don't know. I've absolutely no idea. He's very charming, he's very polite. You don't seem to get much feedback from him. He's not the kind of guy, I don't think, that sits down for a good old chat, you know.

JW: No? [*Laughs*] But why has he gone that way and you've gone this way? You are still sociable, you are still out there enjoying yourself, meeting people?

DB: I don't know. He's American. [*Laughs*]

JW: Say no more!

DB: I don't know. I'm quite a Europhile. I still think of Europe, and specifically Britain, as my roots and where I come from.

JW: So, you have a horror of shutting yourself away?

DB: Yeah.

JW: That would probably be the worst thing that could happen to you?

DB: I'd hate that. Yeah, I would be absolutely lousy on a desert island.

JW: Do you get very lonely? You like company, then?

DB: No, I don't get lonely. I like the vibe. I must have the vibe. I like the buzz. It's my adrenaline.

JW: Oh, God, you haven't got into dance music, haven't you? You can tell.

DB: [*Laughs*] No, no. It's just one gives up drugs and you replace it with society, which is not a bad option. Yeah, when I was doing drugs, that's the time when I was really a recluse, so I've probably come full circle now. Oh, no, that's wrong isn't it, it's half circle.

JW: [*Laughs*] Semi-circle … you'd be back …

DB: If I'd gone full circle, I'd be back in the garage again!

JW: Give you 10 years … [*Both laugh*] What was Phoenix [Festival] like when you played there?

DB: Oh, it's always good. It's terrific. I'm not going on the road next year, I'm taking a year off because I'm going to get some writing and recording done, and I'm going to miss it. I [*Laughs*] really like it. We've only done mainly festivals this year. Twenty-five festivals over the course of this last 10 weeks. It's just been wonderful, and each year it's gotten better and better for us out there.

JW: Does it not get dull when you do gig after gig after gig? What makes it still exciting? Is it the band that you've got on stage or the audience?

DB: Yeah, primarily, I'm doing songs and material that I really, really feel I can do well on stage and kind of mean it, which meant dropping an awful lot of songs that would be expected of me.

It's like a kid in the toy shop – I've got a lot of new material that I like a lot from *Outside*, even *Buddha of Suburbia* and *Earthling*, and I'm concentrating a lot on that material.

JW: Aren't the audience going, 'Oh, go on, please play the classics!'?

DB: No, surprisingly, that's not what's been happening. In fact, because the audiences have been so young, most of them are actually more familiar with things like *Earthling* and *Outside*, which has been just great for us. And I throw in a few things … I'm doing a kind of acoustic version of 'Jean Genie', which is kind of fun. And things like 'Quicksand' from *Hunky Dory* and some more obscurey things, things that weren't singles, but things like 'Fashion'. It's kind of funny, 'Fashion' kind of works now, for some reason. What else do we do? 'Look Back in Anger', we do. They're strange old chestnuts – they're not the songs you'd expect us to do.

JW: You gatecrashed the Radio 1 dance tent this year, didn't you, at Phoenix?

DB: Yeah, I did. Yeah, we did an hour up there.

JW: Were you invited or did you just …?

DB: It was great. Well, by the time we finished, it was packed. [*Laughs*]

JW: People didn't really know it was you on stage, is what I heard.

DB: No, because we kept the lights down so they couldn't see us.

JW: Really?

DB: And we just used our light show, which is formidable; we've got a wonderful light show. They just took it for what it was, and it was tremendous. It was just great. And the Ministry of Sound asked us, and I was able to say, [*Adopts a breathy tone*] 'I'm sorry, we just can't fit you in, we're working in London.' The Ministry of Sound asked us if we'd do a gig down there, but we couldn't do that. But next year maybe.

JW: So, do you feel that you are back in ...?

DB: No, the thing is we're not a dance band, I'm not a dance writer. I merely work with a dance vocabulary, the genre of dance. I like that particular rhythm structure, but what I do is idiosyncratically me. And what we started doing a couple of years ago was trying to do a hybrid of the best dynamics of rock with dance rhythms, and that is something that I've repeatedly done through my life, from soul music through to straightforward disco. It's an area that I really find ... it's really exuberant working there. I like that, and I think we've done it very successfully, and my feeling is that you'll hear more and more kind of hybrid that we've been doing for the last couple of years. You'll find that there'll be more vocals, more melodies coming into dance music.

JW: Who else do you really admire then out of the dance area?

DB: Soul Coughing's not bad. They're pretty good. Out of the dance area, let's see, who do I still like? Oh, really ridiculous things. I mean I still like Scott Walker and still think he's one of the most innovative artists working today. Nobody gives him any credit at all now, I don't think.

JW: What about the bands that are – I hate to mention – but Oasis, that kind of stuff?

DB: They're alright.

JW: Does that not inspire you?

DB: They're okay, you know. They're good at what they do, it's just not my kind of music, particularly at the moment. But who knows, in a couple of years I might be doing it. [*JW laughs*] But I don't think so.

JW: You're going back to The Beatles, going through your Beatles phase.

DB: Yeah.

JW: No.

DB: No. [*Both laugh*]

> <*The show would do a regular feature with guests called 'The Questionnaire', which involved a series of fairly quick-fire questions. 'I can't quite believe some of the questions that I did ask him,' said Whiley years later, 'but he went along with the whole thing.'*>

JW: We'd just like to subject you to The Questionnaire, this stuff that we throw at you. The first gig you ever went to?

DB: Do you know what I did then? I went for a cigarette. [*Laughs*].

JW: I thought it was for your heart, actually. Panic!

DB: [*Adopts an upper-class accent*] Haven't you heard? I have no heart.

JW: [*Laughs*] Actually, the sprinklers will probably go off in here if you light up anyway …

DB: … what, if I touch my heart? [*Both laugh*]

JW: … so we'll probably just get doused.

DB: [*Laughs*] Okay.

JW: Right, the first gig you ever went to?

DB: The first time I ever saw a band live were rehearsals for Peter Jay and the Jaywalkers, who were a sax band back in the sixties. They were rehearsing locally in the church hall. Me and my mate heard all this music coming out of it, so we got in the back and we just stood in the back and watched all these saxophones playing. It was so cool. Actually, they became nearly one of the first gigs that I did see, because they supported Little Richard when he came over. And I saw him at, I think it was the Odeon in Brixton, I saw Little Richard, and opening was The Rolling Stones or something like that. It was the most peculiar show.

JW: Wow! Fantastic.

DB: It was fantastic. But Little Richard was really cool at that time.

JW: Who was it that inspired you, that made you want to get into music?

DB: Little Richard, without doubt.

JW: And you met him?

DB: Yeah, I met him – not until two or three years ago, and the most extraordinary thing was that I never knew in all these years that he has the same eye problem as I do.

JW: Does he?

DB: In the same eye. It was like, 'Oh, wow!'

JW: [*Both laugh*] Oh God! You bonded!

DB: I know, we bonded!

JW: Have you ever met anybody else with the same problem?

DB: That's it. Apparently the guy in *X-Files* has got it as well. So, there's two or three of us out there. We are among you.

JW: If you weren't David Bowie, pop star, what would you be?

DB: [*Laughs*]

JW: Apart from artist.

DB: Yeah, that's it. David Bowie, painter, probably.

JW: Painter and decorator.

DB: [*Laughs*] Painter and decorator. Wallpaper designer, yeah.

JW: If you could pick anybody to sing with that you haven't sung with?

DB: Scott Walker. Yes, I would love to work with Scott in some way.

JW: Excellent. Who are your heroes in life?

DB: I'm always worried about that definition. It's probably very corny, but I guess somebody that's forever inspirational to me would be Buddha.

JW: I thought you were lapsed?

DB: Yes, I am. It doesn't mean that I still don't have great admiration for what he originally said and what he was trying to teach.

JW: Right, so you still follow his teachings?

DB: [*Sighs*] I think as best as I possibly can. I hope that I'm a decent human being.

JW: It is important to you to have some sort of spirituality? Could you not exist without that?

DB: Yes, very. It's a cornerstone of my life, actually. Honestly, yeah.

JW: How often do you dwell on it? Or what does it mean …?

DB: Daily. Yeah. I deal with that, I deal with death, I deal with life every day of my life.

JW: Otherwise you'd go insane?

DB: No, I think it's necessary to do that to retain some kind of balance and equilibrium in day-to-day living.

JW: To keep that sparkle in your eyes.

DB: Oh, you're getting very serious now!

JW: No, no, no. Something I've been dwelling on. What's your most annoying habits? What would your friends say, what's really annoying, this is where we should be calling in your wife, or something?

DB: [*Laughs*] Oh my God! Well, obvious one is I talk too much. I can talk, you don't know. I can really, really talk.

JW: About anything?

DB: Even when I'm straight, I can talk. [*Both laugh*] You just don't know what it used to be like in the seventies. I used to talk, even nobody in the room, I'd just talk and talk and talk. Also, the thing that annoys me is that I'm too willing to play devil's advocate. If anybody starts any kind of … sets up some kind of debate, I'll immediately take the other side, just because.

JW: Just because.

DB: [*Laughs*] Just because, yeah.

JW: I hate people like you.

DB: My son is the same. We're murder together, because we'll argue until the sun comes up.

JW: Even if you don't believe what you're saying?

DB: Oh, yeah, yeah, yeah. Just to see how the mechanics of the argument go, you know.

JW: God.

DB: To see who can win. [*Laughs*]

JW: And who does win out of you and him?

DB: Oh, he does, of course.

JW: [*Laughs*] Just because you let him!

DB: No, actually, not these days, no. [*Laughs*]

JW: Oh, sad. What's the worst thing you've ever done? Something you're deeply ashamed of?

DB: I don't think I'd want to talk about that. [*Laughs*] Too many things come to mind!

JW: What's your poison?

DB: Probably both drugs and alcohol. Two things I don't touch.

JW: Right. And what are you carrying on you right now? What do you have in your pockets?

DB: Alright. [*Rustling noise*] I'll tell you.

JW: Are you a man who carries cash or do you have people that pay for you?

DB: Yeah. Have people that pay for you?! I've got cash!

JW: You're like the royal family now.

DB: There, you see, I've got … I've got [*Slams down a wad of bills on the table*] …

JW: You've got loads of cash!

DB: … about a hundred quid. You see, oh yeah, I always keep a roll.

JW: [*Laughs*]

DB: Listen, ever since I was 16 … [*Both laughing*] ever since I had my first job …

JW: You have a wad.

DB: A wad – down me sock.

JW: [*Laughing*] Down your sock, right, okay.

DB: A couple of credit cards …

JW: Fine.

DB: … and a Voice It …

JW: A 'Voice It'? What's that for?

DB: Voice It is great.

JW: Is that for ideas and …

DB: [*There's a beep as DB presses the record button on the device*] Think of an idea and put it on the Voice It.

VOICE IT: 'Think of an idea and put it on the Voice It.' [*JW laughs*]

DB: See? It's great.

JW: [*Laughs*] Marvellous!

DB: It's like a talking notepad. It's really cool.

JW: It looks smart.

DB: It's great. It's fantastic. And it works! … [*Shakes what sounds like a box of Tic Tacs*] A pack of mints.

JW: Must have chewing gum. Bands always have chewing gum when they come in.

DB: No. I'm not a band though, am I?

JW: [*Laughs*]

DB: That's it!

JW: You still working with Brian Eno? Will you always be?

DB: Yeah, he's gone off to Russia for the rest of the year and he won't be back till Christmas. We keep working with each other, I mean, there's no way that we won't. But there's other people that I hope to be working with. I hope to be doing a bit of work with Goldie next year and I'm doing some work with Trent Reznor from Nine Inch Nails next year.

JW: What's that?

DB: Well, we're doing a bit of … [*Adopts an evasive tone*] a bit of this, a bit of that.

JW: You are such a slippery character. [*Laughs*]

DB: Secret things.

JW: Okay, Goldie, Trent …

DB: Doing my stuff.

JW: Clangs, all these names dropping.

DB: You see, I really need a year off. I've got a lot of stuff I want to get accomplished next year.

JW: Don't you want to have another kid as well?

DB: Yeah, but that only takes a couple of hours.

JW: Does it? That's very impressive. [*Both laugh*]

DB: Or all night, in my case.

JW: That's very impressive. [*Both laugh*] Thank you very much for coming in. I think we owe it to you to play one of your records, seeing as you've chosen stuff that's around at the moment, so pick a track from your history.

DB: Well, it's recent history. This is the track that we do on stage and we enjoy doing a lot. It's called 'Looking for Satellites' from the *Earthling* album.

NEWSNIGHT, BBC TV

INTERVIEWER: JEREMY PAXMAN

This was the interview in which Bowie predicts the impact of the internet. 'We're on the cusp of something exhilarating and terrifying,' he says. 'It's going to crush our ideas of what mediums are all about.'

Paxman was the sharpest of broadcasters, but here he seemingly struggles to keep up with Bowie, who describes the internet as the new arena for thought, communication and revolution. 'It will change our lives for good and bad,' says Bowie. 'We haven't even seen the tip of the iceberg.' All this in the days when dial-up modems made clanging sounds, and an ethernet cable was needed to connect to online service provider CompuServe.

As ever, Bowie was already living in the future. In 1996, he became the first major artist to offer a song as a download-only (back then, it took 11 minutes to download the track). He transmitted a live 'cybercast' of a show and launched his own ISP – internet service provider – in September 1998. Another ISP that launched that same month went by the name of Google. But Bowie's aims dwarfed that particular company's aspirations. As well as offering a way to get on to the World Wide Web, his users were given news feeds, blogs, live online chat forums and a place to share and create their own websites. This was five years before MySpace, six years before Facebook, and seven years before YouTube. Bowie was doing social media before we even knew the term. At the risk of making it all sound like a spoof, he was even one of the pioneers of internet-only banking with BowieBanc.com.

Bowie was always someone who predicted the future. Sometimes he even made the future. But it's amusing to consider that perhaps the furthest he ever got ahead of everyone else was when he was well into middle age.

JEREMY PAXMAN: I was thinking back over your career, and it seems to me that there's been a constant reinvention.

DAVID BOWIE: Of sorts, yeah.

JP: Why did you do that?

DB: I think I was quite happy to buy into the idea of reinvention up until the beginning of the eighties, really. It came about more than anything else that when I was a teenager I had it in my mind that I would be a creator of musicals. I sincerely wanted to write musicals for the West End and for Broadway, whatever. I didn't see much further than that as a writer, and I really had the idea in my head that people would do my songs. And I was not a natural performer – I didn't feel at ease on stage, ever. And I had created this one character, Ziggy Stardust, and it seemed I would be the one who would play him as no one else was doing my songs, and the chances of my actually getting a musical mounted were very slim. So, I became Ziggy Stardust for that period. I liked the idea. I felt really comfortable going on stage as someone else. And it seemed a rational decision to keep on doing that. So I got quite besotted with the idea of just creating character after character. And I think probably there must have been a point in the late seventies – well, I know there was – where I felt the characters were getting in the way of myself as a writer and I endeavoured to kill them off and start writing for me as just a singer-songwriter. I'm not sure if I was ever successful in that, as I do take a degree of theatricality when I go on stage all the time   that's how I deal with the stage situation. I'm still not comfortable on stage.

JP: But David Bowie himself is an invention. Do you think of yourself as Bowie or David Jones, the boy from south London?

DB: Less and less as 'Bow-ie', 'Bough-ie', 'Boo-ee'. [*Laughs*]

JP: How are we to pronounce it?

DB: I don't even know how to pronounce it anymore. I've lost track. I always thought it was 'Bow-ie'. Well, it's a Scottish name, it must be 'Bow-ie', but nobody in Scotland pronounces it like that; they pronounce it 'Boo-ee', I think.

ZIGGY STARDUST

DB: It was some kind of discovery in the eighties, I think, that a lot of what I am is my enthusiasms – that I've always been a very curious and enthusiastic person, again from when I was a teenager. And that it wasn't really up to me to try and identify exactly what that meant. I just had to accept that I was a person … I had a very short attention span, I would move from one thing to another quite rapidly when I got bored with the other. I became comfortable with that, and didn't try to identify myself or ask myself who I was. The less questioning I did about myself as to who I was, the more comfortable I felt. So now, I have absolutely no knowledge of who I am, but I'm extremely happy.

JP: Do you find the business of being in the music industry as interesting and attractive as it is?

DB: I have nothing to do with the industry. I really have so little to do with it. The hub of my creativity comes from what *I* do and where I go. I put myself in places that maybe I've never been before, or I feel there's a certain tension involved. I can't really write or produce much if I'm in a place that's relaxing. I have to have a set of conflicts going around me. Not necessarily of my own doing – I've learned that that is a particularly bad idea.

JP: What do you mean?

DB: Well, I don't create my own conflicts in my own life. I think I might have done that to quite an extent when I was younger, Actually, if things were going too smoothly, being an addictive personality, I would be drawn to create conflicts that would produce the tension necessary to write. Now I find that that I can do it by observation more than being absolutely, deeply involved in a mess to be able to write. [*Laughs*] But the industry side of things, I'm not even sure what that word actually represents to me anymore.

JP: On a personal level, you don't do drugs anymore?

DB: No, absolutely not.

JP: And you don't drink?

DB: I don't drink either, no.

JP: Not even a glass of wine?

DB: No, it would kill me if I started again.

JP: What do you mean it would kill you?

DB: I'm an alcoholic, so it would be the kiss of death for me to start drinking again. My relationships with my friends, my family, everybody around me, is so good and have been for so many years now, I wouldn't do anything to destroy that again. It's very hard to have relationships when you're doing drugs and drinking – for me personally, anyway. And you become closed off, unreceptive, insensitive, all the dreadful things that you've heard every other pop singer ever say. I was very lucky that I found my way out of that. It's been good for me – I've reassessed my life any number of times.

JP: If you were starting out now … did I read somewhere that you said if you were 19, you wouldn't go into the music business?

DB: I think that's probably quite right. I think. I think I'd probably just be a fan and a collector of records. I wanted to be a musician because it seemed rebellious, it seemed subversive. It felt like one could affect change to a form. It was very hard to hear music when I was younger. When I was really young, you had to tune into AFM radio to hear the American records. There was no MTV, and there was no … it wasn't sort of wall-to-wall, blanket music, and so therefore it had a kind of a call-to-arms kind of feeling to it. This is the thing that will change things, this is a dead dodgy occupation to have. It still produced signs of horror from people if you said, 'Yeah, I'm in rock'n'roll,' it was … my goodness. Now it's a career opportunity. And the internet now carries the flag of being subversive and possibly rebellious and chaotic, nihilistic and …

JP: Hmm. [*Sounding sceptical*]

DB: Oh, yes it is! Forget about the Microsoft element. The monopolies do not have a monopoly. Maybe on programs.

JP: What you like about it is the fact that anyone can say anything or do anything?

DB: From my stand, from where I am, by virtue of the fact that I am a pop singer and writer, I really embrace the idea that there's a new demystification process going on between the artist and the audience. I think when you look back at, say, this last decade, there hasn't really been one single entity, artist or group that have personified or become the brand name for the nineties. It was starting to fade a little in the eighties, and the seventies there were still definite artists, and in the sixties there were The Beatles and the Hendrixes. In the fifties there was Presley. Now it's subgroups and genres – it's hip-hop, it's girl power, it's a communal kind of thing, it's about the community, it's becoming more and more about the audience. Because the point of having somebody who led the forces has disappeared, because the vocabulary of rock is too well known. It's a currency that is not devoid of meaning anymore, but it's certainly only a conveyor of information now, it's not a conveyor of rebellion, and the internet has taken on that, as I say. I find that a terribly exciting area. So, from my standpoint, being an artist, I'd like to see what the new construction is between artists and audience. There is a breakdown, personified, I think, by the rave culture of the last few years, where the audience is at least as important as whoever is playing at the rave. It's almost like the artist is to accompany the audience and what the audience are doing, and that feeling is very much permeating music, and permeating the internet.

JP: But what is it specifically about the internet? I mean anybody can say anything … uh.

DB: Yeah.

JP: … and it all adds up to what? I mean, it seems to me there's nothing cohesive about it in the way that there was something cohesive about the youth revolution in music.

DB: Oh, but absolutely! Because I think that we at the time, up until at least the mid-seventies, really felt that we were still living in the guise of a single and absolute created society, where there were known truths and known lies, and there was no kind of duplicity or pluralism about the things that we believed in. That started to break down rapidly in the seventies, and the idea of a duality in the way that we live. There are always two, three, four, five sides to every question. The singularity disappeared, and that, I believe, has produced such a medium as the internet, which absolutely establishes and shows us that we are living in total fragmentation.

JP: You don't think that some of the claims being made for it are hugely exaggerated, I mean …

DB: Of course they are.

JP: … when the telephone was invented, people made amazing claims for it, [*Inaudible*] for example.

DB: I know! The president at the time, when it was first invented, he was outrageous. He said he foresaw the day in the future when every town in America would have a telephone. Now, how dare he claim that? Absolute bullshit. No, you see, I don't agree. I don't think we've even seen the tip of iceberg. I think the potential of what the internet is going to do to society, both good and bad, is unimaginable. I think we're actually on the cusp of something exhilarating and terrifying.

JP: It's just a tool, though, isn't it?

DB: No, it's not, no. It's an alien life form. [*Laughs*] Is there life on Mars? Yes, it's just landed here.

JP: But that's … it's simply a different delivery system there. You're arguing about something more profound.

DB: Oh, yeah. I'm talking about the actual context, and the state of content is going to be so different to anything that we can really envisage at the moment. Where the interplay between the user and the provider will be so in simpatico, it's going to crush our ideas of what mediums are all about. It's happening in every form. It's happening in visual art. The breakthroughs of the early part of the century with people like [Marcel] Duchamp, who were so prescient in what they were doing and putting down – the idea that the piece of work is not finished until the audience come to it, add their own interpretation, and what the piece of art is about is the grey space in the middle. That grey space in the middle is what the twenty-first century is going to be about.

JP: Bowie bonds are the one of the things you are best known for.

DB: Yeah.

JP: You are supposed to have raised 30 million …

DB: Yes, I did.

JP: … by selling rights to your future earnings from your back catalogue. Doesn't there come a point at which there's no point in earning more money?

DB: Do you know how expensive it is to get involved in the internet? [*Laughs*] I think that the majority of the money that I make, I plough back into some new project or other. I also, of course, being working class, always feel that there is never enough to leave my family. There's a kind of survival instinct that, 'Okay, that's going to be fine. I can leave that to all the kids, future and past, and everybody will be okay.' However, I would love to start a new internet company as well, so I'd need a bit more for that. So, you just keep ploughing it back in. I'm not a buyer of things. I think the only thing that I buy, addictively and obsessively, is art. I'm not really a house man or a car man. The only nice car I've ever bought for myself was a 1967 [Jaguar] E-Type, one and a half, I would get the half. I don't have things. I don't have a plane. [*Adopts on an exaggerated working-class accent*] I haven't got very much, Jeremy. I'm not a buyer of stuff. I do tend to regard money as the oil to get other things going. I feel more comfortable with it like that.

JP: Do you have any desire to come back here?

DB: I'd love to come back here, and I will. We haven't decided when it will be, but that's an absolute given. There are a few other things that I want to get accomplished over the next, I'd say, two years that may be quite surprising to people.

JP: What do you make of Cool Britannia?

DB: Oh, lumpen. It's so cliched and silly and ineffective. I don't think it's really changed. I think it's helped the media to get some handle on how to describe these times, but I don't think anybody anywhere else believes it. There's good and bad in everything we do. We're brilliant architects; we've got some wonderful visual artists – and some rubbish artists as well. Music, we've always been good at music. We're not truly a rock nation. Everything that we do in rock'n'roll has a sense of irony attached to it. We know that we're not the Americans. We know it didn't spring from our souls, so as the British always do, they try and do something with it to make them feel smug. That's what we are good at doing.

JP: But when you see politicians embracing rock stars, I mean, personally, I start reaching for my revolver then.

DB: Well, at least I wear a pair of women's high heels when I met a prime minister. [*JP laughs*] I do my bit, still. He didn't even notice, you know.

JP: This was Tony Blair?

DB: [*Nods*] Mmm. I was wearing women's stiletto shoes, and a nice suit and tie. That's the last time I wore a tie, I think. No, it wasn't! I wore a vicar's dog collar, nice black suit, black shirt with a dog collar and a pair of women's high heels. And he didn't bat an eyelid.

JP: [*Smiling*] Thank you very much.

4 DECEMBER 1999

LATER ... WITH JOOLS HOLLAND, BBC TV

INTERVIEWER: JOOLS HOLLAND

On the eve of the millennium, Bowie returned to BBC Television Centre to perform tracks from his 1999 album *'hours ...'*. Ever the pioneer, he had released the album as an internet download, the first major artist to do so. Most people back then had extremely limited bandwidth, and downloading the whole thing would take many well over five hours.

Bowie also used the visit to play one of his old classics, 'Cracked Actor', complete with cigarette in hand throughout. That was something you could still get away with in 1999 – and if you were David Bowie.

JOOLS HOLLAND: You've got a little bit of flu, you said?

DAVID BOWIE: Oh, yeah.

JH: I'm a bit worried about you having the flu.

DB: A little bit of flu there, Jools. Nothing to worry about, though. I should be back on my feet. I'm lying down today.

JH: Now, the first song you played was 'Ashes to Ashes'. Number 1 in 1980. What a great-sounding song.

DB: It's partially the band. The band are fantastic. A very good band.

JH: What inspired that song?

DB: I think I was wrapping up the seventies, really, for myself. And that seemed a good enough epitaph for it, that we've lost him [Major Tom], he's out there somewhere, we'll leave him be. He's up there with Mir [space station]. You know they're going to give him a [*Mimes a long tail*] … they're going to give Mir a copper tail about 11 miles long. Did you know that?

JH: No.

DB: Because it's just about to come back … [*To the audience*] Did you know that?

Audience: No.

[*One man in the audience nods*]

DB: Yeah … because it's coming down to Earth. That guy there [*Points to a man in the audience*] is actually going to attach the tail. It's a copper tail and it picks up the magnetic storms that Mir goes through, and it will lift it back up so it'll be in orbit for another …

JH: When you said Mir, I thought that was a friend. [*Laughter*]

DB: That's right! Mia. Ducky Mia.

JH: Mia Farrow?

DB: No, Ducky Mia. Used to be my old rhythm player. So, he's going to have a copper tail, [*Laughter*] and they're going to keep him going so that he keeps going around the Earth.

JH: I'm very relieved about that, because it was something that was worrying me. A lot of the viewers, you've put their minds at rest.

DB: I think so, because you never know what's going to come down with Ducky Mia. If he landed, it could be catastrophic.

JH: On your record sleeves, you often have characters that you've become. There are some marvellous sleeves there. [*The camera shows nine DB album covers*] It looks like *Celebrity Squares*, but you're in all of the squares there.

DB: [*Laughs*]

JH: Marvellous. Which is your favourite of those?

DB: None of them. [*DB turns round and points in the opposite direction towards the* Liquid Skin *album sleeve for the band Gomez, which is projected on to another wall*] I like that one. That's really good. It's a Robert Longo [American artist and film-maker] kind of thing, isn't it.

JH: Never mind about them. What about you over here?

DB: They wouldn't like you to say that.

JH: What about your record sleeve? That's very strange, *'hours ...'.* [*The album cover shows DB gently holding another DB lying down on a sterile-looking white floor*]

DB: Good God, I've not seen that before. [*Laughter*]

JH: It's you. It's both of you. Do you get involved with the artwork of your albums? Because they are great.

DB: Considerably.

JH: They should be in a gallery, really.

DB: Well, they will be.

JH: Now, you've done a lot of duets with people. A great deal. There's Queen, Mick Jagger and, of course, here, the legendary Bing [Crosby]. [*JH and DB shake hands*] I don't care if I get the flu because I've touched the hand of the hand that touched Bing Crosby.

LITTLE DRUMMER BOY

DB: We did 'Scary Monsters' after that together as a duet, but they never show that. It went so well that I actually took Bing on the road with me and he did the rest of the *Station to Station* tour. But he was bouncing off the walls. He'd take bottles of this Phyllosan stuff – 'fortifies the over-forties'.

JH: And that worked well for him?

DB: He would go out every night and come over to the gig with his posse. [*Laughter*]

JH: Would you call him the wild man of rock'n'roll?

DB: I had to sack him! [*Laughter*]

JH: Was that before or after he died?

DB: [*Laughs*]

JH: Is there anybody now you'd like to do a duet with?

DB: Bong. [*Laughter*]

JH: Is there one?

DB: Not really.

JH: I've got one in my room.

DB: [*Laughs*] Macy Gray … I found it … Macy Gray. [*Cheers from the audience*]

JH: The gauntlet's been thrown down on this programme.

DB: I don't think she'll pick it up quickly.

JH: Is it true that you're a computer-head?

DB: Er, I'm not quite sure how to answer that.

JH: Well, are you surfing the Web, or whatever it is?

DB: Not right now, no. Actually, this is a keyboard. [*Touches the piano and laughs*] This is my new internet …

JH: This is a computer.

DB: Yeah, this is it. You see, you can get straight on to any channel with this. [*DB plays some random notes as if typing and adopts a robotic tone*] 'You've got mail stuff.' [*Laughter*]

JH: In there?

DB: Yeah.

JH: What's the next song you're going to do for us? I'll tell you, in case you're confused, it's 'Something in the Air'.

DB: We're going to do 'Something in the Air'.

JH: Only because I thought, 'Well, I'd better say.' What's that song about?

DB: It's a song about somebody who really can't stand the relationship he's in, so he's kicking out his partner.

JH: In that case, I'm going to ask you to step back over there momentarily while I step over here and introduce a band. David Bowie, thank you very much for joining us!

DB: Thank you very much, Jools.

GLASTONBURY, BBC TV

PRESENTERS: JAMIE THEAKSTON AND JAYNE MIDDLEMISS

Bowie had rediscovered himself, Britain had rediscovered its greatest living rock star, and a gremlin had discovered the off switch.

Glastonbury was witnessing one of its greatest ever performances. Classic after classic cascaded down over a singing city of 150,000 people. 'Changes' followed 'China Girl', then soon came 'Life on Mars?'. For more than decade, Bowie had studiously avoided his own hits; now he appeared to be making up for lost time.

'We had all forgotten who David Bowie was,' said Bowie's publicist, Alan Edwards. Tonight would be the night that we would remember.

And then, five songs in, incomprehensibly, impossibly, the BBC cut the broadcast. They didn't even give a reason. Viewers wondered what on Earth could be so momentous that it would necessitate cutting short one of rock's greatest performances by one of rock's greatest singers. An ageing farmer doing Elvis covers, apparently.

Bowie had spent the nineties dabbling with drum and bass and industrial rock. But with the millennium approaching, he was thinking more than usual about the past and was open to playing Glastonbury, almost 30 years on from his last performance there. With that in mind, Glastonbury's founder Michael Eavis had been invited to a Bowie concert, but, perplexed by the drum and bass sound, Eavis left unimpressed.

Bowie's PR, Alan Edwards, realising he needed to act quickly, 'let it slip' the next night at a well-publicised celeb bash that Eavis was desperate for Bowie to play. As is the way with newspapers, that was rapidly translated into, 'Bowie to headline Glastonbury'. Bombarded by calls from the press, Eavis relented. Although why there needed to be any skulduggery at all is a mystery. Couldn't Bowie's people just have said he was happy to play his back catalogue? Would any promoter turn that down? Let alone Eavis, who once said that there were three singers who stood above all others in the twentieth century: Sinatra, Presley and, yes, Bowie.

There was some ambivalence on Bowie's part, though. 'I find my present situation more than a little confusing actually, as I really don't remember why I agreed to close this year's Glastonbury Festival in the first place,' he wrote in his published diary. 'It couldn't be more inconvenient in a way, now knowing that our pregnancy is well and truly for real. It means losing a clutch of days away from home. Days that I get more and more precious over.'

There were other issues, too. He didn't have a band. And he was worried he wouldn't be able to remember the lyrics, having not sung some of the songs for decades. In his most recent tour, he had felt compelled to take a lectern on stage in case he forgot the words. But for Glastonbury, he was determined to do it right.

'I shall forsake my prop this year,' he wrote. 'If that many people can travel so far, to skid about in so much dung and mud solution, then the least I can do is get the words of Major Tom right.' In fact, he and his band rehearsed 26 songs, only to be told at the eleventh hour that an early curfew meant a £20,000 fine for every extra minute played over the threshold. 'What crap news!!' he wrote. 'This means I have to drastically cut my set by something like 12 songs. What a hopeless task. We love everything!'

These were the songs he kept:

1.	'Wild is the Wind'	12.	'All the Young Dudes'
2.	'China Girl'	13.	'The Man Who Sold the
3.	'Changes'		World'
4.	'Stay'	14.	'Station to Station'
5.	'Life on Mars?'	15.	'Starman'
6.	'Absolute Beginners'	16.	'Hallo Spaceboy'
7.	'Ashes to Ashes'	17.	'Under Pressure'
8.	'Rebel Rebel'		
9.	'Little Wonder'		Encore: 'Ziggy Stardust',
10.	'Golden Years'		'Heroes', 'Let's Dance',
11.	'Fame'		'I'm Afraid of Americans'

In the wings, waiting to go on, Bowie became more than a little nervous. He had contracted laryngitis just a week or so before, and for the first time ever, in rehearsals his voice had given out. It was touch and go whether it would even last the night. For Bowie, there was never any doubt that the show would go on, but the occasion, the size of the crowd, the sense of this being his 'return', combined with fears over his voice, began to get to him as he was about to go on stage. Looking apprehensive, he turned to his pianist Mike Garson and said, 'Mike, go and warm up the audience.' Garson did as he was told, only to find there was no sound coming from his keyboard. After three minutes of silence, surrounded by dozens of frantic sound men and a restless crowd, Garson solved the problem: he'd forgotten to turn the thing on. He started to play 'Greensleeves'. 'Then David walked out and the crowd went crazy,' Garson said.[21]

Here's what the BBC audience heard:

WILD IS THE WIND

CHINA GIRL

DB: Oh, Glastonbury. Glastonbury. You've got a very, very lucky face. All of you. I'd just written this one, the first time I played Glastonbury, 1971.

CHANGES

DB: Mike Garson on piano. The time this one was written, 1975. The guy who played the album with me on that, *Station to Station*, is Earl Slick. This one's from that. It's called 'Stay'.

STAY

DB: Earl Slick on guitar! What a des res – Glastonbury. This one goes back to about the same period as 'Changes'. I'm very fearful tonight as I got struck down by laryngitis earlier this week. So, if I give out and if any of you know any of the words, for Gawd's sake, join in.

LIFE ON MARS?

<*Footage of the broadcast ends here and the BBC cuts to Jamie Theakston and Jayne Middlemiss in front of a fire, both seeming unsure as to why the live stream has ended.*>

JAYNE MIDDLEMISS: The legendary David Bowie there, surely the highlight of the festival so far.

JAMIE THEAKSON: I think so. It's fair to say we've had a Glastonbury moment.

JM: I think so.

JT: I think that's fair to say. Very exciting. We will be going to see more.

JM: We will be going back to David Bowie very, very soon.

JT: Too right, because I tell you why. I've pinched David Bowie's set list from the stage early on. I'm probably not allowed to do this, but it's pretty impressive.

> *<Theakston mentions 'Ashes to Ashes', 'Rebel Rebel', 'Fame', 'Golden Years', 'All the Young Dudes', 'Young Americans', 'Absolute Beginners', 'Station to Station', 'Let's Dance', 'Under Pressure', 'Heroes', 'Starman', 'Ziggy Stardust'.>*

JT: It's some set, let me tell you.

JM: A feast of music.

JT: You can probably hear David behind us on the main stage, which is literally only 40 or 50 yards behind us. There are seven or eight stages at Glastonbury. They're not all as big as the Pyramid Stage, where David is now. Let me let Billy [Bragg] explain …

> *<Bragg heads into a distant field to find Jools Holland playing piano and Michael Eavis singing 'How Great Thou Art', a hymn popularised by Elvis.>*

Via a distant field and some filling, the show meanders on. But none of this was the BBC's fault. Bowie's management had insisted that only four songs were allowed to be shown. They wanted to keep hold of the rights to screen it at a later time, perhaps not realising the significance of the moment in the moment. Perhaps Bowie was peeved at the BBC's often famously low pay rates; at the height of his fame in 1982, he got something like £1,000 for performing *Baal*, Bertolt Brecht's play, for BBC TV. The BBC's defence, though, is clear: as it's funded by the public, it is duty-bound to keep rates as low as possible.

The producer Mark Cooper did his best. Realising within minutes that this was a moment in cultural history, he found and pleaded with Bowie's publicist, Alan Edwards, to allow the BBC to keep broadcasting. Edwards and he made it to the edge of the stage and tried to catch the eye of Bowie's personal assistant, Coco Schwab – who briefly shook her head – and Bowie himself, who unsurprisingly never noticed them. Cooper's efforts did manage to gain a few minutes more, and that meant that viewers did at least catch 'Life on Mars?'.

Under this strange deal, though, part of the encore was allowed to be broadcast. And it was electrifying. Eavis would describe Bowie's performance of 'Heroes' as 'the best Glastonbury moment of all time'. His daughter and co-organiser, Emily, concurred: 'I often get asked what the best set I've seen here at Glastonbury is, and Bowie's 2000 performance is always one which I think of first.' Part of this was just the delight of seeing Bowie back – back on form, back at doing what he did best, and back playing the favourites. But it was also special in its own right. 'Not only the greatest Glastonbury headline performance,' wrote the NME, 'but the best headline slot at any festival ever.'

Near the end, Bowie fell to his knees. 'I haven't been here in 30 years,' he said to the crowd, 'and this is fucking brilliant.'

FRONT ROW, BBC RADIO

INTERVIEWER: JOHN WILSON

'Age doesn't bother me, it's the lack of years left.' That's Bowie's response when Wilson hints that ageing might be one of his fears. Bowie admits that fear permeates his 2002 record *Heathen*, but says it is less a fear of dying or getting old, as a fear of saying goodbye, specifically to his two-year-old daughter Lexi.

'Knowing I'm going to have to leave my daughter on her own doubles me up in a kind of grief,' he says.

The awareness of the preciousness of time appears to have been one of the key spurs in his life. 'Even as a young man,' he once said, 'I was always aware that death was the one absolute certainty about life. It pushed me to a kind of colossal, obsessive activity.'

Despite the optimism he expresses about his daughter and family life, it is clear that Bowie, an artist who often not just predicted but embraced the future, somehow seems to be shying away from what happens next.

'I mean, what a disappointing century this has been so far,' he says. 'I had high expectations about "the future". I had no idea it would capitulate into this awful mess, and this dreadful feeling of an involuntary lack of ability to do anything [about it].'

Despite some of the dark material, *Heathen* was Bowie's biggest-selling album since *Tonight* in 1984, and brought him the added bonus of critical approval.

JOHN WILSON: Let's start with the new album, *Heathen*. Was there an overriding theme or approach? What was the starting point?

DAVID BOWIE: I didn't think there was one. My job seemed to be to start putting together really strong material for Tony Visconti and I to start working on. We hadn't worked together in years – since 1980, really. We did do odds and sods in the mid-nineties, actually, but we hadn't collaborated on something so big as an album. I think the work that we have done is really held in quite high esteem by the people who have got it, and I was dead worried that if we rushed, went into it too fast, during the new album, we may have the chance of tarnishing that reputation in a way.

JW: I suppose Tony Visconti is the key name for fans because you haven't worked together since …

DB: Since 1980 in a major way, and the last album we did together was *Scary Monsters*. We've done so many really good pieces together – *Low* and *Heroes*, of course, *Young Americans* album, even *The Man who Fell to* … sorry, *The Man who Sold the World*, sorry, I'm exhausted.

JW: But was there a conscious attempt to try to re-evoke a sense of those times?

DB: No, that's absolutely what we didn't want to do. That's why it was very important to me to make sure we had some very good musical structures before we went in, so that we didn't lazily dip back into what we'd already done. So, I spent the early part of year making sure we had some quite strong songs to work with before we went in.

JW: And how did you write? Do you still write in the same way as possibly 30 years ago, with a guitar? Does it start with simple words, melodies?

DB: I think I've got different ways of writing now. I seem to have collected different processes. And it really depends on the project at hand. It seems to me I have three basic types. I've got a narrative, literary-oriented kind of album, which is very much about crafted songs. There's something that's more experimental, which is more interested in playing around hybridisations or juxtapositions, and the music is not necessarily secondary, but it's a support to the ideas, so it's more experimental; so you would get things like *Low* out of that, or *Outside*, in the mid-nineties. And there are other things which definitely are written for the stage, and more theatrical things where the motivation and the momentum for the thing comes from what I'm seeing in my mind for the stage itself, and that would produce obvious things like *Diamond Dogs* and indeed Ziggy itself. So, within there, that's a kind of a palette I'll work from. And an album, I'll kind of decide up front if it's going to be A, B or C, and then modified by the other types. So, this one was very much the first – A – narrative, straightforward, with elements of B, but very little C.

JW: But it's less experimental sonically, musically than … *Earthling*, *Outside*, that you made in the nineties?

DB: Absolutely. It is about songwriting in a very straightforward fashion. And that's what I felt that Tony and I should use as a kind of armature for what we wanted. And I think, indeed, that for us, it is a very satisfying album. Even in the mixing stage, we regarded it as a success. It fulfilled all my expectations of what we could do together. And it's not reliant on the past, yet it has a very signature style. You can tell by listening to it that it was made by myself and Tony.

JW: Absolutely.

DB: There's something about it.

JW: But you jumped in when I said 'evoke a sense of the past', and you said 'absolutely not', and yet there are, lyrically, references, aren't there, things that would spark off in the mind of …

DB: You know what, I personally feel that I've consistently written about the same subjects for over 35, nearly 40 years. There's really been no room for me. It's all despondency, despair, isolation.

JW: And spaceships. What is it with spaceships?

DB: Well, it's an interior dialogue that you manifest physically. It's my little inner space, isn't it, [*Laughs*] writ large. I wouldn't dream of getting on a spaceship. It would scare the shit out of me. [*Laughter*] I have absolutely no interest or ambition to go into space whatsoever. I'm scared going down the end of the garden.

JW: There is a song called 'I Took a Trip on a Gemini Spaceship', which is a cover version, isn't it?

DB: It is, yeah. It's actually an old muse of mine, a character called the Legendary Stardust Cowboy who was a stablemate in the late sixties on Mercury [record label], and the chief executive over at Mercury, called Ron Oberman, quietly and conspiratorially put these three singles in my hand sand said, 'Hey, David, you like weird shit, don't ya?' 'Yeah, I love weird shit.' 'Well, this is the weirdest shit we got.' [*Laughter*] And he gave me wonderful, anarchic singles by this Legendary Stardust Cowboy, and I completely fell in love with him, I thought he was just terrific, so much so that I nicked his name for Ziggy Stardust.

JW: And was he a musical influence as well?

DB: Not really. [*Laughs*] Have you heard the records? They are out there. I guess he'd be a comfortable stablemate to someone like Wild Man Fischer or one of those Zappa throw-outs in the mid-sixties.

JW: Art rock?

DB: Well, he's more than that. He has great integrity. He has no idea that any judgements will be made on what he does or delivers. There's an incredible naivety to him. He is solidly outside. He is an outside artist. He is spectacularly outside, and he's on at Meltdown [festival] as it happens.

JW: Which I want to talk about. I mention there are lyrical references to your past, but there is one key moment where, to my ears, you're playing a Stylophone, and that has to be the first time since 'Space Oddity', which is more than 40 years ago. That was a reference?

DB: Actually, no, it's not. Why I started using that is that I did a thing as a cover song for a collection of Who songs, songs written by [Pete] Townshend, a few months ago … last year? Oh, I don't know. My memory is a lousy conveyance of any kind of information. We did the song 'Pictures of Lily', and on there I dragged the Stylophone out. Somebody had sent me one. I wish I could say it was my actual original, but somebody from England had sent me one with the original Rolf Harris boxing on it. I was absolutely delighted. I hadn't seen the thing since '69, '70, whenever. So, I used it as the solo for 'Picture of Lily' – with, I thought, great results. [*Laughs*] I thought it was tremendously impactful. So I said, 'I really should start using this again.' I put it with my collection of old synthesisers … I've got a lot of old stuff … that I've kept over the years that I really dragged out for this album.

JW: But it really is only you and Rolf who have hits with a Stylophone?

DB: Yes, me and Rolf. We're doing a collection next year. We're just going to choose our favourite songs and Rolf and I are going … ah, maybe we won't. [*Both laugh*] Maybe we shouldn't even think about that. Maybe that's a terrible idea.

JW: When you were playing the Stylophone on 'Space Oddity', it didn't have a little picture of Rolf on there at the time, did it? Was it a Rolf Harris Stylophone?

DB: I think that – so my ego wouldn't get bruised, as one does get very bruised at 19 – I think they just sent it to me without any packaging, if I remember rightly. I certainly don't remember seeing Rolf Harris's face on it.

JW: Now, that was … we are going back 30 years, or just over 30 years …

DB: Yeah, we actually recorded it very early '69, then it was all suddenly, 'Oh, the Americans are going to launch a space [rocket] … rush, rush, rush,' and they kind of got it out.

JW: Even within that first single, and it was a classic pop single, you were still adopting a persona, you were still playing a character there. Where did that start from?

DB: No, no. I would disagree there. As the singer, I don't think I'd gotten that far into the idea of characterisation for myself. What I was keen on doing was writing in such a way that it would lead me into writing some kind of rock musicals, which is really, more than anything else, probably what I really wanted to do in the late sixties. I think I wanted to write a new kind of musical, and that's how I saw my future at the time.

JW: Oh, it really was exploring the theatricality of pop?

DB: Yeah, absolutely, it was that. But I was still kind of being only an interpreter of a song at that time. I was still just David Bowie. The real characterisation really didn't kick in till the Ziggy thing.

JW: What I was going to say is that, retrospectively, people were saying that you were playing those characters not as a way of exploring the theatricality of pop but a way of hiding.

DB: Not anything more than shyness, really. I was always quite a shy kid. And I didn't come alive on stage, I just got even more shy; but I found I didn't get so shy if I adopted a character. So it was a convenience, as well as a very bright theatrical idea, [*Laughs*] I subsequently realised.

JW: But taken to an extreme with Ziggy.

DB: No, it was just the first time that theatre of that nature had been seen in rock, so I don't think it was extreme by theatrical standards, at all. But it was certainly kind of new for rock'n'roll. [*Pause*] I don't know, I'll have to read one of the books out on it to get a better answer. There are so many books. Really, I should go and read a book on it. Especially in France, I get followed around, there's always somebody saying, [*Adopts a French accent*] 'Why did you kill Ziggy?' I kind of get bored with it because I've done such a lot of work in 40 years – Ziggy was only going for 18 months, which is not really a very large part of my working life. And I don't think I can say any more than I've already said for the past 30 or so years.

JW: But do you ever look back, obviously you don't want to talk about it, but …?

DB: No! Never. Never. Only with fond amusement. Really, I'm very proud of it and very happy that I did it all, but it's very much not what I'm doing now.

JW: So, on the new album, are you talking about David Bowie now?

DB: Yeah, I think I am.

JW: This is not a reassessment of life?

DB: No, I think these are very real fears and anxieties that were provoked well before that 9/11 thing, that dreadful tragedy. I think living in the city … I've lived here now with my wife for 10 years this time around. Before, I've lived here often so I think I've probably lived in the city more than any other city in the world over the last 40 years. So, I guess you could call it my home. But there is a low-level anxiety that buzzes here at all times, and has been buzzing here ever since I've known it. And I think because of my orientation towards the apocalyptic, it rather hones that and rather galvanises that for me … especially the advent of a new child in my family, my daughter, really focused my fears and apprehensions about what kind of … I mean what a disappointing twenty-first century this has been so far. I had, personally, really had quite high expectations about 'the future'. I had no idea it would capitulate into this awful mess and this dreadful feeling of an involuntary lack of ability to be able to do anything about this impending, possible disastrous, series of consequences, which one has so many suspicions about what are the real reasons and the real causes to them. It's not a pleasant way to live. And I look at my daughter and, sometimes, for the first few days after 9/11, I looked at her and couldn't feel happy, which is a terrible thing to feel. I looked at her and just felt fearful.

JW: There's one song on the album which seems to address those fears, a song called 'Afraid', which is …

DB: [*Laughs*]

JW: Or is that taking it too literally? You are afraid?

DB: [*Continues laughing*] I'm not pliant today, am I? That actually is probably the one song on the album I don't see as being representative of me. Only because that particular character, the progenitor of that particular song, is talking in terms of how, as long as he goes along with the sheep-like mentality of everybody, he won't feel afraid. He believes that his security will be bought if he plays the game, so to speak. So, unfortunately, I have to distance myself from the song and say it was an irony of kinds. It's an interesting deceit, but it's not mine.

JW: But I read it, because it was written in the first person, and repetitively it keeps going over the fear and the neuroses …

DB: Yeah, obviously the idea of fear is very strong within the album. I think one of the major fears that underlines it all for me personally, is a fear there is no spiritual life. One hopes that there really … I'm confronted every day of my life, it's something I've always thought about. I'm a very spiritual person, in as much as I've had this awful bloody journey searching for a spiritual life that makes some kind of … that, firstly, actually, meets my expectations of what a spiritual life should be and what kind of part it should play in my life. Maybe I ask too much. But I keep … I keep coming to a dead end. But, I mean, as I get older my questions are fewer, but I ask them – I bark them more [*Laughs*] than ask them. And I keep approaching them from a different direction each time. But I probably only have three or four questions left. I guess by the time I do my last album, I'll only have one question.

JW: This may be wildly off the mark, but one of the things that I think marks your lyrics over the years has been the questions in there.

DB: Yeah, they're very questioning.

JW: On this album, there are more declarations.

DB: Yeah, they're stubborn, they're naive declarations. If you're not going to do anything for our world, you're not going to have support for your plans in the future … God! [*Laughs*] That kind of bald-faced idiot statement. But it's the frustration, it's the actual frustrations of day-to-day life. You have these ideals but they're usually based on such irrational … they don't fit into reality too well.

JW: Is writing a catharsis – I mean, do you try and work out those fears in the lyrics?

DB: It seems that I do do that, and I can't say that it's actually necessarily an enjoyable situation each time, either. I don't think it's something that I enjoy a hundred per cent. There are occasions when I really don't want to write, it just seems that I have a physical need to do it. It's so much part of my life that I can't see a day going past without me doing something or other, either melodically or lyrically. Sometimes, when I'm forming the songs themselves, they're not particularly … in fact, there's an instance of that in this album, the song 'Heathen'. It came together quite early on in the making of the album and … the words were literally tumbling out for it. I was very alone, very isolated up in the studio, one early … as is my wont, five o'clock or six o'clock in the morning. I was up in the studio on my own waiting for everyone else to get up, and I was kind of putting the day's work together and this thing started appearing for me. I'd already written a melody that I very much liked, and the words started appearing out of nowhere, and I *just* couldn't control them. And I realised what it was, that it was about, and I really didn't want to write it, because I wasn't sure that I really wanted to voice or articulate those particular thoughts at this time. But it just wouldn't stop, and I had to write it, and I was in tears by the end of the thing. It was, it was really… not sure if it was … [*Exhales*] it was a traumatic moment for me. At least, possibly, it was an epiphany. I don't know.

I have to go and look up 'epiphany' in the dictionary and see if it was an epiphany. I think it was a, a traumatic epiphany. [*Laughs loudly*]

JW: But you were revealing something to yourself just by putting the lyrics out …

DB: To myself, yeah.

JW: And what is that song directly about, then? Is it about confronting spirituality?

DB: It was. It has … why I called it *Heathen* is that it's not a dialogue between a man and his God, it's a dialogue between a man and life itself. So, it's almost pagan in some respects, but it definitely has a heathen propensity in that way. It's a man confronting the realisation that life is a finite thing, and that he can already feel it … life itself actually going from him, ebbing out of him, the weakening of age. And I didn't want to write that, you know? I didn't want to know that I do feel that … Who does?

JW: It's something that's marked Neil Young's work, there's a Neil Young song on this album, a very early song. He's been very candid and written about that ageing process, and about growing old and fearing growing old, but it's something that's never really been associated with you, is this …

DB: Well, I've not been his age, have I? [*Laughs*] I mean I am now getting to that stage where I'm sure that … It's not the age itself, you know. I mean, age doesn't bother me. So many of my heroes were older guys. It's the lack of years left that weighs far heavier on me than the age that I am. I feel pretty good, frankly, and I have a wonderful life; I'm so lucky to have found the right woman to share my life with. We have a child and I do what I've always wanted to do. I'm a writer. But yet it's … it's having to let go of it all, you know?

Even more so now, it's so much more poignant. For me, often, there's such a cloud of melancholia about knowing I'm going to have to leave my daughter on her own at … I don't know what age that's going to happen, thank God. But it just *doubles* me up in a kind of grief.

JW: And a lot of the album is addressing that kind of issue?

DB: I wouldn't have this album if we didn't have our daughter. I'm not saying the whole album is about her, but I think it provoked questions that search certain areas of my own discomfort and anxieties.

JW: But would you say it's a more candid, more honest album than especially many of your more recent …?

DB: That's unfair. That's like saying I've done my best to conceal myself on my albums. That's not right. Many of my albums are impressionistic. I don't write in the kind of autobiographical way, I never have done, and it's only recently that I've started to, and this may be something to do with age and that one matures. I don't know. It's all very Graham Greene, isn't it? Although I don't think I'm going to become a Catholic! [*Laughs*] I'm not that mad.

JW: But you are trying to get to the heart of the matter?

DB: I think I'm writing for a different purpose. That's what it is. I think one's reasons for writing change an awful lot through life.

JW: Are you writing more for yourself now?

DB: Yeah, very much so.

JW: Because there's a whole set of expectations that your fans … they are devoted, very loyal, quite obsessive fans, and have been over the years, and they look for certain motifs.

DB: Yeah, incredibly bright, wonderful, intelligent people. [*Laughs*]

JW: But do you ever play to their expectations?

DB: Well, again, that's a contrived statement. [*Sounding peeved*] Come on. I wrote for an audience, yeah. I really wanted to be ... as I say right at the very beginning ... I wanted to write theatre, and I guess I could have just written for theatre in my living room, but I think the intent was to have a pretty big audience to come and watch it. But those ambitions are modified and changed over the years. I mean any writer, I think, especially a pop writer, writes for an audience. Over the years, I found that working *for* an audience – performing for an audience – wasn't anything that I particularly enjoyed. I realised fairly soon on that I wasn't a born performer. I don't like performing very much. I, unfortunately, can do it, which is not great because you're put on tour a lot. I'd much prefer to do a few shows and then get on with my next project. So, I less and less thought about the audience's expectations and, especially now, at this time in my life, I really am writing for myself. I really am writing for myself.

JW: Are you worried at all ... I mean, you talk about the 'ageing process' there and the different questions that arise. Do you ever worry about working within the pop genre?

DB: No, no.

JW: I mean, you talk about being an artist, talk about being a writer, that doesn't worry you at all?

DB: No, I'm totally indifferent to that. And, again, it's not the ageing process ... you must understand, I don't have a problem with ageing. In fact, I embrace that aspect of it and am able to, and obviously am going to be able to, quite easily. It doesn't faze me at all, ageing. It's the *death* part that's really a drag. [*Laughs*] Everything else I quite cope with … quite cope with … I don't know, I'll see when my body starts seizing up, see if I can [*JW laughs*] cope with that as easily I'm saying now. Probably not. I'll probably get very angry and irritable when I can't lift my leg up [*hear DB moving, and what sounds a crack of a knee, and both laugh*] like that.

JW: You're still going to be doing the scissor kicks onstage, are you?

DB: [*Laughs*] Yeah, while I can still do them, yeah!

JW: You've always talked about your music, your words, as an art form. I know you have been painting for 20 years, you've probably been painting for 30 years …

DB: Yeah.

JW: Are you still painting? Is that just another outlet, an expression?

DB: Yeah, it's something that I do enjoy an awful lot. It's not something I've been able to do recently. One of the major reasons is that I gave up my studio here; I've got to find another one… I can write music, in fact I *have* to write music, at home and with my family to be no hindrance at all, but I don't seem to be able to do visual work with my family around. It's very odd; so it's rather slowed me down, because I need to find a new studio. I haven't done anything of any note. I've done some sketching and some charcoal work, but I've done nothing that I've really been able to get my teeth into for 18 months or so. I tell you who I really like in England at the moment is Banksy. I think he's really good.

JW: The graffiti artist.

DB: Hey, Banksy, if you're listening, I really think your work's great. Yeah, I think he's tremendous. I like his work a lot. I think he's going to be quite important, that one.

JW: Are you still following the art movements in Britain?

DB: Yeah, I like to see what people are doing. But I like to see what people are doing in any area, really. One of the joys about being a musician, it was the first career that really I could drag all my other hobbies and interests into. If I'd gone into, oh, I don't know, car design, [*Laughs*] I don't think I would have been able to drag theatre into it in quite the same way, [*Both laugh*] or avant-garde poetry or something.

JW: That's interesting. If you'd started out now at the age of 19, would you be sitting in a bedroom writing pop songs, do you think?

DB: Look, the trouble with futurism is that all it generally is, is an elaboration on the recent past. I'm not sure I can really answer that with any kind of intrinsic worth. [*Laughs*] Alright, I'll stab a guess at it. I'd say, no, I would have probably gone straight into the internet, I would think. I would have seen that as a really viable form of expression somehow. I just don't know … I just love music. Probably a combination. Yeah, it would have been something to do with the internet and music.

JW: And you're still excited by contemporary music? You're still influenced by music?

DB: I love it. I love it. I love it.

JW: Obviously, there are some contemporary influences on this.

DB: Yeah, I suppose there might be. I'm not so sure what they might be. It's the same as when I worked in Berlin … there you are, you see, you've got me doing an anecdote. I see it written time and time again that one of the great influences on the albums that we did there is Kraftwerk. You know what, we are the antithesis of what Kraftwerk were doing. They were working in a very robot-like manner … [*Door creaks loudly as someone opens it*] … Fast, fast, young man. Fast! It's not going to happen, is it? [*The door creaks even more loudly*] Give me a couple of minutes. [*Presumably one of DB's team has entered the studio to gesture to JW that time is up*] Kraftwerk were working in a very minimalist fashion. There was no live drum kit – they were using an electronic drum kit. And they kept away from the idea of blues form or R'n'B form completely. It was a very European sensibility and almost nineteenth-century structure to the music, whereas I was using a very funky band with live musicians, live real-time tempo and kind of swathing it with atmospheric sounds over the top, with myself and Visconti and Eno. It was their provocation, the fact that they were working in a new area, the area itself became something that captivated me, and they are terrifically responsible for my moving into that genre of music. But I wouldn't say that if you put the two albums together, *Low* and *Radio-Activity*, say, there's absolutely no similarity whatsoever. We work within a blues structure, frankly. We were playing blues with strange, sonic sounds over it, if you have to nail it down to something. But it wouldn't have happened if I hadn't heard Kraftwerk in 1974. 'Inspirational' is the word. I tend to be inspired by the work of others very much, and I'll only nick if I can get away with it.

JW: And you do nick?

DB: [*Adopts a Cockney accent*] Nah, not me, guv. [*JW laughs*] I'm as clean as the driven snow.

JW: David, thank you very much indeed.

DB: My pleasure.

FRIDAY NIGHT WITH ROSS & BOWIE, BBC TV

INTERVIEWER: JONATHAN ROSS.

Pete Townshend had joined Bowie the previous year to record a LP of songs Bowie had written and performed in the sixties. The idea was to have fun as a band, and fellow guitarist Mark Plati recalled those sessions as 'a little party'.

Six months later, Townshend returned to the New York studio to put the finishing touches to the record and continue the party, or so he thought. The studio's most famous feature had been a large glass window that looked directly out on to the World Trade Center. Since Townshend's first trip, the towers had been destroyed and Bowie had shelved his album.

'David had completely dumped everything he'd been working on,' said The Who guitarist. 'The new album was darker, grimmer and more about what had changed on that extraordinary day. That event changed him, made him darker, and I don't know that he ever really snapped out of it.'[22]

Bowie was in upstate New York when news of the attack came through. He immediately phoned Iman. 'The Twin Towers were right in front of our apartment,' he said. 'While we were talking, the second one went in and she said, "Oh my God, another one has gone." I said, "You are under attack, get the fuck out of there!"'

Iman put the baby in the pram and ran 20 blocks. Subsequently unable to get through on the phone, Bowie had no idea if his wife and daughter had made it out alive until later that evening.

'It was so, so horrifying,' he recalled. In the days and weeks afterwards, the city's fire crews recalled Bowie being a regular feature at their stations, talking to them and offering support. The resulting album was called *Heathen*.

JONATHAN ROSS: I am so pleased to meet you, sir. Please sit down. And that was great. Well done, band. Fantastic! That was tremendous. Thank you so much for that.

DAVID BOWIE: It's my very great pleasure. Quite Danish this, isn't it? [*DB rubs the leather sofa*]

JR: What? The furniture? Let me start with the big question, David. You are a lovely-looking slim man, if you don't mind me saying so. [*Applause*] Let's face it, you're getting on a bit and you're looking fantastic for your age …

DB: [*Laughs*] I used to say things like that to my mother. [*Laughter*]

JR: You've never been fat in your entire life.

DB: No, no. I got a bit kind of lazy at one point, but I'm back to working out again. I work out a lot.

JR: You do boxing, don't you?

DB: Yeah, I like it. Want to do a couple of rounds?

JR: You know what, I've been doing some boxing, sparring.

DB: Good, isn't it?

JR: It's hard, though.

DB: Yeah, well, that's the point. [*Groans and rolls his eyes, laughter*]

JR: Okay. The new album … we don't have to do this, we're doing this because I'm a fan and I like the new album an awful lot. The new album [*Holds up a CD of* Heathen] …

DB: [*Reaches inside his jacket*] I have a copy with me just in case you'd forgotten to … [*Laughter*]

JR: I have about a dozen copies now. It's fantastic. It's a terrific album. It seems to me that this has been better received than just about any album you've had out in the last five, six, seven, eight years. I mean, it's really done well.

DB: It's difficult to say, you know. Okay, yeah, it's been very positively received, however it seems to be traditional now that every album since *Black Tie White Noise* is the best album I've put out since *Scary Monsters*. [*Laughs*] Inevitably, that's what I get. But this one, it seems to have caught people's imaginations.

JR: Strangely, I do get the feeling that by listening to the album we can get closer to you than we have for many years, in terms of knowing who you are and where you're at, at this stage.

DB: You know, Jonathan, that'll never happen. [*Laughter*]

JR: But David, life for you, you seem more sorted. Obviously, I know next to nothing about you, really, but to the casual observer, you seem more sorted than ever before.

DB: [*Lets out a long, thoughtful breath*] Yeah, I am. I mean, domestically, in my love life, in my work. I guess in all those areas of my life everything is absolutely … I couldn't ask for a better thing, a better place to be located. It's just absolutely fantastic. As a writer though, and I guess that's what you draw on … there's a second part of my life, there's an inner thing, there's a sense of mystery that I'll never be able to fully confront. I need to escape from certain things … look, I'm drawing them in [*Indicates the audience*] like crazy, here. [*Laughter*] I have no idea where I'm going. Yeah, I'm very happy, yeah. [*Starts whistling, pretending to be someone who is covering up being embarrassed*]

JR: Are you aware of this question? Because I kind of do feel, a lot of people do, because your music has genuinely meant so much to me, I believe you have some sort of extra knowledge. I'm sure a lot of fans feel this way.

DB: But I want certainty. [*Laughs*]

JR: I know you're an incredibly well-read man, you're a voracious reader …

DB: What does 'voracious' mean?

JR: So, you're getting to the point where you're coming to terms with inevitable death …

DB: Yeah.

JR: … mortality. This probably should have been at the end of the interview, but anyway. [*Laughter*]

DB: Don't worry, [*Looks at his watch*] it will be. [*Applause*]

JR: Don't go! You know that period back then. What was the period, what were those albums that you say you weren't writing for yourself, you were writing for other people's expectations?

DB: Of the 26 albums I've made, I think there were two where I really wasn't involved, and that was *Tonight* and *Never Let Me Down*, the two follow-ups to *Let's Dance*. Yeah, it was my Phil Collins years, yeah. [*Smiles cheekily and audience laughs*] I tell you that's not … [*Holds up the palms of his hands to calm the audience down*] … let me just explain that a little further, I don't want to get into some deep shit here.

JR: It's okay, he hasn't got any fans left.

DB: Ah, no. [*Grimaces*] I don't like getting into those places. That's terribly unfair. No. There was a period where I was performing in front of these huge stadium crowds at that time, and I'm thinking,

'What are these people doing here? Why have they come to see me? They should be seeing Phil Collins.' They were definitely Phil Collins-type audiences. And then that came back at me and I thought, 'What am I doing here? [*Laughter*] I should be playing to people who don't look like they've come to see Phil Collins.' That's what I'd been used to, up until that point. I don't know the guy …

JR: Well, a certain kind of stadium rock, then.

DB: A certain kind of mainstream feel that I'm not comfortable in. I'm just not comfortable in it.

JR: And did you think your earlier fans felt betrayed because of that period, they felt like this wasn't …?

DB: I had to throw away an awful lot of silly-looking clothes and make-up and buy some really bad clothes and make-up. [*Laughs*]

JR: You had some great looks. I'm not disappointed now because you look fantastic, but I'm hoping that underneath there somewhere there's a lightning flash painted on or something?

DB: I tell you what I did do. My concession to Ziggy … [*Caricatures a distraught German fan*] 'Why did you kill Ziggy?'

JR: Well, why did you kill Ziggy?

DB: [*Caricatures a distraught German fan*] 'Why did you kill Ziggy?' [*Adopts an upper-class accent*] 'You don't understand, there was a war on. Your mother and I, we tried to protect you from all this, but well, if you must know, your sister ran way.' [*Switching back to the upset German fan*] 'Why did you kill Ziggy?' [*Back to the upper-class accent*] 'It was hard for all of us, it was hard for the country, dammit.' Sorry.

JR: You know, I did have a dream once where you were my father.

DB: [*Laughs*] Please, please don't share this with me. [*Laughter*]

JR: Well, it's okay, because you were stern but you were fair.
[*Laughter*] Although the make-up took some explaining at school.

DB: My concession to Ziggydom is that I had those, you know those
platform boots ... not those horrible stack-heel boot things, I hated
those ... platform boots, that's what it was about. That was the great
thing. Solid Japanese platform boots. Red with a black thing on. I've
just had those remade in black patent leather and they look fantastic.

JR: You've got to make sure you wear them both at the same time
or else it looks like you've got an orthopaedic problem, though.
[*Laughter*] David, wasn't that a fantastic ... it must have been a great
period. Just the way bands looked. You look at bands now, you look
at Oasis, and they're like four blokes, you see them waiting for a bus
normally, wearing anoraks. What's that all about? Whereas look,
there we've got Roxy Music, Eno looking mad as a March hare.

<*Bowie laughs at a photo of Roxy Music with Brian Eno looking skeletal
in shiny, tight gold trousers, crimson boots and dyed orange hair.*>

JR: Look at him!

DB: Look at his trousers!

JR: Looks like he's walked off *The Rocky Horror [Picture] Show*. But
wasn't that great? A little bit of lurex, a little bit of Velcro. Look,
there you go!

<*A photo of the band Slade, with guitarist Dave Hill dressed head-to-toe
in silver causes more audience laughter.*>

JR: It must have been great turning up on *Top of the Pops*, though.

<A photo of the band Mud in platform boots, flares and satin outfits of garishly different colours is shown.>

JR: Never knowing who'd be dressed as a clown, who'd be a snowman.

<A photo of Bowie in a feather boa and a knitted, striped, one-legged Yamamoto outfit is shown to cheers from the audience.>

JR: Were there any outfits you experimented and, even you, tried them on at home in front of the mirror and thought, 'You know what, this is too stupid'?

DB: That one! [*Laughter*]

JR: Did one of your aunts knit that for you, David? That looks like a home-knit job to me.

DB: It does, doesn't it?!

JR: Someone had a machine and they said, 'Who wants this? Tell you what, I'll give it to David.'

DB: Avant-garde Missoni job. Actually, it was all Kansai Yamamoto. He has a lot to answer for.

JR: But a fantastic style and incredibly brave. Now, we look back and in hindsight you think you can see why you made those decisions, and you can see why they worked. But at the time, when you did that, when you cut your hair that way or experimented with make-up like that, you really were out there on your own, weren't you?

DB: Makes me wonder why I killed him off.

JR: I was thinking, wouldn't we all be interested in an album which told us where Ziggy would have been now? [*Audience agrees*] Where he would be 30 years on. Don't you think that's a cracking idea?

DB: Ah, nah, I know somebody who will probably write that. [*Laughs*]

JR: Andrew Lloyd Webber! [*Laughter*] When you're writing lyrics, do you still experiment with that cut-up technique? You still use that, which was famously employed on some of those early albums?

<*Footage from* Cracked Actor *film.*>

JR: David, I experimented before the show. You have awakened in me dormant creativity.

DB: Oh, blimey.

JR: Before the show, I thought, okay, you do the cut-up lyrics, I'm going to do some cut-up questions for you. [*DB laughs*] I wrote some ideas down, I cut them up and I placed them together. I still don't know how you did it. Here's one … 'When Ziggy guitar teeth crotch enjoying?'

DB: [*Laughs*] That's Japanese!

JR: No, that makes sense if you think about it. Better than some of your bloody songs, mate.

DB: Japanese makes sense.

JR: 'Nietzsche preacher creature teacher'.

DB: That was not a cut-up.

JR: It was!

DB: You're lying!

JR: I helped it a bit. You don't have to be random, do you?

DB: No, you don't.

JR: Fat old Ziggy.

DB: I like that. I want that one. [*Takes the card with the cut-up words on*]

JR: Here's one you'll like. 'Brian Eno make-up Arthur Lowe Spiderman'. [*Laughter*] That could be a mini-series!

DB: Wonderful! No, these are wonderful.

JR: Here's a good 'un. This is a genuine one. 'Primitive Jagger chimpanzee penis'. [*Laughter*]

DB: [*Adopts the distraught German fan voice again*] Why did you kill fat old Ziggy?

JR: David Bowie is going to perform another track for us now. It's going to be a track from the new album, I believe.

DB: It is indeed.

JR: Is it 'Slip Away' you're doing now?

DB: Yeah.

JR: Fabulous. It's a fabulous album. [*Applause*] I'll see you in a second, David.

SLIP AWAY

JR: That sounded great. Ladies and gentlemen, that was 'Slip Away'. It's from the current album *Heathen*. I think that's grown to be possibly my favourite track on the album.

DB: Oh, great.

JR: You played the Stylophone at the end of that. What a fabulous treat to see that not only back on a top-selling album, but back on TV.

DB: Let's see if we can conjure up something. Have you got one too? [*Laughs*]

JR: I don't only have one, I've got one with a special holster. [*Laughter*]

DB: [*Sings while playing Stylophone*] Ground Control to Major Tom.

JR: I've had this since the 1970s. Mine's got David Cassidy on the back. Don't be jealous, that was before I discovered you. [*Laughter*]

DB: That's alright. How did you get a black and white one?

> <*Ross plays 'Do-Re-Mi' from* The Sound of Music. *Bowie then plays something that sounds like interference.*>

JR: Oh, you're doing the scratching at the back there. Would I be right in thinking, you don't really need all of that, [*Points to the band*] you could go on the road with this alone? [*Laughter*]

DB: Yeah, I think some people have made a profession of this.

JR: It's a great sound. You like playing around, presumably, but yours is cleaner than mine.

DB: This is boys and their toys, beyond.

JR: David, if you want, as a present …

DB: [*Adopts a young boy's voice*] That's really good. Yours is black and white though. I could only get the white one. How many stamps did you have to put in to get one of them?

JR: Would you like the holster to take home?

DB: [*Still in a young boy's voice*] Do I get the holster with …?

JR: Do you want the holster?

DB: Yeah, course I do.

JR: No one goes home from this show empty-handed. [*JR hands over the holster*]

DB: You're kidding me.

JR: Here you go.

DB: Oh, that's so, that's wonderful. [*Applause*]

JR: And I would so love to see you wearing that. You don't have to put it on now.

DB: The cool thing is, you can get it out really quickly!

JR: You can be quick on the draw. You never know when inspiration might strike.

DB: When I'm at a party and someone says, 'You don't happen to have a Stylophone on you, do you?' [*Laughter*]

JR: David, just a little word of advice as well. Wear that naked around the house … it will drive Iman wild! [*Laughter*]

DB: I'll tell you, I'll tell you if that works. [*Laughs*]

JR: Your wife, she is one hell of a beautiful woman.

DB: She'll get a kick out of that.

JR: She's an incredible-looking woman.

DB: Yeah, you're right.

JR: And she could do better. [*Laughter*]

DB: Oh, I couldn't agree with you more.

JR: You are lucky. [*A photo of Iman, David and their baby Lexi is shown*] Look at that, she is gorgeous.

DB: See that little baby?

JR: How old is she now?

DB: Twenty-two months.

JR: That's wonderful. But you're a lazy dad, aren't you? You don't do the nappies and stuff.

DB: Are you kidding me? No, I wouldn't go near that. [*Laughter*]

JR: You see, you shouldn't be proud about that. You should be somewhat ashamed.

DB: No, it's not proud. I'm just resolved that this is not my ... I'm resigned is more the word ... and pretty resolved, believe me ... I want to be there, you know, help her through the dictionary, [*Laughs*] help her build a library up, things like that.

JR: A teacher.

DB: Walking and talking stuff. Now it's like ideal, because ... I had a conversation today that was just unbelievable. It was, approximately: [*Adopts a baby voice*] Daddy.
Hello, darling.
[*In baby voice*] Hello, my Daddy. [*Makes small baby incomprehensible sounds*] [*Encouragingly*] Yeah?

[*More baby noises*]
Then she got stuck on la, la, la. [*Laughter*]

JR: David, you know what? There's a character on *Big Brother* who talks just like that. [*Laughter*] A girl called Jade who sounds just like her. Let's demystify you somewhat, just for my own sake, if not for others'. What is a good day for you, David? In New York, when you're not recording, what's a good, fun family day? What do you do?

DB: Ah, okay. I get up around 5:30, six, just about every morning. I make a lot of European phone calls at that time. That's when I go to the [web] sites, there are a couple of sites that I look after, not technically, but I'm kind of overall operator on them.

JR: This is the internet, of course. You're big on the internet.

DB: Yeah, yeah. I've got my own site, plus I've got an art site. The idea really is to help graduate students find some kind of way to show their work and get known without having to pay huge commissions to dealers, who usually take about 50 per cent of what an artist makes.

JR: That's still a better deal than you had in the seventies, isn't it, with your agency MainMan. You were getting about 10 per cent of your total fee, weren't you?

DB: I wasn't that lucky, Jonathan. [*Laughter*]

JR: Because you made nothing for years, didn't you?

DB: No, I made nothing. I had a lovely wardrobe, though. [*Laughter*] But a fat lot of good it does you when you're trying to find some place to live when you're dressed like that. [*Laughter*]

JR: Can you imagine, a bloke's come to look at the flat. It's Aladdin Sane outside. 'I'm sorry mate, we're full!' [*Laughter*]

DB: He's got a knitted cossie and its leg's missing and its arm's missing, and he's wearing like a fur thing and he wants to know if the room's available. [*Laughter*]

JR: Do you mind talking about your sexuality?

DB: [*Pretends to sniff his armpit*] Sorry, why?

JR: Because what was the deal there? You were gay for a while, then you were not gay.

DB: No, I was just happy. [*Laughter*]

JR: But were you bisexual, were you pansexual, were you trisexual? Because I thought being gay was a bit like the Foreign Legion, once you joined, I didn't think you were allowed back. [*Laughter*]

DB: Well, I was just very … I just got me leg over a lot.

JR: Did you have relationships with these people as well or was it …?

DB: Not if I could help it. [*JR laughs*] I was incredibly promiscuous.

JR: I bet you were.

DB: And I think we'll leave it at that. [*Laughs*]

JR: No, we can't! This is great stuff, David.

DB: No, it might be for you, son.

JR: But everyone wants to know. [*Laughter*] You must have had a great time.

DB: Why would I go into that when I can make a fortune by writing a book about it? Why should I give it to you for free? [*Laughter. DB rubs his fingers and thumb together to signify he wants the money*]

JR: Well, let me ask you this then, David. We'll get to the book in a minute. Should I …?

DB: Don't even think about it.

JR: Should I try… I've never tried the man-love? [*Laughter*] I haven't tried the man-on-man, the man-in-man, the man-with-man. I haven't tried it. I was tempted recently when David Beckham scored that penalty goal. [*Laughter*] Suddenly, I felt a stirring. Should I give it a try? [*Pause*] Father!

DB: Such a serious and a life-challenging and -changing question. The answer that I have for you would probably create such turmoil in your soul …

JR: You know, it probably would.

DB: … that I'm not sure that you could withstand it or, in fact, last the rest of the show, so I'm afraid I have to politely and reluctantly not answer that question. [*Applause*]

JR: Thank you for your concern and I respect you for that. Let me ask you something more specific. Mick Jagger has been knighted, he's Sir Mick Jagger. And we had the big concert at Buckingham Palace and, of all people, Ozzy Osbourne [*DB smiles*] was playing, amongst others. Does it interest you, that kind of thing? Would you like to be knighted? Would you accept that honour if it was bestowed upon you?

DB: Would I …? I think I would suggest that they give it to somebody who would give a damn. [*Applause*] There are some people who feel that maybe it's something that enhances their life and whatever. I'm not sure what I'd do with it. I'd lose it or break it, or put it in a drawer and lose the key. I wouldn't know what it's for. I wouldn't know how it would enhance my life.

JR: Sir David Bowie does sounds peculiar, it doesn't sound quite right, does it?

DB: It's just, I don't know, it's just not on my shopping list at all.

JR: Do you miss things about this country when you're not here? Because I know you're a fan of a lot of the new British comedy. You're a fan of League of Gentlemen, I believe?

DB: Yes, of course.

JR: Harry Hill.

DB: Harry Hill. I love Harry Hill, a terrific, manly, stalwart gentleman.

JR: Can I show you a clip? I don't know if you've seen this clip recently. I remember when it went out. You're on *The Kenny Everett [Video] Show* and, David, you'll forgive me, but it's one of the weirdest things I've seen. [*Laughter*] This must have been what, '80?

DB: Yeah, '80. I think it was the Christmas Eve show … it was New Year's Eve! Coming from '79 into the new decade.

JR: This is the way to celebrate it. David Bowie with Kenny Everett.

<*Footage of Bowie on* The Kenny Everett Video Show.>

[*Applause*]

DB: [*Adopts a Yorkshire accent and quotes from Monty Python's 'The Four Yorkshiremen' sketch*] And you try and tell that to the kids today. They don't believe you. [*Laughter*]

JR: That was so strange. Do you remember doing that?

DB: Yeah. Ah, he was lovely.

JR: He was lovely.

DB: Yeah, a smashing guy.

JR: You've worked with so many great people over the years. I was thinking about that Bing Crosby Christmas special you were on – when you sang 'Drummer Boy' with Bing Crosby, which is just such a fabulous but odd juxtaposition of iconic pop figures.

DB: I don't think he knew he'd sung it with me. He was already at a place where not much … he wasn't kind of reacting to very much around him. I mean he was pretty old by that time, and he was just this little old fella on a stool. [*Adopts a deep voice*] 'Hello, David.' 'Hi, Bing,' 'Hmm? [*Looks around as if confused*]' 'I'm David Bowie.' 'Hello, David.' Oh, dear. It was kind of like that.

JR: It's actually a wonderful piece of music together …

DB: It comes out every year. I mean [*Laughs*] it keeps going into the Christmas chart.

JR: Can I ask you about a period which I wasn't the biggest fan of, David?

DB: [*Laughs*] Go on.

JR: Tin Machine.

DB: Yeah.

JR: Now you were 42, 41, when you started Tin Machine?

DB: Oh, I can't do the math.

JR: Yeah, you were. That whole thing to me screams midlife crisis. [*Laughter*]

DB: Yeah, well it was. It really imploded on itself. We had a lot of personality problems within the band. I didn't realise what it meant to be in a real democracy until I demanded one. [*Laughter*]

JR: See, it doesn't work that way, does it?

DB: Uh oh! Bowie's demanding a democracy, watch out! [*Adopts a deferential tone*] 'Yes, sir. How do you want it run, sir?' [*Laughter*] It was like that, wasn't it? 'We're all going to be equal, okay?' 'Yes, sir!' [*More laughter*]

JR: Your internet site. David, I'm a member of your internet site. I have a BowieNet address. I go on, I log on, it's a fabulous-looking site.

DB: Oh, this is scary.

JR: It's great. I know we have people here involved with it as well. But I'm curious … when you're on the internet … because someone had told me, and I don't believe this is true, that Iman, your wife, limits the time you're allowed to spend on the internet.

DB: [*With a knowing grin*] She doesn't limit anything I do. [*JR laughs*] No, that's not true.

JR: But do you find it best to leave like a Word document open, so that if your wife comes in when you're looking at, for example, fatladybendsoverforyou.com, you can quickly click on the other thing, hence hiding the screen and therefore keeping the relationship intact? [*Laughter*]

DB: Let's go back a little while to an earlier problem that you have. Is this something to do with the man and man-love thing?

JR: No, I'm the least bi-curious guy you could meet, David. And yet I do like looking at pictures of naked ladies, ideally smiling. [*Laughter*]

DB: Good lord!

JR: You must occasionally look at a bit of the old porn on the internet, David?

[*Silence*]

JR: [*Chidingly*] David?

DB: No.

JR: That's a good thing, and as I grow slightly more sober and mature and decide that I would like to impress you, I'm going to stop looking at it as well. [*Laughter*]

DB: You're going to be a better man for it, you know, and your children are going to thank you.

JR: Well, the boy might want to find a few things lying around when he hits 13. [*Laughter*] You've got to pass a few magazines on to your little fella. What about your son? When Duncan was growing up, you must have …

DB: That little fella is 31 years old. [*Laughs*]

JR: Well, he'll hit puberty any day now! Did you ever have a father-son talk to him, like the birds and the bees thing? Because from you that must be quite something. [*Laughter*]

DB: Yeah, I believe it was more of a monologue. [*Laughs*]

JR: [*Pretending to be DB talking to his* son] It's the birds and the bees and molluscs and anything else you fancy, as long as no one gets hurt and it's consensual.

DB: I don't know. He'll have to remind me, I'm sure, but I think I was quite loutish about it, and quite graphic and full of bonhomie and backslapping and [*DB winks*] 'Hey!'. [*Laughter*]

JR: Did you find it tough being a dad first time around?

DB: Yeah, because I was absolutely not prepared for all the responsibilities that are inherently a part of it. Firstly, my son and I get on incredibly well and he's a wonderful man. He's grown up to be just beyond my expectations of what one's own child can grow up to be. He's just terrific, kind-hearted, honest, straight-ahead. He's just a great guy. And I'd like to be around for quite a long time for my daughter, too.

JR: And we would like you to be around for a long time too, not just for your daughter but for us as well, David, if that doesn't seem selfish.

DB: Oh, alright.

JR: Let's celebrate the release of the new David Bowie album, which is fabulous. I don't know if you have a copy, but it's fantastic.

DB: Thank you.

JR: It's called *Heathen*. It's out now. This is a terrific track off it called 'Everyone Says "Hi"'. But before we do that, David Bowie, [*Both rise and shake hands*] thank you so much.

DB: Oh, it's been a pleasure.

PARKINSON, BBC TV

INTERVIEWER: MICHAEL PARKINSON
OTHER GUEST: TOM HANKS

Much has been made of the positive influence Bowie's father had on him, but his relationship with his mother is often painted as fraught and distant. Of course, that certainly is true in part, but it's also revealing to hear that she, too, had a profound influence on his musical aspirations; operatically singing along to the radio on songs like 'O for the Wings of a Dove' and speaking to her young son about her dreams of becoming a professional singer.

Bowie recites, pretty near perfectly, the famous Larkin poem about your parents fucking you up. Parkinson, sensing an opening to this normally off-limits area of close family relationships, tries to edge in.

'So, you didn't like your mum and dad, or what they'd done to you?' asks Parkinson.

'O, wings of a dove!' sings Bowie.

And the door promptly closed on that line of chat.

<Bowie finishes performing. Wild cheers and applause. Parkinson makes a joke about how the audience must be from Brixton, Bowie's hometown.>

DAVID BOWIE: [*Laughs*] Just a couple, yeah. [*Looks out into the audience*] I recognise a lot of people from Hatfield there. [*Laughter*] [*Turns to fellow guest, Tom Hanks, and refers to the actor's earlier anecdote about sinking to the bottom of a swimming pool with bricks in his trunks and breathing through a hose*] Thanks for reminding me, and coming out about the garden hose, breathing through it. I thought I was the only one. [*Laughter*] How did you do it? I did it like that [*Puts his closed fist to his nose and inhales deeply; more laughter*]

MICHAEL PARKINSON: I'm a tad disappointed. I was told you might appear wearing the Little Richard jacket, [*DB laughs*] your great hero, which now you've acquired.

DB: I've acquired that through my wife. It was one of our wedding anniversaries a few months ago. And my idol when I was a kid was Little Richard, and she knew that, so she found one of his old, original stage jackets – 1956 – and she got it for me for an anniversary present. And *Little* Richard – he's huge! [*Makes sweeping gesture with hands*] I can use it as a tent in the garden. [*Laughter*] [*Inaudible*] He must have had really little legs and a big body, because the sleeves are down there on me. I saw him first in 1963, I think it was, I *think* it might have been at the Brixton Odeon – somebody will remember the tour … everybody remembers everything these days – and The Rolling Stones were opening up for him. It was the first time I ever saw them. And they weren't really very well known. There's about six kids rushed to the front. You know, that was their fan base at the time. Everybody was there for Little Richard, and I think Bo Diddley was on the show, and all that. And it was priceless; I'd never seen anything so rebellious in my life. Some guy yells out,

'Get yer hair cut!' And Mick [Jagger] says — and I'll never forget these words — [*Does a great Jagger impression*] 'Wot, an' look like yew?' [*Loud laughter and applause*] I thought, 'Oh my God, this is the future of music!' And sure enough ...

MP: But was it music that engaged you or was it the showmanship of it all?

DB: It was really ... it was really the music. [*Pause*] And the showmanship of it all. [*Laughter*] It was the combination, I think. My mother – she didn't realise what she was starting – but she would always say at breakfast, 'Oh, I could have been a singer, you know,' and then she'd sing. And there was this thing on radio, *Two-Way Family Favourites*, on a Sunday, when I was about six, and every Sunday without fail, this thing by Ernest Lough was sung and it was 'O For the Wings of a Dove.'

MP: That's right, a boy soprano.

DB: A boy soprano? Yeah, he's dead now.

MP: Yes, he's dead.

DB: And he was what, 90, when he died?

MP: His voice went before he died. [*Laughter*]

DB: And my mother was [*Sings operatically*] 'Oh, for the wings, for the wings of a dove. Far away, far away' and all this. [*MP laughs*] She was really good and I thought maybe she would be a singer, she'd be a great singer. So that was one of my first influences, Ernest Lough.

MP: But I mean, there you were in Brixton and then in Bromley – it was just that one moment seeing Little Richard that decided you, this is the life for me?

DB: It was seeing Ernest Lough, actually. I went along to the church and I saw him singing along there and I thought … But there were weird notes in that, and there were other things on the radio that really committed me to the idea of music, because it was the pieces of music that broke my expectations … I remember also in those days, Holst's *Planets* suite got played a lot, especially 'Mars'. [*Hums the menacing violin notes that start the piece*] Those notes were so weird, it didn't follow anything that I knew. Songs like that, and pieces of music where the notes didn't go the right way, really got me. Like 'Tubby the Tuba'. Do you remember?

MP: Ah, I do. 'Sparky and the Magic …'

DB: Nah, that had a regular …

MP: Sorry I mentioned that. [*Laughter*] 'Tubby the Tuba'.

DB: Well, that one was … da da da da da diddle de da [*Goes on for a few seconds*] … then there was this weird bit, don't forget that … da da [*Laughter*] da da da da! [*Pretends to strain to get to a higher pitch; MP joins in*] It was that note. Da! … da da da [*Points down and sings much lower*] duh. It was, like, awkward.

MP: This is the beginning where you got into rock'n'roll?

DB: Yeah, well, I liked Little Richard along with this stuff.

MP: But you mentioned, when you saw Little Richard, an interesting word: rebellion.

DB: Yeah.

MP: What was the purpose of your rebellion?

DB: Oh, I don't think I really ever had a rebellion.

MP: Oh, come on …

DB: No, I think against my mother and father, it was really no wider than that. You know it wasn't against the world generally. [*Laughs*] I wanted to get a lot of the world, as much as I could get.

MP: But what was wrong with your mum and dad?

DB: They fuck you up, your mum and dad. [*Laughter*]

MP: [*Laughs*] That's what Larkin said. But do you believe that to be true?

DB: With my mother, yeah. [*Laughs*] My dad was very … [*Tries to remember poem*] 'They fuck you up, your mum and dad. They may not mean to, but they do, and they fill you full of thoughts they had, and they add some extra just for you.' [*Laughter*] The last verse was good, what was the last verse, do you remember?

MP: No, I don't.

DB: It's 'Man hands misery on to man. It deepens like a coastal shelf. So get out as soon as you can, and don't have any kids yourself.' [*Laughter*] Now, that's an English poem, isn't it.

MP: So, you didn't like your mum and dad, or what they'd done to you?

DB: [*Ignores the question, sings*] 'Wings of a dove …' There's a funny note in that one, you see, 'Wiiiiings … of a dove'. [*Laughter*] Weird, innit?

MP: So, what I'm trying to get at now … I'm even more confused than when I first started …

DB: Oh, you don't know! [*Puts head in hands*] I confuse myself.

MP: And Tom Hanks sitting there is totally confused.

HANKS: No, I'm still going through 'Tubby the Tuba'.

MP: Where does Ziggy Stardust come from?

DB: Oh, Lord [*Closes eyes and covers mouth with hands*] … I don't know.

MP: That was the rebellion, was it, that was creating this alter ego?

DB: The thing is I never really wanted … I never really thought I could sing very well. I used to try on people's voices if they appealed to me when I was a kid, about 15 or 16, I got into Anthony Newley like crazy because, a couple of things about him … before he came to the States and did the whole Las Vegas thing, he really did bizarre things over here. A television series he did called *The Strange World of Gurney Slade*, which was so odd and off the wall; I thought, 'I like what this guy's doing, where he's going is really interesting.' So I started singing songs like him, but I was reading a lot of stuff by the angry young men generation, you know, Keith Waterhouse and John Osborne, stuff like that. So I was writing these really weird Tony Newley-type songs, but the lyrics were about, like, lesbians in the army and cannibals [*Laughter*] and paedophiles and things like that. I thought, 'Yeah, this is my bag! This is what my career is going to be like.' And the first album really is the most extraordinary piece of work in that way. I mean utterly forgettable, [*Both laugh*] but there's no faulting its ambitions.

MP: But what about this androgynous appeal you developed? Where did that come from, that feminine side of you?

DB: Oh, that's just me being camp, really.

MP: But when did you first start being camp?

DB: When I put those clothes on, funnily enough. [*Laughter*] It's amazing what it does to you, the first time you drag up, isn't it Tom?

HANKS: Ah, totally. It gave me a lucrative career, for a while anyway.

DB: No, I tell you what was even funnier, though, was getting my band to put the clothes on. Because my band were all from Yorkshire. I've got to tell you, my father was from Yorkshire.

MP: [*Himself a Yorkshireman*] From Tadcaster, right?

DB: Well somewhere between Tadcaster, Doncaster and York. So, he's from there and my mother's family are all from Lancashire, so when I hear somebody with your [accent], I'm nearly there, you know. [*Adopts a Yorkshire accent*] By heck, I've supped some stuff today. [*Laughter*] I can't help it. I'm trying desperately not to get into your accent, it's really hard.

MP: You do do it very well.

DB: You sound like my dad, you see. It's really off-putting. I won't look at you. [*Laughter*] I will actually, because he was a good man. So, these guys all came from [*Adopts a Hull accent*] Hull. 'We're going play in a rock'n'roll band, I like the songs and all that.' I said, 'Yeah. Do you want to see what we're going to wear?' 'Oh, yeah, right … [*Adopts a Hull accent*] No way! Not bloody likely. I'm not putting that on!' I said, 'No, believe me, you'll look great. It'll really suit you.' I don't know how I did it, but I managed to talk them into doing it, and a couple of nights later, we'd done a couple of shows, all these girls were all over them. Suddenly, the dressing room procedure was really different. [*Adopts a Hull accent*] 'Right, who's got the blush?' [*Laughter*] Heh, Trevor! Have ya finished with that mascara?' It was a phenomenal thing … a little bit of eyeliner.

MP: When you look back on that now …

DB: I look back on that as rarely as possible. [*Laughs*]

MP: But you remember it fondly?

DB: I do, yes, absolutely. We had some wild times, it was a fantastic period. We had no idea what we were doing, really didn't know which way the whole thing was going. I just knew that I was getting bored very quickly. The great tragedy of it, I suppose, in my eyes, was … well, not really, because it was great to let go of it … I tend to grasshopper about, my attention span is very short, as you can probably tell. [*Laughs*] We were only together for 18 months, the whole thing was over in 18 months, the whole Ziggy Stardust thing. And a good halfway through, nine, 10 months into it, I knew it was over already. I just wanted to move somewhere else, a new kind of music. I wanted to write something with a different kind of theatricality that I wanted to bring into it, and all that. The last few months I was really treading water; I couldn't wait to finish.

MP: The amazing thing is that you nearly threw all that away, all that creativity, through drugs. You got through it in the end.

DB: Yeah, well, I guess all that period was pretty fine. It was the later years, the later part of the seventies. My story, in terms of drugs and the alcohol and all that is no different to anybody else's, and it's almost a textbook story.

MP: Except you survived it.

DB: Yeah, well, a lot of us did, you know. I'm not the only one by any means.

MP: Just tell me, because I was fascinated in the research, you saw a guy on CNN, a doctor was talking about the effect that cocaine had on the human brain; I don't know if it changed your mind on drugs, but it certainly had the effect of making you not wanting to take drugs.

DB: Oh, that actually … no, that didn't put me off at all, actually. [*Laughter*] I saw that in the seventies and I said, 'Whoa, too cool!'

It was showing a brain of cocaine users and the holes that were in it – great, huge holes. I thought, 'Yeeaahh, that's me!' It didn't occur to me that this was a bad thing– that didn't come for quite a while later, really.

MP: And what started the change? What was it?

DB: You can't have relationships with anybody. You don't know anybody else exists. You become a really dreadful person, you know. And I just think I got fed up with being a dreadful person, actually. It's as simple as that. I guess I was lucky that I was able to knock it on the head, you know.

MP: And what about being a new father now, because you've got a two-year-old child now, haven't you?

DB: Yeah, I have indeed. Wonderful little girl, Alexandria, and also a wonderful boy, 31 years old. I've got two. I've got also a step-daughter, of course, Zulekha, who is 21.

MP: One imagines, of course, that the 31-year-old, that period of time when you had the boy, that you were an absent father in many ways?

DB: I was, you know. I was on tour all the time. I was very ambitious. I was young, I was keen to go and do these stage things, and I was just whizzing around the world half the time.

MP: Now, of course, you've got a chance to relive that, of course, recapture that?

DB: Absolutely, yeah. I mean I was very lucky in a way. The marriage, of course, went hopelessly wrong very early, but Joe was with me since he was five, six years old, so I was kind of a one-parent family since he was that age.

MP: Are you a New Age father now? Are you a nappychanger?

DB: No, I'm ridiculously Victorian, [*Laughs*] absolutely hopeless at that kind of thing. I've huge admiration for guys who can get in there like that. I just can't. I mean, well, my wife didn't let me, which was great. [*Laughter*] She was like, 'Oh, get out of here!' She was like pinning and wrapping things up. [*Mimes putting on a nappy*] I knew there was some kind of … something was being prepared and, at the end of it all, my little daughter came out! [*Laughter*] It's great. But I'm good at saying, 'This is a book, and we're going to look at this,' and, 'Come to this museum,' and I'm kind of fairly good like that.

MP: How much now is left of the lad from Brixton, do you think?

DB: Not very much, I would think. I never became who I should have been until maybe 12, 15 years ago. I've spent an awful lot of my life, as I think most people in the so-called entertainment industry, actually looking for myself, you know, and understanding what it was I existed for, what was it that really made me happy in life, and who exactly I was, and who are the parts of myself that I was trying to hide from a lot. You know, it's like exposing yourself. And I think a lot of us are, one: dysfunctional – in showbusiness this is, [*Adopts an American accent*] 'showbusiness' – pretty dysfunctional; and, two: in huge senses of denial about who we are and where we exist in the world. There's some kind of traumatism often goes on in our childhoods, I think, that makes us crave some kind of strange affection. Often, you'll find that the person who craves a lot of affection actually isn't terribly good at giving it. I found that all my life, especially in the seventies, I was like that. I really wanted to be very emotionally involved with people. I didn't know how to do it. My parents were like that and, I guess, as I say, Larkin's right in that way, they pass on a lot of faults.

MP: Do you buy that, Tom?

TH: Yeah, I think that's very true. We're in a narcissistic business, constantly figuring 'How do I do that? What do I have to do next? Let's talk about me. Enough about me. [*DB laughs*] What do you think of these shoes? Are these good shoes?'

MP: And what about the kind of problems your children have in dealing with this kind of narcissistic approach, if you like? Because the 'animal' is that … they can observe the effect that fame has on you and the way people react differently to you than they do to other people. That's something you can't really tell them about, isn't it? They have to make their own mind up about that? Is it as casual as that, or are there things you can do?

DB: Well, in my situation, I think my son watched me grow up. It was very strange for him in some ways. Sometimes I feel there's almost a protective quality about him when he's with me.

MP: He's looking after you.

DB: Well, he's not, but he is. You know what I mean? But I also feel the same way. I really want to protect him, too.

MP: Let's hear a classic song of yours, 'Life on Mars?'. But first of all, before we hear that, tell me how you came to write this song.

DB: [*Adopts a Yorkshire accent*] When I was just a little sprog …

MP: Would you do it all in a Yorkshire accent?

DB: No, no, no. [*Adopts a cockney accent*] I can't do any accent. [*Laughter*] I was with a music publishing company and they were passing me songs, lots of them from the – I was going to say from the Orient [*Laughs*] – some of them sounded like they came from the

Orient – a lot of songs from Europe that they wanted me to do kind of English translations. Not translations … a new set of English lyrics for. One of them was this French song that I thought was really very good, and I wrote some *really* terrible lyric. I think it was called 'Even a Fool Learns to Love'. I sent it back again and I thought, 'That's the last I'll hear of that.' Then I hear it on the radio, and I thought, 'That must be my song, but these are different lyrics. And it was Sinatra singing 'My Way'. [*Laughter*] And I was … but I wrote the lyrics, what happened? I phoned them up and they said, 'Oh yeah, your lyrics were rubbish.' 'I know that, but they were the ones I did.' They said, 'Well, we got Paul Anka to do them instead and this is "My Way".' And that really made me angry for so long, about a year. [*Laughter*] Eventually, I thought, 'I can write something as big as that and I'll write one that sounds a bit like it', and so I did [*Laughs*] 'Life on Mars?', which is my revenge trip on 'My Way'.

MP: Well, thank God you did. [*Laughter*] It's a lovely song. Shall we hear it? Your pianist awaits you. David Bowie, 'Life on Mars?'

LIFE ON MARS?

MP: Did you enjoy that, Mr Hanks?

TH: Oh, you know, oh …

MP: That's got to be the ultimate in performing, actually.

TH: Have you ever stayed at the Sunset Marquis hotel in Los Angeles?

DB: [*Sarcastically*] Ah, no. [*Laughter*] Yes, I know it very well.

TH: Legendary place.

DB: Been to a few parties there.

TH: I've gotten lost there a few times. [*DB laughs*] But the patio is split right in half. There's actors on one side and there's musicians on the other. [*DB laughs*] And the musicians are all looking at the actors, 'Look at those actors, they've got it so easy, they just say the lines, there's people who write for them, they don't have to work.' And the actors are all looking at the musicians, 'Look at those musicians, they've got it so easy, they've got to [*Adopts a baby voice*] play the guitar and get up and sing.' [*Laughter*]

DB: And the comedians down at the end.

TH: Yeah, they're all goofing around. They're asking you what you'd like to drink with your sandwiches.

DB: That's absolutely true. Every musician I know either wants to be an actor or a comedian. And comedians likewise want to be actors or musicians. I think there's quite a few actors who'd want to do …

MP: But you're happy doing what you're doing?

DB: Oh, absolutely. Completely.

MP: You find yourself in a kind of lagoon state of life?

DB: Really? That's really nice, I like that. With the hosep …
[*Mimes putting a hosepipe into his mouth to breathe to laughter*]

MP: David, after this, what? You're on tour at present …

DB: I'm going home. I'm missing my wife and baby like crazy. Have a good long writing thing [*Laughs*] … afterwards … [*Laughter*] … whoops, I didn't want to go there. Then Christmas comes and we'll be going through all that. I think my daughter's ready to really take the tree in now, you know. At two and a half, it'll make sense, won't it?

MP: Well, thank you for talking to me tonight. I've very much enjoyed it and hope to do it again sometime.

DB: It's been great meeting you both. It's been lovely.

MP: David Bowie! [*Applause*]

LATER ... WITH JOOLS HOLLAND, BBC TV

INTERVIEWER: JOOLS HOLLAND

Bowie would often get up early, around 5 am. As such, he liked to get home earlier than might be expected of a typical rock star. In his later years, he would often pop backstage to say hi to a band *before* they went on stage, as he'd most probably be in bed reading a book by the time they finished.

On this night, some of the bands on *Later ...* had overrun, so by the time Holland got to Bowie, the singer was noticeably irritable. Even before Holland got to his first question, Bowie was overtly looking at his watch saying there was something on TV he hoped to watch.

Despite the initial tension, Bowie relaxes quickly to talk about the cacophonous noise of the Legendary Stardust Cowboy which, he said, was so uniquely atrocious that he had fallen in love with the Texan singer immediately.

JOOLS HOLLAND: I'm very excited that you're here with us this evening. A marvellous band. [*Points to DB's band in the wings*] A marvellous new album that we're going to be …

DAVID BOWIE: [*Making a big show of looking at his watch*] I had a good night's viewing planned, so we've run a bit late, so I might have to …

JH: You want me to rush this?

DB: Yeah, let's get this done.

JH: Okay.

DB: I'll catch the next Miss Dynamite …

JH Well, just hang on for a moment, hang on.

DB: … and The Coral and then …

JH: Ah, well! Who in the room … we've got a big selection in here. Anybody here that …

DB: It's pretty cool, isn't it?

JH: What do you think it says?

DB: Beenie Man, The Coral, Miss D. What does it say? It says 'now' to me. [*Laughs*] I tell you one interesting thing that, apart from all the crap in the charts here, artists like Miss D and The Coral there give some strong indication that there's still a pulse in British music.

JH: There is still a pulse. You're a big influence of course, have been …

DB: I like British music, yeah.

JH: You're a big influence on it.

DB: Oh, am I?

JH: I'm afraid you are. [*Laughter*] We brought you here to tell you that.

DB: Oh, is that it?

JH: Yes. You have got this *Heathen* record out and it's a very good record.

DB: Thank you very much.

JH: I've had it in my car, up loud, and it works very well on the dashboard.

DB: It's easier to put it in a CD player, but a car will do. [*Laughter*]

JH: It does the job. You've got old Tony Visconti producing it.

DB: And he is old as well.

JH: Is he?

DB: Yeah.

JH: Why did you decide to go back with him? He did lots of your early things.

DB: Yeah, we stopped arguing. We started getting on as friends and all that. And we'd already done a lot of really good stuff together, so it was worth a chance of going back in and seeing what else we could do between us. I'm really pleased we did, it was a good move. It's a good album.

JH: His strings are great, aren't they?

DB: Fantastic.

JH: Also, as well as doing your own songs, you have covered quite a few interesting ones, like The Pixies and Neil Young. But I'm more interested in a man who I was a big admirer of a few years ago, The

Stardust Cowboy. Not many people know him … how did you find him? Who is he?

DB: [*Laughs*] He made positively the most cacophonous, awful records that had ever been made in the late sixties, and he was a stablemate of mine on the label in America called Mercury Records. One of the record executive guys over there said, 'You like weird stuff, dontcha, Dave?' And I smacked him, because nobody calls me Dave. [*Laughter*] So he said, 'You like really weird shit, dontcha, David?' And I said, 'Yeah.' And he said, 'Well, try this.' And he gave me a stack of singles by this guy and I thought they were unbelievably atrocious, but in that wonderful way that you couldn't stop listening to them, they were so awful.

JH: If he were to do 'Your Cheatin' Heart', it would be [*Pounds the piano with his fist and barks out*] 'Your cheatin' heart will tell on you!'

DB: Without the melody. [*Laughter*]

JH: It is like that, isn't it?

DB: Yeah, yeah. Well, his first one was called 'Paralyzed'. [*Plays random notes on the piano while shouting like a Sergeant Major*] 'Wah oh two, wah oh ya, here it comes, ah yeah, paralyse!' [*Laughter*] And it continues, and there's a bugle solo in the middle, which is to die for. [*Laughs*] And he won me over. His name, 'Stardust', became part of the Ziggy Stardust name.

JH: Is that right?

DB: That's where I got the name from.

JH: Interesting stuff coming out tonight. Actually, let's go back. I'm going to take you into the time capsule. We're zooming down here.

DB: Oh, shit. [*Laughter*] I bet I've got silly hair.

*STARMAN (*Top of the Pops*)*

JH: What a treat!

DB: Nearly 30 years ago. That blue guitar … it was just a regular guitar … I gave it into the garage where I went, and I got them to do the blue that I'd seen on sports cars that they'd done metallic blue. And they did that for me. It's very nice. I smashed that up a couple of years later when I was drunk, unfortunately. [*Laughter*]

JH: Oh, over somebody? Or just in the general smash-up …

DB: I was pissed that I hadn't spent my money on a car, a decent car, blue, the same colour.

JH: Out of interest, what's your favourite song on *Heathen*?

DB: I think probably '5.15 The Angels Have Gone'.

JH: I like 'I Would Be Your Slave'.

DB: Yeah? You like that?

JH: I like that very much.

DB: Thank you.

JH: But what I want to know is what are you going to play for us in a moment?

DB: '5.15 The Angels Have Gone'. [*Laughter*]

JH: How very, very convenient. [*Laughter*]

JONATHAN ROSS, BBC RADIO

INTERVIEWER: JONATHAN ROSS

Did David Bowie really keep pigeons in a loft on the roof of his New York penthouse? No, surely not. But he had such an ability to make the seemingly unbelievable so credible that you end up half believing him. In researching this book, I actually called up his PR team to try to check if the following 'David as pigeon-keeper' story had any basis in fact! Even though it's highly improbable, we never did get to the bottom of it.

This is Bowie free-styling, talking about Elton kaftans (or djellabas, which he calls 'jubblys') and the deluxe multi-keyboard Stylophone (again, all make-believe), playing a didgeridoo (possibly true?) and still leaving time to give a shout-out to his schoolfriend George Underwood, who was about to exhibit his paintings at a London gallery. Bowie was as charming as ever.

JONATHAN ROSS: Top quality! He's back again! All the way from Brixton, the 8th of January 1947 to New York today, where he is sitting on the end of a telephone – no doubt dressed as a Turkish potentate – David Bowie! David, how are you?

DAVID BOWIE: I'm wearing a jubbly.

JR: You see, a jubbly, that's a Moroccan kaftan, isn't it?

DB: No, that's the Elton kaftan.

JR: Oh no, you can't go that way.

DB: Morning, everyone, how are you?

JR: David, it's a room full of David Bowie fans, because we've got Siouxsie and Budgie from The Creatures here.

<All exchange hellos and light-hearted banter.>

JONATHAN ROSS: Hey, David, the new single sounds fantastic.

DAVID BOWIE: Thank you very much.

JR: Congratulations! And I'm not just saying that. I would have said it, even if I didn't like it, but I actually do like it.

DB: [*Laughs*] I know you would!

JR: But I do like it, which is fantastic. This is a taste of the album? This is what it's going to be like? It's more …

DB: Yeah, I suppose, I don't know. It's just a collection of songs; there's no real through-line to it. I like it a lot, though. I'm going on the road, so I'm looking forward to touring it.

JR: And is this you working with Visconti again, Mr Tony Visconti?

DB: Yeah, and this time a lot of the stage band that I've had over the last eight, nine years are pretty much the musicians on it, so it's pretty much representative of the stage, I suppose.

JR: Siouxsie and Budgie, you must have seen David live. You've played on his tour … Because the Glass Spider Tour – that was pretty much your worst tour, wasn't it, David?

DB: That was actually pretty much the way that we're planning this next tour. [*Laughter*]

SIOUXSIE SIOUX: Inflatables!

DB: It was singularly responsible for bringing abseiling [*Laughter*] into the rock'n'roll arena, which has some merit to it, really.

JR: David, am I imagining it or, on the tour, did you have a bloke come out on crutches at one stage?

DB: That's right.

JR: I remember a dancer coming out on crutches and remember thinking, 'Okay, he's lost me!'

DB: Well, he couldn't dance.

JR: Should have got Rolf Harris.

DB: Yes, you had Rolf on your show this morning.

JR: Oh, we had Rolf on and he brought two pristine Stylophones with him and we jammed.

DB: Did he bring one of those multi-keyboard Stylophones?

JR: No! No!

DB: When Harris and I kind of came up with the Stylophone thing in the sixties, they thought they were in for huge sales. [*Laughter*] So they started bringing out all these incredible, complicated Stylophones.

JR: I like to think that in an alternative universe somewhere, that's the only instrument left.

DB: I tell you what, I did bring a didgeridoo, because I do play didgeridoo.

SS: Can you do the cyclical breathing?

DB: Hold on, give me a second, because you've got to light the fire and heat the water up before it starts working. [*Laughter*] I've got it mainly going here. Hold on a second. [*Sound of a didgeridoo being played really well comes down the phone line*] Bowie then pants heavily.

JR: Incredible.

SS: And he's out of breath, so he did it himself.

[*Inaudible chat*]

DB: Then you finish off the phrase and you go … [*More didgeridoo sounds*] Pretty impressive, isn't it?

JR: Thanks for sharing that.

DB: I can do that all morning.

SS: Did Rolf bring his extra leg?

JR: Nah, he didn't have his extra leg with him.

DB: I saw you, Siouxsie, and you were really excellent, many, many years ago.

SS: It would have to be many years ago.

DB: I was clutching my copy of *The Scream*, I think, probably.

SS: Ah! Those were the days … many years ago.

DB: And what I loved was that little Apache dance that you did on stage. I used to love that. I probably nicked that for a few gigs.

SS: Well, I was into my Indians.

JR: I always thought you were like one of those chickens standing on a hot plate. [*Laughter*]

SS: This cheeky Jonathan Ross, what are we going to do with him? I'm sitting next to him … I think I'll pinch him.

JR: Ouch! David is now 72, okay. He's in incredibly good shape. When he was here last time, he did a lot of kangaroo hops for us. You remember that, David? You came in, and we were talking about the original Legendary Stardust Cowboy, and you'd seen him hop around on stage, or something, and you did it and I could not believe how flexible your knees are.

DB: My knees are talk of the town.

JR: Do you still do the boxing training, you still do the stretching?

DB: Yeah, I do. I don't like to talk about it too much because I'd be hopeless in an actual match.

SS: Jonathan's offering to be a punchbag when you next join him …

JR: You know we had Ricky Gervais, who I know David is a fan of as well. Ricky was over here. Did you see the celebrity boxing he took part in, David?

DB: No!

JR: He boxed someone. [*Inaudible*] I propose we put him in the ring with you.

DB: That's not a bad idea, is it? He could just tell jokes at me, I'd collapse.

JR: Nah, you're faster. Come on, you'd be able to jab him, get in there.

DB: Yeah, I could jab.

> <*Ross says goodbye to Siouxsie and Budgie, and plays a song by The Bees.*>

JR And we have David Bowie live with us from New York City. David, thanks so much for calling. I really do appreciate it, genuinely.

DB: Not at all. That was lovely, that piece.

JR: It's a nice track. They're a great band. You've always had a ear for new music. Who are you listening to at the moment?

DB: I don't know. I guess I've gotten a bit stuck into me own thing at the moment. I'm listening, obviously, to the new Grandaddy's album, which I actually like. I know it's not received that much …

JR: I haven't heard the Grandaddy's. It's alright? It's good, yeah?

DB: Yeah, it's not bad. It's called *Sometime*.

JR: Do you like The Kings of Leon?

DB: Yeah, nah, bit too hardrock thing for me.

JR: This is what interests me about you. Sometimes you veer – sometimes you're doing the hard rock, you've had periods in your career where you've done the hard rock-y stuff; you've had your soul period, you've done that kind of stuff.

DB: It's kind of a bit quirky, my rock. I don't think I've done straightforward R'n'B rock since 'Jean Genie'-type stuff.

JR: I've got in front of me an old, early CD release of *The Man Who Sold the World* with the extra tracks on, but I was thinking of 'Running Gun Blues' and 'Black Country Rock' on that. Had a real Led Zeppy feel to it.

DB: Yeah, I guess that was the harder stuff; that was really the first kind of flames of the [Mick] Ronson thing, really. Terrific.

JR: How much does what you are listening to, though, colour what you are producing in any given time?

DB: That's hard to say. I guess other people would say more than I would. I hope it doesn't, particularly. I think I go back to the past an awful lot.

JR: I'm interested that the new album has some cover versions on, because *Pin-Ups* [a covers LP] was such an incredible album, and a huge success for you, as well. But you are doing two covers on the new album, is that right?

DB: Yeah. One from Jonathan Richman and the Modern Lovers called 'Pablo Picasso'.

JR: Now I didn't have you figured as a Jonathan Richman fan.

DB: Oh, he was terrific. I guess he's still terrific. He's up in Boston somewhere, still writing.

JR: He is still terrific. He does quite a lot of Spanish-language stuff as well now.

DB: Does he really? Well, we plonked a Spanish guitar on our version of 'Pablo Picasso'.

JR: I think that was from the first Modern Lovers album wasn't it? Along with 'Ice Cream Man' and …

DB: … and it was covered at some point later on by John Cale and The Velvets.

JR: I can't wait to hear your version of it.

DB: It's totally … it's completely unrecognisable, actually.

JR: Otherwise, why do a cover, I guess. And you do a George Harrison song, as well.

DB: Yeah, ironically that was unwitting, because for me it was always a Ronnie Spector single. I think it was the last single produced by Apple Records back in '74 or something, and Harrison produced it for her with Phil Spector, and I got it around that time because I was totally gaga over Ronnie Spector; I always thought she was absolutely fantastic.

JR: She's still a fine-looking woman.

DB: Oh, she's a terrific-looking woman, yeah.

JR: Incredible voice as well. Does she still perform?

DB: Yeah, a couple of years ago she did one of the last things that Joey Ramone produced, he produced a little kind of EP with her, and she still sounds absolutely great. So, I covered it as a Ronnie Spector song, and it kind of really only dawned on me afterwards that I'd actually done a tribute to George, which is, I guess, a lovely thing to have happened, really.

JR: Presumably, you're going to be playing the new material live when you come back. The last tour that I went to see, you played all of the new *Heathen* album and all of the *Low* album, back to back. What are you plans for this new tour?

DB: We're not going to duplicate it because that worked out so well, and I didn't want to ruin that by repeating the same thing. We're doing an awful lot from *Heathen* and from *Reality*, the new album, and I've certainly pulled out a lot of interesting things from the past and the near past as well, going back to things like [The] 'Motel' and 'Battle for Britain'. But there again, I'm also putting in things like 'Suffragette City' … [*Inaudible*] And, on Monday, we're having a crack at 'Win' from the *Young Americans* album.

JR: Oh yeah! Fantastic!

DB: 'Loving the Alien', we're doing, I think. So, some interesting things we're doing.

JR: The new European tour is kicking off on October the 7th in Copenhagen. In the UK, Manchester, the 17th of November.

DB: When are we doing the Orpington Civic?

JR: Now, hold on a second, David. I know why you're choosing 17th of November.

DB: Why's that?

JR: You know why.

DB: I haven't got a clue, Jonathan.

JR: David …

DB: Because it's your 15-year marriage anniversary.

JR: No, that's August 23rd. Don't be silly.

DB: Listen, congratulations on that.

JR: Thank you. 17th of November – it's my birthday.

DB: Oh, Jonathan! How awful of me to forget.

JR: Don't pretend you didn't know. We know you've built your calendar around it.

DB: Actually, yeah, you guessed.

JR: Ain't that sweet. David decided to kick off his UK tour on my birthday as a kind of gift for me.

DB: I didn't realise …

JR: Don't say you didn't realise. Don't spoil the moment! [*Both laugh*] I can't wait for the new album. Presumably, you've recorded most of it, or all of it, now?

DB: It's all finished, all mixed and we're actually into rehearsals right now.

JR: Which internet site can I go to to find a bootleg copy of it?

DB: Actually, you will have a problem at the moment. This week, I shouldn't say this, it's tempting fate, this week there's nothing up there yet.

JR: Well, fingers crossed, because often they do sneak out early.

DB: Don't go to Kazaa.

JR: No, we won't do that. You must be enjoying this at the moment, because *Heathen* was such a huge hit for you, deservedly so.

DB: Yeah, it's fantastic. I can't think of anything better at the moment. I'm producing music that I really feel proud of, I've got a fantastic band, and the tours that we've been doing have been going down a storm.

JR: And, of course, home life seems to be going great, as well. How's the baby?

DB: That's even better. Well, the loveliest thing is that we've just built a pigeon shed on top of the roof here, which is really good. So I'm up here at the moment in the pigeon shed, feeding the pigeons, and I've got a little Bunsen burner here so I can make coffee. Moby's place, which is just over the road, he's about two streets away, he got me on to this thing, keeping pigeons.

JR: Do you send pigeons to each other?

DB: Yeah, song ideas. We kind of tie them to the legs of pigeons and send them backwards and forwards.

JR: If you had a very robust pigeon you could send him over with an iPod strapped on, [*DB laughs*] and then you could swap music that way.

DB: That's innovative, Jonathan. Almost as good as abseiling.

JR: A different way of file sharing. What happened to that giant glass spider you had on that tour? Where's that now? Is that in storage somewhere?

DB: That's down in the basement. [*Laughs*]

JR: You should let the kids play with it. That's for Alexandria when she's a bit older. 'Dad's got a glass spider downstairs; if you're very good, I'll let you go and slide on it.'

DB: It's her birthday in a few days' time.

JR: How old is she now? Three?

DB: Will be, yeah.

JR: Wow, that's gone quickly.

DB: Extraordinary, isn't it?

JR: Are you having another one?

DB: No, no, no. She's great. She's absolutely fantastic. All we want.

JR: David, I couldn't be happier for you, I really couldn't. I'm so enjoying the new music you're making, as always I'm enjoying all your old stuff.

DB: Do tell me, how is Ricky? Because I hear from him occasionally.

JR: Ricky Gervais is fine. He is, as always, not the easiest man to look at for any period of time, [*DB laughs*] due to his just general grotesqueness. He looks rather like a sketch by [Thomas] Rowlandson, doesn't he? He's got that kind of look.

DB: He does somewhat, yeah.

JR: He's got the Brueghel feel about him. But he's a lovely fellow, as you know, a thoroughly decent bloke.

DB: Yeah, I like him very much, indeed. I've turned on so many Americans to that series [*The Office*]. They don't get it immediately, they're not sure if this is supposed to be [*Adopts an American accent*] 'the reality thing', or whatever, but once they do … the whole band love it now.

JR: Are you watching other British comedy, other British TV at the moment?

DB: Not really. That's about it, I suppose. Not really watching that much. I seem to be a bit too busy for all that.

JR: Have you seen the new series of *Bo' Selecta!*?

DB: No, I saw the first series, which I *kind of* liked bits of. I like the Michael Jackson skits, very funny.

JR: I'm curious, because someone like you who lives in New York, you're tapped into a lot of what's going on here.

DB: I get to see everything and, of course, I listen to your show lots, because we can pick up these days on the internet any radio that we want.

JR: You know what, I was watching *The Man Who Fell to Earth* the other day, as I often do. I really love the film. The scene when your character is sitting there watching dozens of televisions. In actual fact, what we have with the internet, that's not that far …

DB: It's not that far from the truth. Nic Roeg really had some extraordinary ideas in that film that came to pass: the Kirlian photography and the idea of the sound on the chrome-looking ball, kind of anticipated the CD. He had some extraordinary things in it. Listen, can I just make … my mate George Underwood. You know George.

JR: Yes, George Underwood who designed the *Ziggy Stardust* …

DB: He did the *Ziggy Stardust* thing, he did *the Space Oddity* album way back then. He's got a show of his paintings at the Portal Gallery [Portal Painters] starting on the 20th of October, I just wanted to say that.

JR: And that's here in London somewhere.

DB: Good luck, George!

JR: That's very kind of you.

DB: He's a great painter. In class one day, our English mistress – this is like when we were 10 or something, maybe a bit older, and she said – she didn't like him at all because he was making jokes all the time, disrupting the class – and she stood him up one time and said, 'Underwood, I want you to make a sentence using the phrase, "herd of cows".' So, he said, "Men from Mars have never heard of cows." [*Both laugh*]

JR: I'm surprised you didn't cut that out and put it in the lyrics.

DB: It's smashing, isn't it?

JR: David, we've got to go because we've got to play a track and we've got to say goodbye. In September, you're going to come on the talk show?

DB: I'd love to.

JR: That would be fantastic.

29 NOVEMBER 2003

PARKINSON, BBC TV

INTERVIEWER: MICHAEL PARKINSON

OTHER GUESTS: CLIVE JAMES AND VICTORIA BECKHAM

Reality will be Bowie's last album for 10 years. This interview catches him in the middle of his tour and in fine fettle. He and broadcaster Clive James crack jokes about 'Big' Little Richard and poetry. Bowie gets a little touchy when Parkinson suggests New York is a dangerous place. No more than pretty much anywhere else, Bowie suggests.

Bowie has rediscovered his love of playing live – perhaps inspired by the success of the *Heathen* tour – so much so that many of the new songs written for this album were composed with a specific view to playing live.

Producer Tony Visconti was back on the control knobs, with Bowie saying how their relationship had immediately slipped back into 'stunningly comfortable'; and the reviews were again overwhelmingly positive. Bowie looked great and sounded great. But he had embarked on what would prove to be his final tour.

DAVID BOWIE: Picking up from something you said, I always wanted to be 5 foot 2, Black musician ... Little Richard.

MICHAEL PARKINSON: That's what you wanted to be, is it?

DB: But surgery wouldn't have helped at all. [*Laughter*]

CLIVE JAMES: I met Little Richard. He's not little. He's about 7 feet high!

DB: It's the other Little Richard! [*Laughter*] That's his big brother.

CJ: Big Little Richard.

DB: Big Little Richard, yeah. But he's got funny eyes, did you notice that? He's got these, [*Points to his eyes*] he's got my eyes.

MP: Has he?

DB: Yes, it's a deal we made. Swapping eyes. Nice book of poetry. [*Looks over to CJ, who had been reading out some of his poetry*] That first poem was really funny, that's really good.

CJ: That's music to my ears.

DB: 'The book of my enemy has been remaindered' ... yes!

CJ: [*Laughs*] It was a true emotion, yeah.

DB: It's a very rock'n'roll kind of sentiment in that. 'Buddy's album? [*Looks upset*] Oh no, really, nobody's buying it? [*Turns away and looks delighted*] Yes!!!' So, a really horrible but very human trait.

MP: Did you ever think of ... did you ever write poetry yourself?

DB: No, no, I'll just stay with the rock lyric, it's what I do best. The poetry that I have written always looks like it needs a melody with it, and that's what it ends up as ... this time it'll be a [*Adopts an upper-class accent*] po-em. It goes down like a poem, but then I end up reading it [*Taps his leg on the floor*] like that. But I can't write on tour, because I'm touring at the moment.

MP: I know that.

DB: It's not anything I can do on tour.

MP: I can't imagine that you … how old are you now?

DB: I'm going to be [*Looks up to think*] … 70, in three weeks' time. Something like that.

MP: [*Laughs*] You are not 70!

DB: So, I'm doing better than both of you, yeah? [*Looks at MP and CJ; laughter*] You know, I thought about that, it's only 13 years for me to be 70, and that's only as long as I've been married to my wife. So, I looked at how long is that going to feel from now till 70 so I went [*Makes whizzing noise and spins fingers*] backwards through time to when I first met my wife. Do you know, it's not long.

MP: It's not, is it?

DB: No. It's really just round the corner.

MP: As you get older, things gallop away from you. Like the years gallop away from you.

DB: They certainly do. Friends and everything. [*Mimics galloping away; laughter*]

CJ: But there's one big advantage, which he's not going to need, and you're not going to admit to, and that's the bus pass. I just got mine.

DB: Buy your own bus, it's easier. [*Laughter and applause*]

MP: How very rock'n'roll! Did you ever imagine touring as long as you've been touring?

DB: No, I had this poetic, romantic, kind of juvenile idea that I would be dead by 30. All artists think, 'I'll be dead by 30 – I'm going to get TB and die' – loss of blood, Aubrey Beardsley and all that. But you don't, you get past that, and then suddenly you're 30 and you're 40, and then you're 50 and 57, and all that, and it's a new land. I'm a pioneer, me and my kind.

MP: That's right.

DB: Christopher Isherwood … 'Me and my kind.' Just sort of scraping the edge of what this thing is about being a rock'n'roller at the age of 57. But my revenge is, all these bands below us, they've got to do this. So, they're saying, 'Yeah, they're really old,' but secretly, they're thinking, 'I better watch how he does it, because I'm going to get there soon.'

MP: [*Laughs*] Because there's no precedent …

DB: Travis! [*The band had just played. DB adopts a Scottish accent to mimic singer Fran Healy*] 'I bet he dyes his hair. That's never natural blond.' [*Laughter*]

MP: That's true, you're the first generation, of course.

DB: It's not a wig, either. [*Pulls at his hair*] Do you know, it's funny we were talking about 'toops', toupés … I wonder if I should name him? No, I better not.

MP: Go on.

DB: Celebrity. No, I can't do that, it's not my thing. My hairdresser used to work for him and was sacked because he didn't glue his toupé down properly for stage one night. And he has a fan in front, like we all do, to keep us cool. And the fan was going, and he was doing something very attractive and highly sensitive on the guitar and his 'toop' is like a dancing furry animal on the top of his head. And the audience were like in fits, they were falling into the aisles ... and this sensitive, very socially serious kind of writer was ... he went apeshit after the show.

MP: I've sat opposite and peered at some of the best toops in the business, as you can imagine, and I used to have an irresistible urge to pull one off. [*Laughter*] I used to sit on my hands at times, because I'd sit there thinking ...

CJ: You have to make sure they've got one, because sometimes [*Laughter*] they'll look as if they've got one ...

MP: I could see the canvas! This was in the days when the toops were not like they are now.

CJ: You see, Ronald Reagan did not wear a toop. They used to take him at night, while he was asleep, and dip him upside down in a bathful of ink [*Laughter*] so that his hair was black. Someone once said he was prematurely orange, but I tell you one thing for sure, he did not wear a wig. He just looked as if he wore one.

MP: You could make a very bad mistake.

CJ: Whereas I saw Charlton Heston once in Hollywood ...

DB: He wasn't really a president, he just looked as if he were a president. [*Laughter*]

MP: What's the difference between touring now and touring as that manifestation, as Ziggy?

DB: The big difference probably is Jordan's breasts are even bigger now [*Laughter*] than in Ziggy's day. Well, you know, this god came to me and say, 'Let there be Ziggy,' and I said, 'What's he going to look like?' 'Like Eddie Izzard without the breasts.' [*Laughter*]

MP: You're just jealous.

DB: It's hard … Eddie wasn't around. Eddie came to the show the other night and, you know what, we didn't talk about high-heeled shoes, we talked about machine guns and different types of artillery.

MP: Was he in female mode?

DB: No, no, no. He was in Eddie mode, I suppose – simple nail varnish and a cashmere sweater. [*Laughter*] And he was thoroughly charming. But he's violence-crazy, you know. He's totally into the army thing. He loves talking about operations and how you defeat the enemy … with lipstick and handbags. [*Laughter*]

MP: But what was Ziggy about? What was that gay Martian?

DB: The premise was, men are from Mars, I'm from Bromley. [*Laughter*] I'm just a bit different from other men in that way, and I just saw the world in another kind of fashion. I don't know … it was about pushing together all the pieces and all the things that fascinated me culturally, everything from kabuki theatre to Jacques Brel to Little Richard to drag acts. Everything about it was a hybrid of everything I liked, because it seemed to me that rock'n'roll was such a fundamentally American thing that they believe in, and they still do believe it to have an intrinsic American value, and I knew it wasn't English. We weren't really rock'n'rollers, we were kind of just playing around with the idea of rock'n'roll. And I thought, let's take that to the next stage … how far can you talk about rock'n'roll but with using rock'n'roll? – it got quite arty, in that way.

MP: It was very, very theatrical as well. What's been curious is that you've never explored that avenue, musical theatre.

DB: No, I've been approached several times, but it's been the usual thing about cobbling together a lot of my songs and developing a rather dodgy storyline to go along with it. I don't want to do that. I quite like the idea of writing something musically theatrical for *a* stage, maybe a travelling stage, like a rock'n'roll tour in some way. But I don't like musical theatre very much, believe it or not. I actually don't get off on it. I think it's pretty crappy, both on Broadway and in London. I don't think it's got much to give.

MP: But when you're talking about travelling theatre, there's an echo, isn't there, with your father?

DB: Yes.

MP: Tell me about your father.

DB: Well, he was orphaned very, very young. He was about four years old in fact, so he never knew his parents. One was killed in the First World War, and his mother died tragically not long after that. And he went into care, then he went to live with one of his aunts. But he was left all this money when he was about 16 years old, so he bought [*Laughs*] a theatre troupe. [*Laughter*] Oh, what a wise idea! [*More laughter*] He toured it into the ground. It never made a penny, but the little that he had over, he opened up a nightclub for boxers and wrestlers and gangsters in London, [*MP laughs*] which also folded up very quickly. Then he got an ulcer, a duodenal ulcer, and then he had a dream! And the same god that told me about Ziggy said, 'Go into children's homes.' So, he started working for a charity organisation from that point, and worked there, Dr Barnardo's, for the rest of his life.

MP: He sounds a remarkable man, actually.

DB: Not now – he's dead, [*Laughter*] but he was remarkable.

MP: And also an influence on you, because … there are echoes …

DB: I tell you what, he had all these books from … was it Readers Book Club, or one of those things? And they all had the same cover, but in different colours, but they were quite wonderful books. So, I got my first taste of Hemingway and things like that, because you get one every two months or something, they come through the post, and I'd read them after him. So, between him and my half-brother, I got quite a good reading background.

MP: He was a Yorkshireman, too, of course. You missed that most important part.

DB: Yeah, Tadcaster.

MP: Let's go back to what Victoria [Beckham] was talking about. You've gone through all this celebrity bit with knobs on.

DB: I didn't like it, yeah.

MP: You talk in the past tense.

DB: Yeah, yeah.

MP: You've still got it.

DB: No, you see, it's just a personal choice, I guess, but I kind of opted out of it. I'm not a secretive person, but I live a quite private life, my wife and I; and we just find that we're happiest in a place where we can remain and live our life, on a day-to-day basis, very anonymously. We actually find that in New York – it's very easy for us, and it's a way of living that we like.

MP: It's better in America, isn't it, for people like yourselves?

DB: Some parts of America. I think New York, downtown, where we are.

MP: You are more anonymous there than anywhere else?

DB: Yeah, well, one thing … it's always been kind of an artistic area, I guess – there's a lot of painters and musicians and writers there. The flavour of it is more … a little more cosmopolitan feeling and fairly sophisticated in that way. They don't really go, [*Lifts his hands up in shock*] 'Funny hair! Make it sign something.' [*Laughter*] You don't get that down there, but you do in LA and you do in Paris and, my God, you get it in London, don't you? [*Looks at Victoria Beckham*] It's a nightmare in this country, really. But I love the audiences and [*Adopts a schmoozing American accent*] 'Hey! I love your little people.' And all of that. But I can't stand the intrusion of the press, so I just don't put up with it.

MP: Having said all that about New York, of course, I mean it's a dangerous place, because John …

DB: [*Forcefully*] It's a dangerous place here.

MP: But John …

DB: This place is very dangerous.

MP: But John Lennon …

DB: A lot of really dangerous stuff happens in this country.

MP: Yeah, but talking about the celebrity …

DB: Well, no, you're emphasising something that happened once, many years ago.

MP: Of course, of course.

DB: [*Pretends to look quizzical*] What happened to George Harrison? Oh, I don't know. Or the Queen, somebody … You know, it's not just New York. That's rubbish. It's like saying the terrorists will only ever attack New York. You know, I wouldn't bank on that.

MP: Hear, hear. But you knew Lennon, didn't you?

DB: Yeah, very well.

MP: You met him through Liz Taylor.

DB: I met him through Liz Taylor. She handed to me what she purported to be a script. This thing called the … I can't even … *The Blue Bird*? 'Fire Bird'?

MP: *Blue Bird.*

DB: I know it wasn't Stravinsky. Far from Stravinsky. It was *Blue Bird*! She said, 'Read this, make it with me, be my leading man.' And it was such, [*Puts his hands to his mouth in horror*] such an awful script. I was so excited when she handed it to me. 'Oh, Liz Taylor's giving me a script, and we're in Hollywood. And I'm … [*Puts his hand to his heart*] 13 years old …' You know. No, I wasn't, that's a lie. [*Laughter*] And I got through this thing and it was absolutely awful; but she did invite me to a wonderful party that she threw, and I met Lennon there and we went on to a great relationship over the years. Terrific guy – very, very funny guy.

MP: Do you have any plans at all [for acting]?

DB: No, no, no. My crushing fear is that I would have to study acting and all that. I'd love to be a film star. I kind of fancy that because you get the name on the poster, big picture, they airbrush all the lines out.

It's fantastic. 30-foot tall. But you've got to do all this work to do that. [*Laughter*] Nah, let's be just kind of rock'n'roll. That's where my heart is, and I like doing that work. It's accumulated so many methods of working itself out – rock music – and it's taken on board so many other kinds of information from other musical styles. It's really growing and developing.

MP: Okay, well you are part of all that. Thank you for being my guest.

DB: It's my absolute pleasure.

MARC RILEY, BBC RADIO

INTERVIEWER: MARC RILEY

Bowie's last ever radio interview (which follows this one) would be for a relatively obscure late-night show for jazz aficionados. Naturally. What else should we have expected from the Master of the Unexpected?

But this interview with Marc Riley marks one of Bowie's last, if not *the* last, interview before his heart attack in June on stage in Scheeßel, northern Germany. He would perform publicly only a handful more times; with Alicia Keys, Arcade Fire, Dave Gilmour and to introduce Ricky Gervais with 'Little Fat Man'. His heart attack would not only end his touring life – it would also, in effect, mark his retirement from public life.

Two days before Scheeßel, Bowie had complained of severe chest pains while performing in Prague. In hindsight, two things stand out from that night in the Czech Republic. Firstly, why didn't the hospital doctors take his condition more seriously? Secondly, that Bowie performed through a heart attack, such was his determination to not let his audiences or bandmates down no matter the personal cost, and it's worth detailing the events as they happened.

During the Prague set, Bowie was in such pain, he had to leave to let the band play two songs without him. Coming back on, he told the audience, 'Let me tell you what's happening here. I've got a severely pinched nerve … and I'm having intense pains across my shoulder and into my chest. So, I'm going to keep going as best as I can … but I must let you know, I'm in terrible pain, okay?' The crowd applauded him in gratitude.

He managed two more songs, 'China Girl' and 'Modern Love', before having to vacate the stage again. An announcer, in Czech, asked the crowd to wait patiently for 10 minutes.

When Bowie came back on yet again, bassist Gail Ann Dorsey said that he was now so unwell that they had to find a stool for him to sit on. 'I do apologise,' said Bowie. 'This doesn't usually happen, so look at it as a bonus. [*Bowie laughs and the audience cheers*] They just gave me some pills to try and take the pain away, so we'll see how it goes. Anyway, let's keep going. How you doing?' he asks the audience to another round of cheers and applause. He manages another song, but as the chords to 'Changes' start, he says, 'I'm sorry, folks. I just can't continue. I'm in too much pain. I have to bid you goodnight. I'm so sorry.' With that, he leaves the stage a final time.

He was taken to hospital, but incredibly doesn't seem to have been checked over for a heart attack. Given the symptoms Bowie described of *both* shoulder and chest pain (pinched nerve pain is usually localised to one specific area while heart attacks often have more diffuse pain), any standard hospital procedure would likely be to rule out the most dangerous possibility with an electrocardiogram, which takes five minutes, or a blood test, which provides results within 10 minutes. Neither of these appear to have been done.

So, convinced he was simply suffering from a trapped nerve, Bowie, still in pain, travelled to Germany. Two days later he was back on stage, and no doubt still on painkillers. The band noticed his subdued performance, but only at the end of the set, after a three-song encore which culminated in 'Ziggy Stardust', did Bowie leave the stage. He bowed, walked to the wings and went down the steps, where, at the bottom, he collapsed.

Bowie had performed through a heart attack. Not once, but twice. His career is full of courageous acts – time and again, in front of the whole world, he had dared to be different. But this time he exhibited another sort of bravery. It is no exaggeration to say that he put his life on the line for his work. 'He just hated to cancel shows,' said Dorsey. 'There were nights where he was so sick, he had a bucket at the side of the stage where he'd go to puke between songs.'

Within hours of his collapse, he was undergoing an angioplasty, the insertion of a small metal tube, for a blocked artery.

How severe the heart attack was, we don't know. But the recovery time following a mild heart attack treated with a stent is usually measured in one to two months. Bowie pretty much disappeared from public view for two years. He may, of course, have taken the opportunity to take a break from public life, or his family may have insisted he take things easy. Or it may be that this heart attack had caused significant damage and he really did need significant time to recover. Bowie himself seemed to suggest as much to the BBC's Courtney Pine in that final radio interview the following year when, 15 months on from his collapse, he said, 'I've been working out a lot this year and I'm back on course, I think.'

Almost as a premonition, Marc Riley asks him in the interview that follows, 'Aren't you exhausted?' Bowie would end up doing 112 shows on this tour, the longest of his entire career. 'No, I'm really not,' replies Bowie, who sounded, not only as fit as a fiddle, but also to be genuinely enjoying himself, despite the tour's length.

But away from the dark clouds of his health that would overshadow some of his final years, this interview is one of his funniest and most enjoyable. Riley is a highly amusing and quick-witted host, but Bowie has no problem keeping up. He even creases Riley up by just reading out the promo jingle, 'Hi, I'm David Bowie and this is 6 Music.' To make that line funny takes some doing.

Here's how Marc Riley remembers that day:

Myself, producer Michelle Choudhry and Jim Simmons (the man whose job it was to get it all down on tape) went to a hotel room on the south bank of the Thames. David was his usual smiling, disarming self, and as we sat down, he launched into a playful fairytale!

'So, there's a knock on door (oh yeah?) yeah … and I opened it, and there was John and Paul … (really!?) … really … and we got to talking and they asked me if I'd like to form a group with them … a supergroup (wow!) I know… (and what was this supergroup to be called?) … erm …David Bowie and The Beatles …' I am paraphrasing here, but you get the drift.

Luckily, Jim had already pressed the buttons on the recording equipment, and this typically playful exchange ended up being the start of the interview. When I say 'interview', I have to say, David was not even remotely interested in talking about his latest record or tour … he wanted to talk about seahorses being found in the Thames for the first time in decades, and simply wanted to have a laugh and make me feel like a kid in a sweet shop. Job done.

At one point I said to him, 'You've been on the road for a long, long time … you must be exhausted.' He took a slight exception to this and replied, in an old man's croaky voice, 'I'm 57 and I can still hold a pen.' Sadly, the truth was David did actually look tired and somewhat ashen. It was only a few days later that he had the heart attack whilst on stage in Germany.

I shared a radio studio with David Bowie five times and introduced him on stage three times. As a result, I count myself a very fortunate man.[23]

DAVID BOWIE: Frankly, I'm glad you two [Riley and Radcliffe] split up, you see. [*Laughter*] Oh, are we rolling?

MARC RILEY: Oooh!

DB: Oh, shit, I'm sorry, man, I didn't mean to say all that. So then, Paul said to John …

MR: Ooh, go on. You were there, were you?

DB: You know what, that was funny. It was New York around 1974, and I think it was around the first time they'd gotten back together again, because I got a knock on the door one night at the Pierre Hotel. I'd taken over a suite, virtually, for months and months. I was kind of living there. I'd just gotten one of the new Sony reel-to-reel video tape things, black-and-white thing, and I was doing Cecil B. DeMille things, cutting out little figures and stage sets. [*Laughs*] I could re-film things off the set and then have characters appear on my little set. It was incredibly involved. Fortunately, I was doing cocaine so I could stay up most of the night and complete these things. About three in the morning, there's a knock on the door, and John was there and he had got Paul with him! That's the two of them being out on the town for the evening. He said, 'Can we come in? You won't believe what I've got here.' I said, 'I thought you two had …' 'No, no, we're gonna … all that's going to change.' It was great. We spent the evening just rapping and talking. There was a kind of a strange thing between us, a little bit of distance every now and again, but that must have been the first time they'd been back together since the big bust-ups.

MR: Did they not ask you to drum for them or anything?

DB: They actually asked me if I'd kind of join the two of them and become a trio with them and we'd change the name to something else.

MR: A power trio?

DB: Yeah, David Bowie and The Beatles. They liked the idea there'd be two, like DBB – I think that's why – they wanted to call it DBB.

MR: DBB?

DB: Yeah.

MR: See, now, 6 Music, it's an exclusive, you're getting this first. David Bowie and The Beatles, combined.

DB: Yeah, but the next morning it just never came to anything.

MR: It's always the way, isn't it? Scousers.

DB: That's it. You can't trust them.

MR: Can't trust them.

DB: No.

MR: When this goes out in Liverpool, we'll cut this bit out. You can do that with technology, can't you?

DB: Not on that machine, unfortunately. That's one of the newer ones. You can't play things backwards like you used to be able to in the old days.

MR: No, you can't.

DB: I'd say to Tony Visconti, 'That's great, now turn it over, put it on backwards.' 'It's going to take me about four days to do that.' Thirty years ago, I could just turn the tape over and play it backwards.

MR: Is that why your records aren't as weird?

DB: [*Laughs*] Yeah.

MR: Is it? You see you reinvented rock'n'roll by turning the tape upside down, you can't do it anymore. No razor blades, no little white chinagraph pencils. It's all changed.

DB: Well, my guitar player, Gerry, has got a little, fabby machine that he can play solos backwards … which is an extraordinary thing … live! It says nothing in rock can ever be new again. It knows all the solos he's ever going to play, because it's been programmed with a thorough history of rock, so it can predict what he's going to play. A little notice comes up on digits on the machine – it says, 'You're just going to play the same old thing, aren't you?' And Gerry hits that 'yes' button, and it just plays.

MR: Easy as that?

DB: Yeah, easy as that.

MR: Amazing. Do you know what, I think we're probably like four minutes into the interview and, this being David Bowie Day on 6 Music, we've not even said hello.

DB: Oh, God, not a David Bowie Day.

MR: Yes!

DB: That's the third one this month.

MR: I know, well, they are racking them up. We went for a Tiny Tim Day. [*DB laughs*] But he's not alive anymore, is he?

DB: [*Laughs*] Yes, he was on BBC 5 the other day, a classical thing. David Bowie Day. Didn't I tell you that [Ralph] Vaughan Williams said he wanted to kind of do a duet with me? DBVW, it was going to be called.

MR: [*Laughs*] Was it?

DB: Yeah, but he's got this new recording contract with Sony [*Laughs*] and they said, 'No, we're not going to go with that.'

MR: Do you not want to talk about the tour?

DB: I don't want to talk about Vaughan Williams. I fell out with that Vaughan Williams big time!

MR: Oh, he's a nightmare, Vaughan. Vaughan Williams Day – forget it!

DB: Yeah. Stay with his 'Thomas Tallis'. See if I care.

MR: Leave him! Forget him!

DB: Me, I'm an Elgar man, me. El-gaar.

MR: [*Deliberately confusing the name with Elgin*] Oh, his marbles, his marbles, I remember.

DB: [*Laughs*] 'Elgar's lost his marbles' – it was the one thing he wrote on LSD. Did you know that LSD is actually Roman, isn't it … lira, Solari and dinari, isn't it?

MR: No, it's English. It's pounds, shillings, pence.

DB: No, it's not, it's L, S, D. If it's pounds, shillings and pence, wouldn't it be PSP?

MR: PSP? That's a horse tranquiliser.

DB: It is. I did a lot of PSP, actually, about 30 years ago.

MR: [*Laughs*] Come on, then, tell us.

DB: God! I remember, I wrote a lot of things with Dylan. Actually, not many people know that me and Dylan were going to do a duet thing one time. We got it in our heads that we could do like an Art

Garfunkel thing. But the next morning, I didn't hear another word from him. The whole financial system – that's what I was getting to, of course – was devised by the Italians, the Lombard family and all that crowd who came over, and gave us LSD. It was all in Italian.

MR: Now, you've been working non-stop for three and a half years.

DB: [*Laughs*] Yeah, it feels like it.

MR: Yeah, I can tell.

DB: [*Adopts an accent*] Oh, I do, I need a holiday! [*Laughs*]

MR: I've only come to cheer you up, David. You do a couple of interviews and it's drudgery – but we talk about Vaughan Williams.

DB: Oh, me and a bucket and spade, and back up to Scunthorpe.

MR: Scunny. No, you have, you've been all over the place. It started when you recorded *Heathen*, then you toured *Heathen*.

DB: Not very much, though. It wasn't a big tour, though, was it?

MR: It wasn't a big tour, but then you did *Reality* on the back of that pretty much straight away, and then you've been touring for …

DB: It's now 10 months. I've got another two to go. And then, good behaviour, I should be alright.

MR: Are you exhausted?

DB: No, I'm really not.

MR: You must be!

DB: No, absolutely not. Why I must be?

MR: Is it not like, you're constantly on the road …

DB: It gets irritating, and it gets irritating to be in America when you're not in New York, and you're out in the middle there and every time you walk out the door it's another shopping mall. It's the same shopping mall! That's the problem. It's not even a different one. It is absolutely the same. Branding in the States is beyond what we've got over here. We think we've got a lot of Starbucks and all that, but you just have no idea, until you get to the States, what branding can do to the culture.

MR: Just saturation. Do you get the opportunity to go out and see the other countries … when you go to Japan …?

DB: Oh, yeah! All the time. I did a lot of that here, whilst I've been here. I went out the other day and just walked around for five hours. I got the Tube …

MR: Did you go out on the Tube?

DB: Oh yeah, yeah, yeah. I always do when I come here. And I went somewhere and I just walked around for four or five hours. It's kind of depressing how much is going and how much is being put up, and how shabby some of the newer stuff is, as well – a lot of the office blocks and things.

MR: Did you ever manage to get back to Brixton?

DB: Oh yeah, yeah. I haven't taken the baby yet, but I took the wife last time we were … went to Brixton. That was really lovely. I thought the atmosphere was really cool. Don't get me wrong, I think there's a lot that's great here, a lot of it I like very much indeed. I like the atmosphere, I like the vibe in the streets here, actually – again, outside of the West End, which really has gotten really touristy. Poor old Trafalgar Square.

MR: And places to park, et cetera, et cetera.

DB: Uh? [*Seemingly mishearing*] Oh, the parks are lovely, though. The parks are still great here. I do miss that in the States. Central Park is one thing, but we don't have … like that huge bloody lake in St James'[s] Park with all those birds on it. No two birds the same! It's absolutely amazing.

MR: Multicultural.

DB: And you can't eat any of them.

MR: Well, I'm vegetarian anyway.

DB: Whereas in New York, you see it in the water, you shoot it and eat it and cook it! Right there in the park!

MR: [Laughs] Is that your philosophy?

DB: It's the law there in the States. Not many people know that, Marc. If you see anything moving in Central Park that's not wearing a hat, you can shoot it and eat it.

MR: What if it's a bird wearing a hat?

DB: [*Laughs*] Well, then lucky bird! Except I did notice the ducks have little wellington boots on, with people faces on.

MR: Do they? You see, I've not noticed that. I'm just walking around looking at the buildings. You see, I'm from Manchester, we don't have big buildings. You do manage to get out and see things and go to galleries and stuff? Do you not get pestered to the point where you just don't bother?

MR: No, no, absolutely not. No, I dress up as Tony Blair and nobody ever says anything to me.

MR: Can you still officially vote?

DB: Me? Officially vote? Or do you mean physically, can I physically still vote?

MR: Well, both.

DB: I can hold a pen. [*Adopts an elderly voice*] I'm 57, I can still hold a pen! [*Claps*]

MR: Excellent. Good work, fella. Alright, so you don't want to answer that.

DB: Yeah, I can vote here.

MR: Can you? And do you?

DB: No, because I don't think it's my place. I don't live here.

MR: You could vote and then perhaps you could make the world a better place?

DB: It's my option to not do that. But there again, I'm not an American citizen, so I can't vote there.

MR: And what was the high point of the tour?

DB: High point of the tour for me was actually doing this interview. I've been looking forward to this ever since we did Madison Square Garden.

MR: Yeah.

DB: I tell you what makes it worthwhile, actually, is the unexpected, in terms of, professionally, the shows. You play a place like Moline – now, do you even know what state Moline is in?

MR: I've never heard of it.

DB: I've been there and I can't even remember what state it's in. But we did Moline, and it was just simply wonderful. The audience were so receptive to not just things that they knew but things they'd never heard of and probably will never hear again. [*Laughs*] That's happened a few times in the oddest places. Hershey – where they make the chocolate – just dynamite, it was just such a great show.

MR: Well, no disrespect to you, but that's that thing, isn't it, surely if you live in a hick town, when David Bowie comes to town, I mean that's going to be …

DB: Yes, I guess it's narrow of myself and short-sighted and narrow and blinkered to not think that they really actually are open-minded to like other stuff than maybe Ziggy Stardust and whatever. But they really were. I mean we were playing quite hard stuff. We were kind of pushing them a bit and playing really heavy things off *Heathen* and all that: 'Sunday' and 'Heathen' and '[Bring Me the] Disco King', to see if we could really get them rattled. But they were fantastic. They just liked it all.

MR: You're doing the same thing with festival audiences, aren't you?

DB: I love festivals. I love the fact that it just puts you in contact with other bands. But you really are restricted because of the curfews in these places. The other night it was so frustrating. We could only do 90 minutes. I squeezed another 10 minutes out of it.

MR: When you played the Isle of Wight Festival?

DB: Yeah, at the Isle of Wight Festival. But we would gladly have done the full two, two-and-a-half-hour show, but it gets kind of frustrating because it's cutting our choices of what we can do. We are working between 55 and 60 songs now, which is really a lot of material. I nailed it at about a third very well known; a third more obscure, lesser-known material and from other sources; and then a third probably off the last two albums and some of the nineties stuff. It's a pretty good selection, and I try and make it feel like that, about that proportion every night, and it means everybody's happy, including my band.

MR: Because in the arena tours, obviously the people there, they're Bowie fans, they really are, they're up there with the Elvis fans, they really are, aren't they? It's a strange … I mean, I know a lot of them [*DB laughs*] and they know everything that you do.

DB: Oh, they know much more than I do. They always get the words right, because they mouth them back at me. And when I'm stumbling and thinking, 'Oh, what's that?'…

MR: You should train them up to do the words just slightly before you need them.

DB: It's funny because you can be doing a song … I put back in, foolishly, I hadn't done it for quite a few shows, 'Let's Dance' the other night. And I got to the line, [*Laughs, then sings*] '*Something* like a flower'. I couldn't for the life of me remember what the flower was doing. Was it wilting like a flower? No, it wasn't wilting, that sounds daft.

MR: You were doing this during the guitar solo?

DB: Every time it came to the line, every time, I couldn't remember it. [*Sings*] 'Hmmm like a flower!' And I was looking frantically for somebody I knew in the audience who would know, and I couldn't find anybody. It's like out of spite they decided to keep their mouths shut on that one.

MR: Evil.

DB: But at 'Motel', suddenly all the mouths are going again. But I knew all the words to that one.

MR: These people, they are quite an amazing bunch of people, the Bowie fans, because they do eat, sleep and breathe David Bowie. Your effect on their lives … I remember seeing you on *Lift Off with Ayshea* [*DB laughs*] and it really was … I loved Ollie Beak, that was the only reason I watched it, but of course you turned up.

DB: Ollie Beak, my God.

MR: And Molly White.

DB: Yeah, yeah. Molly White, but he was a … there was a music link …

MR: … folk singer.

DB: Didn't he used to work with Nancy Whiskey?

MR: Did he?

DB: Oh, that's Chas McDevitt.

MR: Do you always get them two mixed up?

DB: Yeah, Molly White and Chas McDevitt, it's a perennial thing with me.

MR: And Ollie Beak, who was an owl.

DB: But Molly White was a skiffle man, wasn't he?

MR: Yeah, that's right.

DB: Do you ever do a tea-chest-based thing?

MR: No.

DB: That came from the 'porch base'. You know the tea chest in skiffle … you get an old tea chest – you know, the thing they bring the tea in – and a broom handle and you stuck that through the top and then you nailed a piece of catgut, like you would use on a ukulele, a long piece down from the top of the broom down to the tea chest. And it would go, 'Dum dum dum dum'.

MR: Was it not bore [sic] out of poverty?

DB: It was borne out of poverty. And actually, where it came from, it came from what they used to call 'porch base' in the States, in the South, where they would nail some catgut to the support of a porch and take it down to the actual porch itself, and that would act as the sound box and it would be thumping through the porch, 'Boom boom boom boom'.

MR: Do you know I read once, actually, one of these tea-chest-based things is played on 'Wild is the Wind', is that right?

DB: No, that wasn't true.

MR: We'll cut that bit out or still put it in, it doesn't matter. That's fine.

DB: If you took all the cut-out bits and put them together, you could have alternative interviews, couldn't you?

MR: I think the legal side, the implications of it forbid …

DB: You don't want those tea-chest-based players suing you.

MR: No.

DB: Remember Archie Andrews?

MR: No.

DB: No? It was a ventriloquist doll.

MR: That was Lord Charles.

DB: Yeah, but no, it was our version. It was on Sunday radio. I often wonder …

MR: Oh, no, I've talked about this. A ventriloquist on the radio.

DB: I always thought that was absurd. I always wondered if Jimmy Clitheroe was, in fact, a ventriloquist's dummy.

MR: Yeah, there's a good letter in *Viz* about Jimmy Clitheroe, [*Laughs*] which I'll tell you about later.

DB: Tell me now and it can be on the alternative show. [*MR laughs*] You can't clip it out? [*Laughs*]

MR: You've got BowieNet, and that allows your fans …

DB: Have I?

MR: You have. You instigated it. It's your beast. It's your fault. It's like *The Truman Show*, it is like reality TV, isn't it, because everything you do, they know. In the days gone by, when you'd go off to America for two years, we'd read about you in the *Daily Mirror* every now and then, and think 'Come back, come back, you sod.' But now you've got journals, you've got reviews of every gig, you've got the set list …

DB: It brings everything down to the mundane, doesn't it?

MR: Well, no.

DB: Well, it does.

MR: Do you think so?

DB: Yeah, which is fine by me.

MR: Well, I suppose your everyday life to you might be mundane if you're working, and obviously …

DB: It is, basically, isn't it? All life is pretty mundane. Did you see that they found a seahorse in the Thames? Now, that's not mundane. They used to have a lot of them –20, 25 years ago – in the Thames, but because of the pollution, they all died off. They just found one, which means that the water is really cleaning up in the Thames, because it wouldn't live here otherwise. Isn't that lovely?

MR: Yeah, that's a great story. They also found, about four or five years ago, a lot of Japanese crabs. They did. Not making it up. [*Laughs*] They found a new species of crab in the Thames. So we can sell that bit to Radio 4! [*DB can't stop laughing*] They should just send me in here for 12 hours and we could do all the BBC networks. Okay, so have you got any plans?

DB: [*Still laughing*] Oh, ah, this is hurting! Plans for the future?

MR: We need to know. Because you've been all over the world. Have you written it like you wrote *Aladdin Sane*, as you've torn across America?

DB: No, I've written nothing, absolutely nothing. Visconti and I have already started booking time in the studio to go back in again. I suppose I'll take two or three weeks off with the family when I've gotten off the road. The last thing we do is … we were going to be doing Iceland, but we're not doing it now. I love Iceland. Isn't it great?

MR: It's a strange place.

DB: I love it.

MR: I went there whale-watching. It was a 24-hour trip.

DB: Yeah?

MR: And we saw one puffin.

DB: I'd love to see one puffin. [*Laughs*]

MR: Yes, very good. Okay, where was I?

DB: We were in Iceland. I think it's now the south of France, I think that's our last show, and then, from there – because there's a big festival down there – the next two months, it's like Norway, Finland, Sweden, Germany, France.

MR: Monte Carlo.

DB: [*Laughs*] Monte Carlo, you're right. Are we doing Italy? I can't remember. Spain definitely. And then we finish in France and I go home. Have a couple of weeks, take them up to Scunthorpe. Then back in the studio.

MR: Do Lexi and Iman go out on tour with you or do they stop at home?

DB: Yes and no. I'll leave it at that.

MR: Okay. It's none of my business, anyway.

DB: We'll cut that bit out.

MR: Yes, Michelle, our producer …

DB: So how's life with you, which is more important?

MR: Oh, I'm great, thank you very much.

DB: Are you enjoying it?

MR: Yeah, great. I'm semi-retired at the moment.

DB: [*Laughs*] Are you?

MR: I'm doing about two and a half days a week and a Saturday show, and we play whatever we like, which usually incorporates you and Lou Reed and John Cale and Iggy Pop and some new, great music. I'm really enjoying it. I mean, you know what the atmosphere was like at Radio 1. It was a good job. Me and Mark worked for 13 years together, but at the end we were doing it with our eyes shut. And I'm here now, and I wouldn't have been if I'd still been at Radio 1, so I'm happy. David, before we stop, would you mind doing something? You do know it's a David Bowie Day on …

DB: No.

MR: It's on 'David in the Park' – it's you, all day.

DB: When do we do T in the Park?

MR: The 10th of July. It's my birthday, I'm sure you'll remember. [*Both laugh*] That's sort of what brought this on. We're putting out a concert that you did in London, Ontario.

DB: Oh yeah, yeah, that was another great show.

MR: Right, yeah, I've heard it!

DB: That was really good.

MR: Yeah, well we've got an hour of that.

DB: Have you?

MR: Yeah, so we're putting that out, there's a documentary going out, we're putting this out, sessions – it's 'wall-to-wall Bowie', which is what it says here; that's the tag line.

DB: Why don't you …

MR: Have you got anything rare you want to give us?

DB: I was going to suggest that you maybe use some of the seahorse and Chinese crab material as well.

MR: We're definitely using that.

DB: You could have a nature corner.

MR: [*Laughs*] Yeah, we will. That'll be in. It'll all be in, David, even this bit. Just at the top, there's a little tag line, if you wouldn't mind doing it?

DB: [*Adopts a pacy American advert accent*] 'Hi!' It's one of those, is it? Okay. 'Hi, this is David Bowie and this is BBC 6 Music'. Let's try, 'Hi, I'm David Bowie and this is BBC 6 Music.'

MR: And the bit below … 'wall-to-wall me'.

DB: 'Jim's question.'

MR: [*Laughs*] No, not Jim's question. You can answer that if you like.

DB: 'Wall-to-wall me. Bowie Day on BBC 6 … Music.' Can't we do Jim's question?

MR: If you've got time and you don't mind. This is Jim, and he's doing a programme about …

DB: [*Reads out question*] 'David, please would you be kind enough to tell us which film soundtrack album is one of your favourites?' Okay, yeah. *Mishima* by Philip Glass.

MR: Okay, brilliant.

DB: Good, good.

COURTNEY PINE'S JAZZ CRUSADE, BBC RADIO

INTERVIEWER: COURTNEY PINE

Bowie had always wanted to make a jazz album. He would eventually get there with *Blackstar*, but the signs were present well before.

While still Ziggy, he hired jazz pianist Mike Garson. When he set his sights on soul, he turned to jazz saxophonist David Sanborn. He and Nile Rodgers bonded not over disco or rock but over their jazz favourites. And when Bowie was trying to work out what to do in the mid-eighties, he worked with jazz guitarist Pat Metheny for 'This Is Not America'. Come the nineties, on the cusp of making *Black Tie White Noise*, he told drummer Erdal Kizilçay that they were about to make a jazz album. The LP didn't quite turn out that way, but it did employ jazz trumpeter and David's namesake, Lester Bowie.

Bowie – David that is – had revealed his intention to Kizilçay as the two were about to head off to a gig. The performer they were to see that night was jazz saxophonist and clarinettist Courtney Pine.

COURTNEY PINE: How are you keeping, man?

DAVID BOWIE: Thanks very much for asking, Courtney. Yeah, I'm doing fine. I've been working out a lot this past year and I'm back on course, I think.

CP: Good, good. Alright, let's talk about the saxophone. Is it true that your first instrument was a saxophone?

DB: I'm not sure if the saxophone is my *first* instrument, but I've tortured one a few times, [*CP laughs*] specifically an alto, which was the first one I ever had. I saw the Little Richard band in a film, I think it was called *Disc Jockey Jamboree*, [the film was actually *Mister Rock and Roll*] and he had a really large sax line-up, all wearing white suits; so I'm not sure if it was the white suit or the saxophone that got me first, but I decided I really, really wanted to join Little Richard's band when I grew up. I was about 12 years old, something like that, between 10 and 12.

CP: Now tell me about the first instrument you actually had.

DB: I got my dad to help me out on the higher purchase system – five shillings a week – to get me an alto sax. What we did was, we went up Tottenham Court Road, there was a big musical instrument store up there. I chose one that was white plastic, I think. I think it was made by Selmer's. It was the same kind that Johnny Dankworth played.

CP: Yeah, you had one of those?

DB: That's where it all came to great tragedy for the jazz world! [*Laughs*]

CP: Can you remember hearing jazz for the first time?

DB: My late brother introduced me to jazz, really. I remember the first two albums, big favourites of his, and he passed them on to me. One was by the MJQ [Modern Jazz Quartet] and the album was *Fontessa*, which was an Atlantic album. I think it was their first one for Atlantic. And the second one was by a band, pretty much unknown, it was the George Redmond Group [George Redmond Quintet]. They were part of the West Coast cool jazz, [*Sings a soft jazz melody*] 'Doo do doo do do do doo'. There's a track called 'Babette' on that album, *Moods in Jazz*, and the baritone player on that was Bob Gordon, who was pretty well known around the time. Actually, you can still get that album now, because I lost my copy and I had to get it again. There's a label called V.S.O.P., it's called *Moods in Jazz*, and a really, really beautiful album. So, those are the first two jazz albums I really heard.

CP: What about gigs you went to see on your trips around the world? Anything interesting?

DB: Over in the States, the first two major jazzers that I saw in the very early seventies was Charlie Mingus at the Village Gate, which was stupendous, and Stan Kenton, the full Stan Kenton Orchestra, at the White Night Club in Chicago. And that was really sad because I think there were more people on the stage than there were in the audience. [*Laughs*] Only about 10 or 12 people in the audience. Kenton was great. He said bring everybody up to the front, so we all moved up to the front, and they still played like the place was packed, you know. That was just tremendous. I met Milt Jackson, as well, in the eighties over in Switzerland, of all places. It was at the Montreux Jazz Festival, and it was wonderful. I had a dinner with Milt Jackson and Quincy Jones and a few other members of their band. I was just like … like a fly-on-the-wall thing. I just sat back and listened, and they were talking about a virtual history of jazz. It was an astonishing evening, really memorable for me.

CP: I've got to ask you, you worked with jazz musicians, you worked with pop/rock musicians. Do you find there's a difference at all between the two stylists?

DB: I tell you, Lester Bowie got a lot drunker [*Both laugh*] than most rock musicians. It was terrific. I mean, I was working with Nile Rodgers, and we decided that we just couldn't resist, we had to get Lester to work on a few tracks with us. Ten o'clock in the morning, man, he was like, first thing he wanted was a six-pack. [*Laughter*] Straight down with them. Let me see, overall, I was always surprised that jazz musicians were so into the idea of doing rock. I guess it's a real change for them. But it was always really cool to work with jazz musicians on a rock session because they really put everything into it.

CP: Yes. What are you listening to at the moment? Do you have an iPod? Are you into technology, and all that?

DB: Oh yeah, yeah, yeah. Let me see. I tell you who I like a lot is Matthew Shipp.

CP: Yeah, the pianist Matthew Shipp.

DB: There's a track of his I really like called 'Rocket Shipp'. The album's called *Nu Bop*, yup, that's right. Oh, oh, oh, I tell you what I've ordered! Have you heard about the new Dizzy Gillespie–Charlie Parker album?

CP: Oh, they've re-released something, have they?

DB: No, no. This is spectacular. Seven 12-inch acetates were found, and it runs to about 40 minutes. It's a town hall recording, New York, in June 1945.

CP: Oh, my goodness!

DB: It's probably the very first, really major, live performance of the Dizzy Gillespie Quintet. Isn't that amazing?

CP: I've got to get that CD! Now, let's play some Matthew Shipp and we'll talk some more with David in a moment.

ROCKET SHIPP (Matthew Shipp)

CP: What about when you were a teenager, did you go to Ronnie Scott's?

DB: There was a club locally in Bromley called the Bromel Club, it was the Bromel [Bromley] Court Hotel. It had a fantastic guy who was the promoter there. I used to see people like Joe Harriott, and Shake Keane used to play down there, and sometimes I think Shake Keane used to read some of his stuff.

CP: Wow!

DB: It was fantastic. Tubby Hayes with Ronnie Ross used to play down there. And then you'd get people like Graham Bond with Dick Heckstall-Smith.

CP: Wow!

DB: It was just a wonderful place. Anybody who went to Ronnie Scott's in London, definitely they hit the Bromel Club. The Bromel Club was really cool. Earlier on, when I was about 12, I phoned up Ronnie Ross because I knew he lived near us in Orpington. I said, [*Adopts a high-pitch tone*] 'I've just bought a saxophone and I'd like to learn to play.' And he said, 'Well, I don't teach.' [*Laughter*] I said, 'Oh.' He said, 'Were you serious about it?' I said, 'Oh, yeah!' And he said, 'How old are you?' 'I'm 12.' So, he said, 'Well, look, come on over on Saturday mornings.' So I shot over there, got the bus over there on Saturday morning, and he gave me lessons for about six weeks, [*Laughs*] which was very cool of him. He wouldn't take money or anything, he was just so cool. It's a lovely memory to have, actually.

CP: Yeah, Ronnie Ross is gone now. He was one of the greatest British baritone players we've ever had.

DB: I saw at the time, who also became one of my idols, was Gerry Mulligan. And I got to see him at the Madison Square Garden, and Gerry Mulligan was playing with an all-star band and I got to meet him afterwards, and that was just wonderful.

CP: Listen, I've got to ask you about something because I get to see many, many concerts … you've done a few in your time … and I remember seeing you at a Phoenix Festival when …

DB: Oh God, yeah!

CP: … you were playing drum and bass.

DB: That's right, yeah. [*Laughs*]

CP: And nobody seemed to realise, and I can remember walking through the audience wanting to tell everybody, 'That's David Bowie!'

DB: Yeah, nobody … well, very few people had a clue. I guess the first couple of rows knew because it was … they weren't big on lighting in that tent, [*Laughs*] which is great. I actually preferred it that way.

CP: Well, for me it really worked.

DB: It was great, we thoroughly enjoyed it. We did a few gigs like that and enjoyed every one of them.

CP: Is there any chance of a jazz record?

DB: [*Laughs*] Oh, yeah! I should start losing sleep if I were you! [*Both laugh*] I tell you what, the only way I'd love to do one, I'd love to do one with you!

CP: Oh, man.

DB: What else?!

CP: That's no problem! You work with a phenomenal bass player, Gail Ann Dorsey. And we worked in a band together.

DB: Yes, she's absolutely wonderful.

CP: She's a great jazz bass player, as well.

DB: Yes, she is. Actually, the band is pretty cool in that respect. I mean, there's some very good players. Mike Garson, my pianist, is also a really excellent jazz player.

CP: Yes. You going to be thinking about a new album soon?

DB: Yeah, I started writing already and it looks pretty weird, so I'm happy. [*Laughs*]

CP: Uh-huh. What are your fans going to be expecting?

DB: Oh, they don't expect anything these days. I think they just wait and see what I put out. It's the luck of the draw. Sometimes it works really well and sometimes it's godawful, but that's the way it goes, and I like that.

CP: If there was one jazz track that really, really moves you, what would it be?

DB: Oh. Oh, that's hard isn't it?

CP: It's a very difficult question.

DB: Oh! 'Hog Callin' Blues' by Charlie Mingus.

CP: Oh, wow.

DB: Now, I saw Mingus, let's see, 1972, '73, at the Village Gate. It was just amazing, a wonderful performance.

CP: Yeah, yeah! Well, David, it's been a real pleasure talking to you, and here's to more in the future.

DB: Likewise, likewise, Courtney, and I really look forward to seeing you again, man.

CONCLUSION

Bowie sometimes had a reputation as a cold and difficult interviewee. The interviews in this book show just the opposite. If the subject matter was light, he was funny; if it was deep, he was erudite. He was also extremely interesting. His never-ending curiosity in everything from the history of art to the latest technology meant he was one of the most fascinating interviewees not just in rock music but in any walk of life.

He clearly thought deeply about everything. Bowie never thought of himself as an intellectual, and occasionally you glimpse his insecurity about his lack of education. But what comes across is that he was, though he would have protested, a genuine intellectual: a man who read widely, created deeply and spoke eloquently.

Sometimes, in earnestly trying to understand the interviewer's intent or to give as honest as answer as possible, he could come across as evasive or awkward. But he was always excessively polite, always the gentleman, and certainly never rude. A fellow rock writer once told me about the time he once met his hero, Lou Reed. The reporter was shown to Reed's table only for the singer to ignore him as he ate his meal, before a series of one-word answers and refusals to engage. In the end, the reporter, who adored Reed, could stand it no more and tears came into his eyes. 'Why are you so horrible to me?' he said in anguish. It seems clear from the conversations collected here that Bowie would never have played that game.

There was, of course, the awkward moment on *Wogan*. But if one assumes that Bowie was simply wanting to be seen as just another member of the band rather than 'David Bowie the Superstar', his behaviour comes across, even here, as an honourable effort to deflect attention away from himself for the greater good.

But the one thing that really stands out from these interviews is how he becomes increasingly comfortable in himself. In fact, it is Bowie who often tries to put the awestruck interviewers at their ease, not the other way round. The further into the book you delve, the more apparent this becomes. The man who tried on so many different skins throughout his life had finally become comfortable in his own.

SOURCES

1   George Underwood's quotes are from an interview with the author.

2   Bowie's comments are from *The David Bowie Story*, George Tremlett (Futura Publications, 1974).

3   Lol Tolhurst's quote is from his autobiography *Cured: The Tale of Two Imaginary Boys*, Lol Tolhurst (Da Capo Press, 2016).

4   Woody Woodmansey's quotes are from an interview with the author.

5   Bowie's 'Good heavens, whatever next' quote is from a 2002 interview reprinted in *David Bowie: The Golden Years*, Roger Griffin (Omnibus Press, 2016).

6   Cameron Crowe's quote is taken from his reply during a Television Critics Association winter press tour for the Showtime series *Roadies* when asked if he'd had any experience with Bowie.

7   Nic Roeg's quote is from article 'David Bowie – the Inside Story of the Man Who fell To Earth', Rob Hughes (*Uncut*, April 2015).

8   Quote appears in *Apollo Memories*, Martin Kielty (Neil Wilson Publishing, 2005).

9   Ibid.

10 Keith Richard's quote is from article 'Bowie's Best Songs' (*Uncut*, June 2008).

11 May Pang's quote is from *David Bowie: The Biography*, Wendy Leigh (Gallery Books, 2014).

12 Bowie's quotes about Lennon come from his address to Berklee College of Music students at a graduation ceremony in 1999.

13 Bowie's quotes about Ōshima come from *Loving the Alien*, Christopher Sandford (Da Capo Press, 1998).

14 Bob Geldof's quotes are taken from an article that he wrote following Bowie's death: 'David Bowie Special' (*Daily Mail*, 16 January 2016).

15 Willie Williams's quote is taken from davidbowie.com.

16 Terry Wogan's quotes come from his autobiography *Is It Me?*, Terry Wogan (BBC Books, 2007).

17 Jon Brewer's quote is from article 'Beside Bowie', Andy Greene (*Rolling Stone*, 2 February 2018).

18 Trent Reznor's quote is from article 'David Bowie Tribute' (*Rolling Stone*, January 2016).

19 John Peel's quotes are taken from an interview with him on programme Radio! Radio! (BBC Radio 1, 1986).

20 Jo Whiley's memories are from her Radio 1 show talking in the days after Bowie's death (BBC Radio 1, January 2016).

21 Mike Garson's comments are from 'Bowie at Glastonbury' (Somersetlive. com, 28 June 2020).

22 Pete Townshend's comments are from a 6 Music interview (BBC Radio 6 Music, 10 January 2021).

23 Marc Riley's comments are from an interview with the author.

ABOUT THE AUTHOR

Tom Hagler is a reporter on the BBC's World Service and an expert on David Bowie. Author of the exhaustively researched book *We Could Be: Bowie and his Heroes*, as a journalist Tom has covered major events and conducted interviews with a wide range of politicians, musicians and major cultural figures, with a roll call as diverse as President Joe Biden, Kofi Annan, Buzz Aldrin and Grandmaster Flash. He was previously a reporter for the *Sunday Telegraph* and *The Sunday Times*.

ACKNOWLEDGEMENTS

My thanks go to my publisher, Joe Cottington, whose idea this book was in the first place. Thanks for thinking of me, Joe! A big thanks also goes to Woody Woodmansey, George Underwood and Marc Riley for sharing their memories. And, lastly, thanks to Becky and my boys for not complaining (too much) at me being such a Bowie bore.

PICTURE CREDITS

INDEX

Jones, Haywood ('John') (father)
13–14, 31, 238, 359, 363,
365, 399–400
Jones, Joey (son), *see* Jones,
Duncan
Jones, Mary ('Peggy') (née Burns)
(mother) 14, 16, 238, 359,
361, 363, 365
Jones, Quincy 429
Juke Box Jury 5–6
'Jump They Say' 216, 217
Just a Gigolo 78, 91–7, 93

kabuki 41, 94, 398
The Kenny Everett Video Show 353
Kerr, Wesley 171–4
King, Jonathan 185
King, Rodney 215
Kizilçay, Erdal 427
Kraftwerk 77, 145, 335–6

Labyrinth 135
'Lady Stardust' 272
Lang, Fritz 75
Lard, *see* Riley, Marc
Larkin, Philip 359, 363
Later … With Jools Holland 253–8,
309–14, 373–7
'The Laughing Gnome' 127,
128, 185, 188
Led Zeppelin 26, 385
Legendary Stardust Cowboy
324–5, 373, 376, 383
Lennon, John 3, 111–12, 124,

128, 129, 144, 260, 401–2,
408, 409–10, 439
'Let Me Sleep Beside You' 14, 16,
264
'Let's Dance' 136, 149, 150, 153,
154, 165, 166, 188, 317, 319,
418
Let's Dance 135, 196, 205, 216,
241, 341
'Life on Mars?' 61, 62, 315, 317,
318, 320, 369–70
Lift Off with Ayshea 419
The Linguini Incident 135, 197–8
'Little Drummer Boy' 312
Little Richard 13, 140, 168, 291,
360, 362, 393, 394, 428
Live Aid 157–60
'Liza Jane' 5
Lloyd, Wendy 248
Lodger 154, 206, 251, 267
'London Bye Ta-Ta' 20
long hair 6–12, 33, 57, 377
Lough, Ernest 361–2
Love You Till Tuesday 50
'Loving the Alien' 165, 387
Low 47–8, 77, 81, 83, 141, 206,
256, 283, 322, 323, 336, 387
'Lucy Can't Dance' 222, 223
Lulu 29, 72
The Lunchtime Social 281–97

Madison Square Garden 262,
416, 432
MainMan 350